Windows NT Performance Monitoring, Benchmarking, and Tuning

201 West 103rd Street
Indianapolis, Indiana 46290

Mark T. Edmead
Paul Hinsberg

Windows NT Performance Monitoring, Benchmarking, and Tuning

Mark T. Edmead, Paul Hinsberg

International Standard Book Number: 1-56205-942-4

Library of Congress Catalog Card Number: 98-86489

Printed in the United States of America

2001   00   99   98   4   3   2   1

Interpretation of the printing code: The rightmost double-digit number is the year of the book's printing; the right-most single-digit, the number of the book's printing. For example, the printing code 98-1 shows that the first printing of the book occurred in 1998.

Composed in Bembo and Rotis Sans Serif by Macmillan Computer Publishing

Trademarks

Warning and Disclaimer

Executive Editor
Linda Ratts Engelman

Acquisitions Editor
Karen Wachs

Development Editor
Christopher Cleveland

Managing Editor
Caroline Roop

Project Editor
Brad Herriman

Copy Editor
Kris Simmons

Indexer
Tim Wright

Technical Editor
Will Adams

Proofreader
Sheri Replin

Production
Steve Balle-Gifford
Louis Porter, Jr.

Contents

About the Authors

Mark T. Edmead is president of MTE Software, Inc., a San Diego Microsoft
Solutions Provider specializing in Windows NT Backoffice consulting. Mark has over
20 years experience in software product development, system design, and project management. Mark is also a senior Windows NT trainer for Learning Tree International
and a past instructor at the University of California San Diego. Mark has presented
papers at SANS (System Administration and Network Security) conferences in
Monterey, San Francisco, and New York. He has also presented at the DECUS confer-
ence on NT optimization and tuning. Mark is a guest editor for *SANS Network
Security Digest*, contributing editor for the *SANS NT Digest*, and contributor to the
SANS Step-by-Step Security Guide.

Paul Hinsberg is currently owner and operator of a consulting corporation, CRSD
Inc., in Pleasanton, California, which is just east of San Francisco. CRSD Inc., focuses
on Microsoft BackOffice products, chiefly NT/SMS and SQL, as well as internet
connectivity including Firewall development, WAN architecture, and internet solutions. Paul is a Microsoft Certified Systems engineer and has degrees in Physics and
Mathematics, as well as a Master in Business Administration (MBA). In addition to
consulting he teaches and writes course materials for Learning Tree International, an
international hands-on technical training company.

Dedication

I'd like to dedicate this book to my children Philippe and Gabrielle.
They are too small to understand what I do for a living.
I was too busy working on the book to spend a lot of quality time
with them, so I will make it up to them now that the book is done.
Mark Edmead

This is for my wife Priscilla, a woman who has continually
amazed me with her compassion and beauty every day
of our 10 year marriage. I also dedicate this to my three children,
Michael, Michelle and Rey. You remind me each and every day
that playing and learning are the real treasures of life.
Thank you all for your patience, encouragement, and love.
Paul Hinsberg

Acknowledgments

Mark Edmead

First I'd like to thank the editorial team at Macmillan, especially Linda Engelman, Karen Wachs, Chris Cleveland, and Brad Herriman. This is my first book writing experience and it was overwhelming to say the least. Everyone at Macmillan was understanding of my traveling schedule (especially Karen who always asked, "Can you get that chapter done by Friday?"). I'd like to thank my co-author Paul for his invaluable contribution (the book would not be the same without him) and Will Adams, for his insightful technical review, comments, and mentoring. Other people who helped me with useful technical input are the NT trainers at Learning Tree International including Jeff Dunkleburger, Gregg Branham, Jon McDonald and John Flynn Mathews. This book could not have been written without the support from these and many other people. Thank you all.

Paul Hinsberg

Writing this book has been one of the most difficult experiences of my life, and if Michael had not of been so persistent, I probably wouldn't have completed my portion of this work. I would like to thank my co-author for enduring the same hardships and making this possible. Of course, without the wonderful people at Macmillan none of this would have been possible. Much thanks to the technical reviewers for helping to make this a better book.

Tell Us What You Think!

As the reader of this book, *you* are our most important critic and commentator. We value your opinion and want to know what we're doing right, what we could do better, what areas you'd like to see us publish in, and any other words of wisdom you're willing to pass our way.

As the Executive Editor for the Networking team at Macmillan Computer Publishing, I welcome your comments. You can fax, email, or write me directly to let me know what you did or didn't like about this book—as well as what we can do to make our books stronger.

Please note that I cannot help you with technical problems related to the topic of this book, and that due to the high volume of mail I receive, I might not be able to reply to every message.

When you write, please be sure to include this book's title and author, as well as your name and phone or fax number. I will carefully review your comments and share them with the author and editors who worked on the book.

Fax: 317-581-4663
Email: networktech@mcp.com
Mail: Linda Ratts Engelman
MTP
Macmillan Computer Publishing
201 West 103rd Street
Indianapolis, IN 46290 USA

Introduction

Out of the box, Windows NT Server and Workstation will perform well under a variety of conditions. However, Microsoft did not attempt to evaluate every possible condition or install NT in every possible network environment. In the real world, administrators and users expose the operating system to a myriad of configurations, and load it with software ranging from DOS games to 32-bit architectural engineering software. In these real-world situations, NT may need some assistance in tuning itself for optimum performance. This book demonstrates a variety of techniques for detecting and resolving performance bottlenecks and other issues. It was written to answer many of the questions NT users and systems administrators have been asking themselves, including:

- Does my system have a resource bottleneck and how do I find it?
- What system areas are available for optimization?
- Where do I begin in my optimization process?
- Do I need to modify the Registry and if so, what Registry keys can I modify to get the best performance?
- How do I measure my system's current performance?
- Is setting up performance for a domain server the same as for an application server?
- How do I improve memory, processor, disk or network performance?

Luckily for us, Windows NT does have the ability to be "tweaked" in order to gain better performance. The purpose of this book is to give the reader a methodical look at how to determine the current performance baseline of the system, and the practices to systematically improve overall system performance.

This book is targeted to those who need detailed information on how to get the most performance out of their Windows NT Workstation and Server. This is not a guide to pass an MCSE test. The book will be a resource on those occasions when performance issues arise. You will also want this book handy when you get a new server in or need to install the newest enterprise software. This book delivers the techniques and steps needed to perform the analysis of and adjustments to NT systems to get them running at their best. The best way to learn a new topic or to fully understand the techniques is to learn by example. With this in mind, this book also presents real case scenarios of the topics covered.

The book starts with an overview of the NT system from an internals point of view. Understanding the NT architecture is key to understanding what can be done to improve specific system components.

Microsoft ships several versions of Windows NT. The Workstation product is mainly used as a desktop operating system while the NT Server product is the high-end performance OS used in such roles as domain server, application server, or file and print server. Microsoft also introduced the Windows NT Enterprise Server, which incorporates many new technologies and enhancements. Many of the optimization and troubleshooting techniques discussed in this book will most likely apply to all NT products. However, when appropriate, differences between the Workstation and the Server product will be highlighted and discussed. Unless otherwise noted, the discussion on the NT Server will include the NT Enterprise server as well.

In regards to system performance, the system hardware cannot be ignored. NT is, after all, installed on a computer. The computer is divided into various resource components, namely the memory, processor, disk, and network. Each one of these will be covered in detail to give the reader an understanding of the inter-relationship between them.

A primary feature of this book is the coverage of the performance monitoring and data gathering tools, specifically the Windows NT Performance Monitor. Mainly, how to use the Performance Monitor to automatically gather the system resource data we want for further analysis later. Once we have the collected data, we discuss what the numbers really mean. We will use Excel to help us interpolate the data and to sophisticated resource planning and forecasting.

This book will also cover in detail, the different system components and how to solve specific performance problems. More importantly, it will cover WHY they occur as well as how to fix them. The last section deals with specific system settings for optimal Workstation or Server performance, registry settings, and performance tradeoffs.

Throughout this book, commands, switches, and arguments are shown in upper case within the text, and in lower case (except environment variables and script labels) in the example scripts. However, this is merely a convention and, except where noted, commands and switches are not case sensitive, and can be entered as desired. The only exception to the rule is Registry entries; often these can be potential problems for variation in case, so you should always try to match the case of any Registry entry mentioned here, or in any other text for that matter. Environment variables and script labels are shown in upper case in scripts to offset them from the lower case commands.

When describing the syntax of a command (rather than showing an example), items that must be entered exactly are shown in uppercase. Placeholders that must be replaced by appropriate values are shown in lowercase italic. Optional items are shown in brackets. Vertical bar characters separate alternatives, where one item from a list must be selected. For example, the AT command syntax is:

AT [*computer*] /DELETE [/YES | /NO]

This example shows one possible use of the AT command. It shows the AT command itself, followed by a computer name prefixed with two backslash characters. The computer name is shown in brackets, and is therefore optional. This is followed by the

/DELETE switch, and then optionally followed by the /YES or /NO switch. The following examples show valid AT commands:

1. at /DELETE
2. at /delete /yes
3. at \\mothra /delete

Also note that the numbers in lines of code are for reference purposes only. They are not to be included in any code commands or instructions.

Understanding Windows NT Architecture

This chapter covers the following topics:

- **The User and Kernel Mode.** This section provides an overview of the Windows NT architecture with respect to the layered operating design.

- **NT Executive Components.** The NT kernel layer consists of several key components that are the working components of the operating system. This section explains each NT Executive component and how it operates.

- **NT View of System Resources.** Your goal is to understand how the system resources and their operation affect Windows NT performance. This section reviews each of the system resources and how they can affect the system operation.

For you to understand what it is you are optimizing, it is best to better understand what you are working with. Makes sense, right? Let's begin by looking under the hood, so to speak, and understanding Windows NT from the inside out. Understanding the many components of NT is the key to optimizing NT performance.

Windows NT is the most powerful operating system available from Microsoft today. Some features of Windows NT include the following:

- Symmetrical Multiprocessor (SMP) System
- Supports multiple processes and multiple threads
- Secure operating system
- High performance and recoverable file system
- 3D graphic support
- Runs on different hardware platforms
- Can run DOS, 16-bit Windows, and OS/2 applications

Although NT has many more features, the features in this list set Windows NT apart from earlier operating system versions from Microsoft. When Windows NT was first released, it represented a major departure from the old 16-bit operating systems Microsoft was known for. The main goal was to develop an operating system that was extensible, portable, reliable, and compatible with existing programs and that also provided good performance.

The User and Kernel Mode

The first order of business is to look at the operating system layout. Windows NT has a layered architecture. The two layers, or modes, of NT are User and Kernel, as illustrated in Figure 1.1.

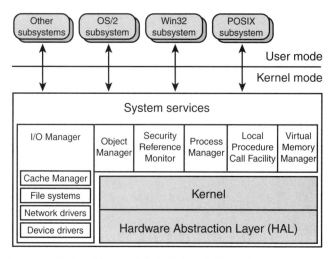

Figure 1.1 The User and Kernel layers of the Windows NT architecture.

Applications run at the User layer. NT supports various application types, including DOS, Windows 3.1, POSIX, OS/2, and, of course, Windows NT. The components that make this possible are the environmental subsystems.

The NT Executive components that run in the Kernel layer are discussed in the next section. The Kernel layer protects the hardware from the User layer. That is, applications running in the User layer do not have direct access to the hardware. This is why certain Windows 3.1 and DOS applications that access hardware directly (such as games) do not run in NT.

This interaction between layers in NT is different from other operating systems. In DOS, for instance, programs are monolithic applications. Once you run a program in DOS, you typically cannot do anything else until that program ends. If the program has a problem and halts, the whole system stops with it, forcing you to completely reboot the system. Perhaps the program tried to illegally access a reserved memory area or even tried to write over the operating system. Again, your system will halt and possibly get corrupted. The same problem applies to Windows 3.1. Windows 3.1 should not be called an operating system because it's instead a graphical shell that runs on top of DOS. Again, if a Win16 application (we call a Windows 3.1 application a Win16 application from now on) illegally accesses a memory address, you will encounter a General Protection Fault (GPF). Although you can perhaps recover from this and return to work, more often than not you have to reboot the system.

One of the problems with the DOS architecture is the way system calls are made. Operating components were not designed to support concurrent calls, and if one of the system components fails, it brings down the rest of the OS with it.

Now that you know the basic architecture layout of Windows NT, it's time to move on to a detailed discussion of the internal components of the operating system. This understanding is key to determining what components could affect performance if the system is not configured correctly.

NT Executive Components

The Windows NT Executive is the name for a number of subsystems and components of the operating system that execute in the Kernel mode. The main role of the NT Executive is to provide a set of fundamental operating system functions that define a common interface. Some of the functions provided by the NT Executive include process and thread management, I/O, security, memory management, and interprocess communication. The NT Executive components play an important role in NT and consist of the following:

- Virtual Memory Manager (VMM)
- Process Manager
- Object Manager
- Security Reference Monitor
- Local Procedure Call Facility
- I/O Manager
- Hardware Abstraction Layer (HAL)
- Microkernel

When discussing optimization, we don't need to cover all of these components. We are interested in the VMM, Process Manager, Object Manager, and Microkernel. The other components are, of course, important to the operation of the operating system; however, in the context of performance and optimization, the four components mentioned are the key players. The following sections explain these NT Executive components in brief.

Virtual Memory Manager

The Virtual Memory Manager (VMM) is an interesting component. When launching a Win32 application, the VMM allocates 4GB of virtual space for that application. This memory is divided so that the operating system uses the upper 2GB and the application uses the lower 2GB. Because the actual physical memory cannot meet the full demands for every application to access the full 4GB range, the OS virtualizes the memory allocation using the physical RAM and a file, which resides on the hard drive.

> Here is an interesting fact: The VMM will try to reserve 4MB of physical memory for its own internal operations. If your system has 16MB RAM, you can immediately subtract 4MB for the VMM, leaving you with 12MB.

In Windows NT 5.0, it will be possible to allocate 1GB for the operating system and 3GB for the application. Microsoft is making this enhancement because applications are getting larger and more room is needed. This feature is also available in Windows NT 4.0 and Service Pack 3.

You can resolve many memory performance issues by adding more RAM. Unlike Windows 3.1 and even Windows 95, where adding more RAM does not dramatically improve performance, Windows NT uses all the RAM that you give it. As you can see from Figure 1.2, Windows 95 uses memory effectively until the RAM reaches about 24MB. After that, the improvement curve drops. In contrast, in Windows NT, the performance curve keeps improving as more RAM is added.

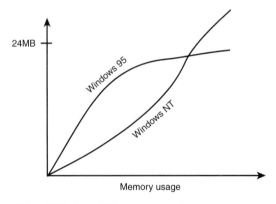

Figure 1.2 Windows 95 and Windows NT memory performance.

Figure 1.3 illustrates the layout of how the VMM interacts with the pagefile.

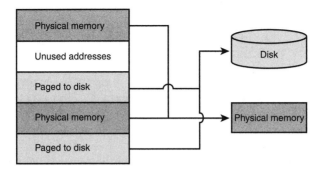

Figure 1.3 VMM interaction with the pagefile.

Windows NT uses a virtual memory pagefile called PAGEFILE.SYS. This file is automatically created by Windows NT during installation, and by default, it is located in the root directory of the drive it is on. The placement of the pagefile and the number of pagefiles on the system affect memory performance. In addition, because the pagefile resides on the hard drive, the drive performance also affects memory performance.

Process Manager

The Process Manager is responsible for preparing the environment and associated resources when a new process is created and then deleting the process from memory when the process terminates. The Process Manager initializes the process's address space with the executable program. The process's address space includes the heap, stack, and code segment. The Object Manager will then create a handle for the process. This handle is important because you can use it to get information about the program. Each process also has at least one thread of execution. A thread is a path of execution through a process. The process will die when that initial thread terminates. With a multithreaded operating system such as NT, a process can have more than thread. The Process Manager is also responsible for the creation and termination of threads.

Object Manager

The Object Manager is responsible for obtaining and maintaining handles to objects in the system. The Object Manager works closely with the Security Reference Monitor to control access to these objects. Objects in the NT system include shareable resources, which consist of processes, threads, files, and shared memory.

I/O Manager

The Input/Output Manager is responsible for servicing I/O requests to the hardware from other subsystem components. The I/O Manager is really a driver packet request dispatcher. The I/O Manager is not responsible for the actual I/O processing, but it creates a request packet that represents the actual I/O operation and then passes this packet to the appropriate driver. Once the I/O operation is complete, the I/O Manager disposes of the packet.

The I/O Manager defines a model around which all drivers are designed. The model calls for all NT drivers to be portable and written in a high-level language. That is, drivers in NT are typically written in C and not in Assembly language as are most drivers in Windows 3.1 and Windows 95. These NT drivers are designed to require few or no changes to make them work on other processor platforms.

With respect to performance, the I/O system can be implemented using asynchronous I/O. Before defining asynchronous I/O, let's instead define synchronous I/O. With synchronous I/O, when an I/O service is called, the driver completes the operation (such as a data transfer) and returns a status code to the program. The return of a status code indicates that the I/O operation is completed before control is returned to the caller application.

Asynchronous I/O operations, on the other hand, allow an application to issue the I/O request and continue executing while the device driver performs the operation. Asynchronous operations can significantly improve an application's execution speed. In fact, most of the native NT services are asynchronous by default. This default feature gives the I/O system the maximum flexibility to perform other tasks while slower drivers perform I/O operations. Other drivers written by hardware vendors to support their devices may be synchronous drivers. Using such drivers can cause performance problems because the execution of the rest of the driver code is suspended until the pending driver operation is completed and the status code is returned.

Microkernel

The Microkernel is the heart of the operating system. This component manages all the system kernel objects and threads. NT is a multithreading operating system, and the system threads and services are managed and controlled in the Microkernel. The Microkernel is brought into memory and does not participate in the paging scheme as do other applications. That is, it cannot be paged out of memory. Because NT is an SMP operating system, this architecture enables the system to run kernel threads on any available processor. SMP operating systems share the workload equally. SMP operating systems can execute both kernel (system) or user (application) threads. Asymmetrical systems, on the other hand, use one processor for kernel threads and the other processors for application threads.

The kernel (system) threads have higher priority than application threads. This is good because you would not want an application to completely overpower the operating system. A crucial component of the Microkernel is the Dispatcher. The Dispatcher is responsible for thread management. The Dispatcher uses a priority scheme to determine the order in which the threads should execute. The Dispatcher schedules threads in order of priority. If a thread with lower priority is executing and the thread with higher priority appears, the system will preempt the lower priority thread and execute the higher priority thread.

This thread-scheduling mechanism is implemented using a thread dispatcher database. This database is a list of all threads waiting to execute. On a multiple-processor system, the database also includes which processor was executing the thread at the time it was preempted.

The NT View of System Resources

It is important to think about how NT views its resources. These resources consist of the memory, the processor, the disk, the network, and the I/O bus architecture. Other resources, such as video card performance, are important to the effective operation of a Windows NT system; however, these basic four resources form the foundation for any NT system, regardless of whether it is an NT Workstation or NT Server. When you want the best performance out of your NT system, you will look at these four resources first. The question is always "Which one of these resources should I look to optimize first?" The answer lies in understanding what each component does and how it relates to the role of the system. That is, what is your system going to be doing? Is it running many applications? Is it validating user logons? Will it accept client print jobs?

Optimization is also the art of alleviating resource bottlenecks. A bottleneck is when a resource takes up most of the time performing a function. When a resource spends a lot of time doing a particular task, it usually does not give the other resources time to perform their duties. The sections that follow discuss each of these resources in detail to help you get a better understanding on how they work and how they interact with each other.

Memory Resources

Memory is a crucial resource component in the NT environment. Memory is needed not only by the running applications, but also by the operating system. When an application is executed, the application is loaded into memory and allocated a certain amount of physical address space. The entire program does not reside in memory, only a portion of it. The rest remains on the hard drive in a file called PAGEFILE.SYS.

When the program executes, the entire program is not loaded in memory, just a portion. When the information the program needs is not in memory, the OS must "page" and get the information from the hard disk. This process is called *demand paging*. The more the system has to page and get the data from the drive, the worse the performance is. In fact, the two types of paging are hard-page faults and soft-page faults. With hard-page faults, the OS must go to the hard drive for information. Soft-page faults, on the other hand, occur when the OS gets the information from memory, not from the disk.

Hard-page faults have a worse impact on performance than soft-page faults. Excessive paging, especially with hard-page faults, is bad. The goal when optimizing memory performance is to minimize paging as much as possible.

The earlier section on the Virtual Memory Manager touched briefly on its general characteristics and its relation to the pagefile. The virtual memory mechanisms define the way the VMM translates virtual addresses into physical addresses and more importantly, how it brings these pages into physical memory. Three policies define how and when paging is performed: fetch, placement, and replacement.

A fetch policy determines when the VMM brings a page from disk into memory. In some cases, the fetch policy loads the pages a process will need before they are needed. On the other hand, demand paging policies load a page into physical memory only when a page fault occurs.

Placement policies determine where in physical memory to put the virtual page. If the physical memory is full at the time the page fault occurs, the replacement policy determines which virtual page must be deleted from memory to make room for the new page.

> When a page replacement is required, the oldest page in the working set is moved to the paging file to make room for the new page. Because the replacement scheme is only applied to the working set of the current process, other processes are guaranteed that their pages will not be replaced by other processes.

Again, the main goal for performance is to minimize paging. NT attempts to keep the number of page faults low by giving each process enough pages in its working set to avoid excessive paging. NT also automatically trims the processes' working sets so that excess or unused pages are available for other processes.

CPU Resources

A processor can execute one instruction at one time. These instructions are the instructions of the application, which when executed, are transferred from the hard disk to memory and then to the central processing unit (CPU) for execution. One of the benefits of NT is that it can support more than one processor or CPU. NT is, in fact, a Symmetrical Multiprocessing (SMP) System. The operating system can run on any free processor or on all processors at the same time while sharing the same physical memory.

On a single processor system, multitasking and multiprocessing is achieved by switching quickly between the tasks. True multitasking (and multithreading) can be achieved by adding more processors. In this mode, each processor can truly perform different tasks at the same time. Windows NT can run both operating system code and user application code on any available processors.

The current version of Windows NT Workstation (version 4.0) supports two processors, and the NT Server product supports up to four processors. Each processor can have more than one cache memory. In fact, each processor can have what is called a Second-Level cache. Caches keep the most recent information the processor has used. Access between the cache and the processor is much faster than if the information is stored in RAM. A Second-Level cache (L2) is usually an external cache, depending on the architecture of the processor. Although a First-Level cache requires one processor cycle to retrieve data, L2 cache requires two cycles.

The type (and speed) of the processor is also a concern when you optimize the system. The processing speed is the speed at which the processor works internally to communicate with other external components. Processing speed is determined by the processor clock speed and the number of instructions the processor can handle on average per clock cycle. NT runs on different processor types, the most common of which is the Intel chipset that is known as a Complex Instruction Set Computer (CISC) architecture. NT can also run on Reduced Instruction Set Computer (RISC) machines. Because of the reduced number of instructions required in a RISC machine, RISC processors run at increased clock speeds and can achieve very fast execution times. RISC systems are typically more expensive than CISC systems, making the cost prohibitive for many companies.

Hard Disk Resources

Windows NT supports a variety of disk subsystems, each of which has benefits and drawbacks. The driver technology affects system performance, and depending on the tasks your NT system will perform, you should closely consider the disk architecture.

Some of the disk subsystems available include IDE (Integrated Drive Electronics), EIDE (Enhanced IDE), and SCSI (Small Computer System Interface).

> You should also remember that the disk performance does affect other NT components, including the Virtual Memory Manager. Remember that the PAGEFILE.SYS resides on the disk, and when the system needs to page, it gets the information from the hard drive.

Windows NT supports various file systems, including the file allocation table (FAT) file system, the high-performance file system (HPFS) from the OS/2 world, and the new file system called NTFS, which stands for NT file system. NTFS adds the following features:

- Recoverable file system
- Support for large volumes and files (17 billion GB)
- File security
- Fault-tolerant drivers for NT Server
- Built-in file and folder compression

The use of the file system type also affects the performance.

Network Resources

Networking is built in to Windows NT, which includes a basic peer-to-peer network server that communicates using the Server Message Block (SMB) protocol. This SMB protocol is what makes NT compatible with the old Microsoft Network and LAN Manager. As with many other operating systems, NT is designed to follow the Open Systems Interconnect (OSI) seven-layer model. Chapter 4, "Determining System Performance Objectives," discusses more on the specifics of each layer.

You should be familiar with two components of the NT networking architecture: the network redirector and the network server.

The redirector provides the facilities for one NT machine to access other resources on other machines on the network. The Windows NT redirector, for instance, can access remote files and printers. Because the redirector uses the SMB protocol, it is completely compliant with DOS, Windows, and even OS/2 systems. You can think of the redirector components as the "client" side of the client/server architecture. This means that as the client, the redirector wants to connect to a server resource somewhere on the network.

The network server is also compliant with the SMB protocol. You can think of the network server as the "server" side of the client/server architecture. This means that the network server is responsible for accepting and processing requests from client machines. Because NT is SMB-compliant, it can accept requests not only from other Windows NT systems, but also from other systems running LAN Manager software.

To communicate with different types of network systems, NT needs to allow for the installation and use of different transport protocols. In Windows NT, transport protocols are implemented as drivers. To avoid the problem of letting a particular transport protocol know which type of input the protocol driver expects, NT implements what is called a transport driver interface (TDI). TDI is a single programming interface that redirectors and other high-level network drivers use. It is the TDI that allows redirectors and network servers to be independent from the transport layer of the OSI model.

I/O Bus Architecture

When an application is loaded and running, the program will more than likely need to make some type of request to either get or receive data from a peripheral. In fact, this requirement exists even before the program runs. When a program executes, the operating system must first get the program from the hard drive. Part of the program is then transferred from the disk (or whatever media the program resides in). Most Intel-based systems provide the option of installing interface cards into different bus types. The system contains a bus controller that is responsible for servicing the request to and from the peripheral device.

The I/O architecture plays an important role in system optimization. Regardless of how much memory you have or how fast your processor is, if the data is moving to the peripheral at a slow rate, that will become your bottleneck.

Intel systems provide an 8-bit, 16-bit, or 32-bit bus. Obviously, the 32-bit bus is the ideal implementation. The slower of the available bus architectures is the ISA (Industry Standard Architecture) bus. The ISA bus has a transfer rate of 5MB/sec. ISA includes both a 8-bit and 16-bit I/O bus. A Peripheral Component Interconnect (PCI) bus, on the other hand, is a 32-bit bus, which means that it can address the full 4GB. The PCI bus is also a 133MB/sec bus, which is a significant improvement from the ISA bus architecture.

Be on the lookout for a faster PCI bus architecture. Currently, developers are working on a new PCI bus that will increase the speed to 166MB/sec.

Summary

To understand the available choices for optimizing the system, it is important to know the NT architecture. NT is installed on a computer system, and you have many choices for various computer system resources, such as memory, processor, hard disk, network, and I/O bus architecture.

Windows NT was designed with an eye toward modularity and robustness. Unfortunately, NT was also designed with backward compatibility in mind, which means it carries all the excess baggage necessary to run existing DOS and 16-bit Windows applications.

Subsequent chapters in this book address in detail optimization of the Windows NT system. This first chapter prepared you or refreshed your memory about the internal workings of NT. You will see how these NT features can sometimes adversely affect NT performance. Luckily, you can make changes to the NT system to overcome these deficiencies and make NT work as the system it was intended to be.

Using the Performance Monitor

This chapter covers the following topics:

- **The Performance Monitor.** Introduction to the Performance Monitor and the capabilities it provides.

- **Performance Monitor Objects.** A detailed description of PM objects and what information they provide.

- **Performance Monitor Instances and Counters.** A detailed description of PM counters and how you can use them to collect resource information.

- **Performance Monitor Interface.** Detailed information on the various ways to use the PM to view information.

- **Performance Monitor Service.** Information on how to use the Performance Monitor to collect data even while the user is logged off.

- **Issues with Using the Performance Monitor.** Supplemental information on how the Performance Monitor works. Also tips and tricks on using the Performance Monitor.

A user in your organization is complaining that his NT system is not performing as well as he thinks it should be. You ask him such questions as "What sort of performance problems are you experiencing? What are you doing when experiencing performance problems? What do you mean when you say the system is running slow?" Your job is to determine what the system is doing and what is causing the performance degradation.

Where do you begin? You should begin by collecting information about the system. This is analogous to going to a doctor for a checkup because you are experiencing health problems. The doctor takes measurements of various body components and records them. Perhaps the doctor takes your temperature, blood pressure, blood cell count, and so on. All of this information gives the doctor a look at what your system is doing. These tools provide the doctor with an "inside" view of your body. You need to do the same thing for your system.

To "see" how well (or how poorly) your NT system is operating, you need a way to "look" inside the operating system and take some measurements of different components. The more data you have to work with, the better your diagnosis will be. The Performance Monitor is the basic tool of choice available for looking at the internal performance of the NT system. The Performance Monitor works by looking at what we call NT objects. These objects can provide detailed information on the system.

Before jumping into the finer details of the Performance Monitor, you should gain an understanding of NT objects and how they relate to monitoring performance. Chapter 1, "Understanding Windows NT Architecture," covered the main resource objects that you should consider when optimizing NT: memory, processor, disk, and network. These objects are not, however, the only resource objects available. Other resource objects include threads, servers, and process objects. (See Appendix A, "Performance Monitor Counters," for a complete list of Performance Monitor objects.) Depending on the particular optimization task you face, you need to look specifically at certain objects, just like a doctor looks at your heart to get specific information about how it is performing.

> The NT Kernel Executive component called the Object Manager is responsible for the management of NT resource objects.

Performance Monitor Objects

The Performance Monitor defines two types of objects:

- **Core objects.** Core objects are those built into Windows NT. Examples of core objects include the memory, the processor, and the logical disk objects.

- **Extended objects.** You sometimes install extended objects when you add services or programs to Windows NT. For instance, when you install the Network Monitor Agent and Tools, several network extended objects are added.

The following list shows the Windows NT core monitoring objects, which include the base resource objects discussed in Chapter 1, as well as the remaining core objects:

- **Cache object.** The Cache object type manages memory for access to files. This is also known as File System Cache or simply System Cache.

- **LogicalDisk object.** This object provides disk partition data and other counters of disk space.

- **Memory object.** This object includes counters to monitor both physical and virtual memory. The physical (or real) memory is allocated in pages. If virtual memory exceeds the real memory then paging will occur.

- **Objects object.** This object monitors certain system software objects and can be used to monitor or detect unnecessary use of computer resources.

- **Paging File object.** This object is used for the Virtual Memory Manager operations. The pagefile is the file used by the VMM, and it resides on the physical disk.
- **PhysicalDisk object.** This object refers to the hardware disk unit.
- **Process object.** This object represents a running program. A process has at least one thread of execution. Process objects are not schedulable entities.
- **Processor object.** This object refers to the central processing unit used to execute instructions.
- **Redirector object.** This object manages network connections to other computers.
- **System object.** The System object includes counters that represent the activity of all processors on the computer.
- **Thread object.** The Thread object is the basic object that executes instructions in a processor. A process has at least one thread. Threads are schedulable entities.

After you select the object that you want to investigate, you need to select a counter. The Performance Monitor counter offers you the ability to analyze in detail the actions and operations that affect the performance of the object selected. Counters are the measurable entity for the object. It is these counters that give you the measurement granularity you need. Not only are the objects important, but it is also important to know specifically what about those objects you want to monitor.

Case Study

You believe that the problem with the computer system is related to the fact that the system is running low on memory resources. Because memory resources are low, you suspect the system is paging more frequently. Because you suspect memory problems, you need to monitor the Memory object in the Performance Monitor. But monitoring the Memory object is not enough. You need to determine what it is that you want to specifically monitor about the memory object. One of the counters available for the Memory object is the Pages/sec counter. This counter provides a value for the amount of pages (that is, paging from memory to the disk) per second. Monitoring this Pages/sec counter gives you the granularity needed to pinpoint the potential problem.

You should be aware that to get an accurate picture of what is happening, you most likely need to monitor more than one object. Based on this scenario, you decide to monitor the memory object and, more specifically, how many times the system pages. Based on what you know about paging, you know that the hard disk is involved because the page file resides on the hard drive. You should probably monitor disk performance as well. Understanding the relationship between the different computer resources is crucial. This subject is covered in more detail in Chapter 4, "Determining System Performance Objectives."

Now that you understand the relationship between Performance Monitor objects and Performance Monitor counters, this next section covers the various types of counters and how you can use them.

Performance Monitor Counters

Windows NT defines two types of counters. One is the *rate* counter. The rate counter is basically a calculated number that requires at least two measurements. Most rate counters have a "percent" or "per second" in the name such as Pages/sec. The other type of counter is the *raw* counter. The raw counter displays the most recent measurement.

In Windows NT 4.0, the rate and raw counters have been replaced with the averaging and instantaneous counters, which are defined the Microsoft Windows NT 4.0 Resource Kit as follows:

- *Instantaneous* counters display the most recent measurement.

  For example, Process: Thread Count displays the number of threads found in the most recent measurement.

- *Averaging* counters, whose names include per second or percent, measure a value over time and display the average of the last two measurements. When you start these counters, you must wait for the second measurement to be taken before any values are displayed.

  For example, Memory: Pages/sec, shows the average number of memory pages in the last two reads during the second measured.

- *Difference* counters subtract the last measurement from the previous one and display the difference if it is positive.

As noted in the preceding list, Windows NT 4.0 defines a new type of counter called a *difference* counter that works by subtracting the last measurement of an object from the previous measurement. If the resulting difference between the two measurements is positive, the difference counter displays the number. If the resulting difference between the two measurements is negative, the difference counter displays a zero. The Performance Monitor does not by default include any difference counters. Other applications install difference counters, which you can then monitor within the Performance Monitor.

The last item regarding Performance Monitor counters that you should be familiar with is the instance value. If your system has more than one processor, more than one physical disk, or more than one network card, you can monitor each one independently. With the Performance Monitor, you can select which instance of the particular object you want to monitor (see Figure 2.1). When more than one object is available (two processors, two network cards, and so on), the first instance is displayed at instance 0, the second instance is instance 1, and so on.

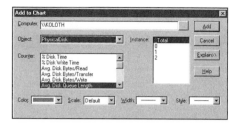

Figure 2.1 Selecting an object to monitor.

Suppose your server is experiencing hard disk performance problems. You have two physical disks installed, configured as drive C and drive D. It is possible to monitor each disk individually by selecting which instance of the physical disk you want to monitor. Then for each instance, you can select perhaps the % Disk Time counter, which provides the percentage of elapsed time that the selected disk drive is busy servicing read or write requests.

Performance Monitor Interface

The Performance Monitor ships with both NT Workstation and NT Server. The best reasons to use the Performance Monitor are not only to optimize performance, but also to analyze resource bottlenecks, troubleshoot system problems, and accomplish capacity planning. Capacity planning enables you to anticipate your system growth requirements based on your user's needs. Capacity planning helps you predict how new hardware and software will affect the overall performance.

The Performance Monitor interface is intuitive and user-friendly. You start the Performance Monitor by launching it from the Administrative Tools folder. The Performance Monitor provides four views or ways to look at the information: the Chart, Alert, Log, and Report views. You should choose the best view for your specific monitoring requirements. The following sections examine the four Performance Monitor views and determine the most appropriate view to use in a given scenario.

The Chart View

The Chart View provides a real-time look at the objects (and counters) you are monitoring. This view is also the default view when you start the Performance Monitor. The Chart View displays 100 data points at one time and enables you to chart many counters at once.

The two different display options available with the Chart View are the Graph and the Histogram Views. The Graph view (see Figure 2.2) is ideal for viewing the behavior of different counters. This is the default view. You can use the Histogram View (see Figure 2.3) to compare the same counters on the same or different machines.

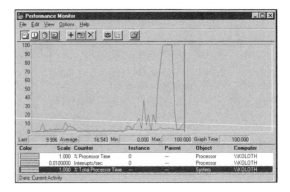

Figure 2.2 The default Graph view of the Performance Monitor Chart view.

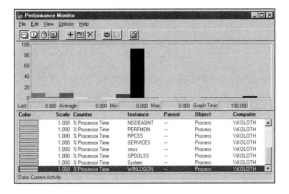

Figure 2.3 The Histogram view of the Performance Monitor Chart view.

Because you can use the Performance Monitor to chart objects from remote computers, you can set up the Chart view to track local and remote objects at the same time. This is particularly useful when you need to track the same object across different machines. Assume, for instance, that you are interested in tracking and comparing the processor usage of two machines. You can then compare the two values and see how they differ from each other.

Case Study

Suppose you have two similarly configured NT machines. One of the machines is exhibiting performance problems, which you believe are related to the processor. Using the Performance Monitor, you can select to monitor the Processor object on both machines at the same time and look at the % Processor Time counter. Figure 2.2 shows the two objects viewed in Graph view, and Figure 2.3 shows the objects in Histogram view.

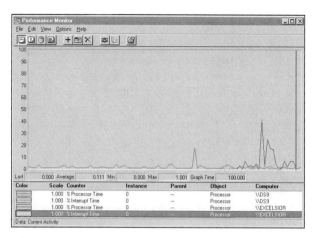

Figure 2.4 Monitoring processor performance for multiple machines in the Performance Monitor Graph view.

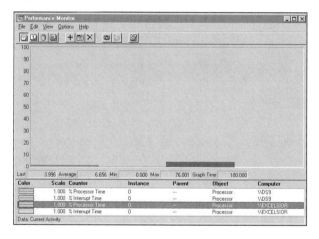

Figure 2.5 Monitoring processor performance for multiple machines in the Performance Monitor Histogram view.

By customizing the chart, you can monitor the current performance of the selected counter and instances. This is useful when you want to determine why a computer (or a running application) is slow. In some cases, the problem you are trying to find is intermittent, so the Chart view provides a real-time view of the NT system. More importantly, the Chart view enables you to discover the need for an increase in system capacity.

For example, say you want to find out how your system performs when a particular software package is executed. You want to know the impact on the processor (what percentage of the processor is used), memory (how many pages per second), and the disk (how many disk reads per second). You can determine the impact of the software by selecting the Processor, Memory, and LogicalDisk objects to monitor (and the appropriate counters and instances) and then looking at the change in values while the application program is running (see Figure 2.6). Perhaps the program is processor intensive. In this case, Figure 2.6 shows in the Chart view how the Memory Pages/sec counter increases while the application is running. It indicates that the program pages significantly during startup.

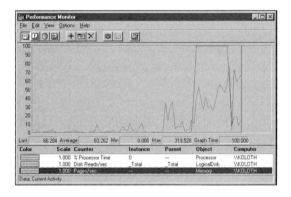

Figure 2.6 Tracking application impact on memory usage in the Chart view.

Because you can monitor several counters at the same time, you can select a different color, width, and style of the line for each counter. You can modify the scale for any displayed value so that it is easier to compare two values.

Too many counters make reading the Chart view difficult. It is better to open several copies of the Performance Monitor and select a few counters in each than to have one copy running and display all the counters displayed.

If you need many counters displayed, you can select an individual counter by clicking it on the bottom part of the display and pressing either the Backspace key or Ctrl+H. This highlights the currently selected counter in the chart as shown in Figure 2.7.

The Alert View

The Performance Monitor also provides the Alert View as shown in Figure 2.8.

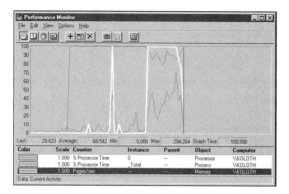

Figure 2.7 Highlighting a particular counter.

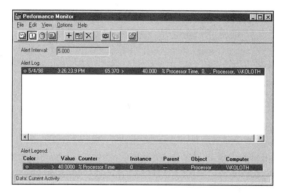

Figure 2.8 Performance Monitor Alert view.

The Performance Monitor Alert View enables you to continue working while the Performance Monitor tracks events and notifies you when a counter exceeds a given value. The user interface enables the notification to occur the first time a counter exceeds the given value or each time it exceeds the value.

An alert is an event that is triggered when a specific criterion is met. Assume, for example, that users have been complaining that the new client/server ordering system has been slow since the new upgrade. Because client/server applications tend to be processor intensive, you want the Performance Monitor to notify you when the processor is more than 80 percent busy. To set up this alert, you do the following:

1. Select the Processor object from the Alert View dialog box.

2. Select the % Processor Time as the counter to measure.

3. Enter the value for the criteria (in this case, 80).

4. Select the Alert If Over radio button.

As with the Chart View, the Alert view allows you to measure several counters at the same time. When a counter meets the trigger criteria, the date and time of the event are recorded. The log reaches a limit of 1000 recorded events before discarding the oldest one.

The Alert View also enables you to run a program when an alert condition happens. For instance, you can send an administrative alert or you can record the alert condition in the Event Viewer using the Resource Kit utility LOGEVENT.EXE. When the event occurs, you can specify that the program run every time or just the first time that the event occurs.

> LOGEVENT.EXE is a utility that allows you to record an event in the Windows NT event log and view it using the Event Viewer.

Unfortunately, you cannot set alerts on two conditions of the same counter for the same instance. This means that you cannot set an alert to be triggered when the % Processor Time exceeds 90 percent and set another alert for when the % Processor Time falls below 10 percent. In addition, you cannot set an alert on more than one instance of an object with the same name. If two processes with the same name are running (such as two copies of MS Word), you can only set an alert for the first instance of the process. Although both instances of MS Word appear in the Instances box, only the data collected from the first instance will trigger the alert.

The Log View

Performance Monitor provides the Log View for long-term collection of system data. You can use the Performance Monitor to log the objects that you want to a file on the hard disk. This log file is useful because you can reopen it at a later time on the same machine or on another machine. This logging feature is particularly useful when you need to diagnose problems from several computers. You can set up the Log view on these machines and then have the users send you the log files for you to analyze at your machine. Figure 2.9 shows the Log view in Performance Monitor.

With the Log View, you select the objects that you want to log, but you cannot select what counters or instances to monitor. With the Log View, it is all or nothing. You can only select which counter and instance to monitor when examining the data from the log file. Also, when reopening the log file, you can reopen it as a Chart, Alert, Report, or even as another Log view. These log files can become more useful when you use bookmarks. You can add bookmarks to major points of interest so they are easy to find later.

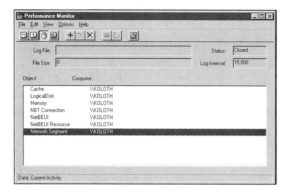

Figure 2.9 Performance Monitor Log view.

Case Study

Suppose a user in an organization is complaining that the system is running slow. More specifically, she complains that the disk access (reads and writes) seems to be taking a long time. Based on what you know now, you realize you need to collect information about the hard disk. In this case, the Chart and the Alert Views are not ideal because the Chart View requires you to constantly look at the chart for information.

The Alert View might work if you want to know when a particular threshold is met, but what you really want is to record the information for later analysis. Because you can collect data remotely, you can open the Performance Monitor on your machine and select the user's LogicalDisk (or perhaps PhysicalDisk) object in the Log view. Notice that all the counters and all the instances for the remote computer's LogicalDisk (or PhysicalDisk) are collected (see Figure 2.10).

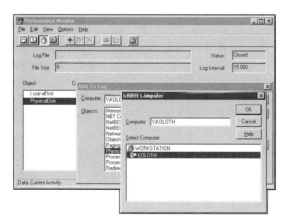

Figure 2.10 Selecting a remote computer to monitor in Log view.

The Log View provides not only the capability to log performance data but also the capability to take the log file and view the contents on any other NT computer with the Performance Monitor. This feature is ideal because you can have users send you their log files for offline analysis. When viewing the log file, you can "play" it back as a Chart, Alert, Report, or even as a Log View as shown in Figure 2.11.

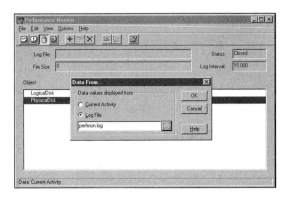

Figure 2.11 Viewing user log files in Performance Monitor.

One of the weak points of the Performance Monitor is that although you can log performance information to disk, it is not very useful beyond that. The Performance Monitor is not an analysis tool. In addition, you cannot print the information. What you can do is export the log file in a comma-separated (.CSV) or tab-separated (.TSV) file. Then, you can import the file to other applications such as Excel. Applications such as Excel give you more flexibility in analyzing the recorded data as you will discover in Appendix A.

In the previous case scenario, you used the Log View to capture the disk information from a remote computer. During the setup of the Log View, you enter the name and location of the log file. However, you have a potential problem. The Performance Monitor log file can become quite large. The size of the log file depends on the amount of objects you monitor, the log interval, and the duration of the log. With this information, you can predetermine the size of the log file. You can use the information provided in the Performance Monitor Log View to calculate the resulting size of the log. Instead of configuring the Log View to collect automatically, you need to configure it to collect the data manually. The specific steps for determining the size of the log file follow:

1. Select the Log View. Add the objects you want to log. Remember that you will be logging all the counters and instances related to this object (see Figure 2.12).

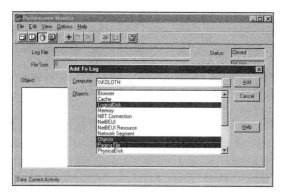

Figure 2.12 Adding objects to log.

2. Select the Options menu and select the Log menu item. From there, you can switch the update interval to manual update mode and enter the name of the log file (see Figure 2.13), and click Save.

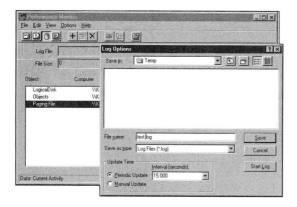

Figure 2.13 Entering the log file name and setting the update interval.

3. Click the "camera" toolbar button (see Figure 2.14). This will take a sample collection.

4. Record the size of the log file from the File Size text area after you take a sample collection. This is the amount of data required to collect the objects.

5. Click the camera again. Record the new file size. The difference between the second and the first value is the amount of space required for each update (see Figure 2.15).

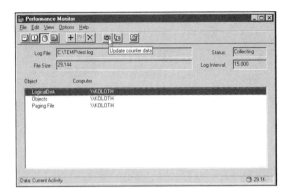

Figure 2.14 Taking a sample collection.

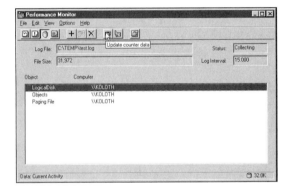

Figure 2.15 Determining the file size space required for each update.

6. Now, you can calculate the disk space requirements. If the size difference between the two collected is 8KB, for instance, every time data is collected the file size will increase by 8KB. Therefore, if you want to collect this data every minute for 24 hours, the log file size will be 8KB × 1 minute × 60 minutes/hr × 24 hours, or 11,520,000 bytes.

Based on these values, the disk space requirement calculations are as follows:

Sample Size = Initial Value–First Value

Number of Samples = Sample Interval × Length of Sample Period

Space Needed = Sample Size × Number of Samples

Bookmarks

One useful feature of the Log View is the capability to add bookmarks to the log as illustrated in Figure 2.16.

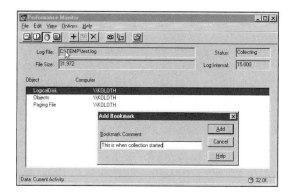

Figure 2.16 Adding bookmarks to log files.

The Performance Monitor automatically adds administrative bookmarks to the log, for instance, when logging starts. Bookmarks are ideal when looking for a particular event in the log file. Suppose you are logging the Processor, Memory, and Disk objects. While these objects are being logged to disk, you want to record in the log certain events as they occur so that when you look at the log file again, you will be able to find them quickly.

The Report View

The last view available in Performance Monitor is the Report View as shown in Figure 2.17. The Report View displays values in a report format. The Report View is ideal when you want to compare actual values and when you need to perform calculation and statistical analysis based on these numbers.

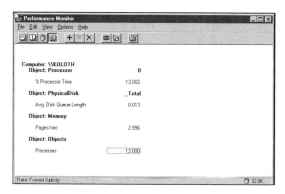

Figure 2.17 The Report view for Performance Monitor.

When is it best to use the Report View? One feature of this view is that it constantly displays changing counter and instance values for selected objects. Instead of a chart or a graph, the values appear in columns for each instance. If the counters you are monitoring are averaging counters, the report shows the average value during the Time Window interval. If the counters are instantaneous counters, the report shows the value at the end of the Time Window interval.

We just introduced a term called the Time Window interval. The *Time Window*, selected from the Time Window command from the Edit menu, enables you to view selected portions of data from your log (see Figure 2.18).

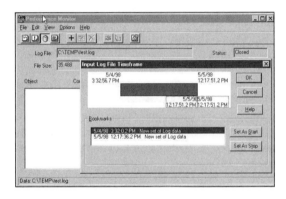

Figure 2.18 Viewing log file data in the Time Window.

The Time Window is only available when you are reviewing logged data, not when collecting in real time. When you change the Time Window interval, the Performance Monitor will recalculate all values, including minimum, maximum, and average values, to match the selected time interval. The Time Window is available in with the Chart, Alert, Log and Report Views. So how do you use this Time Window? Let's look at the following scenario.

Case Study

One of your users has been logging performance data for more than two days. The client/server ordering system may be the cause of the processor performance problems. In the scenario described earlier in the chapter, you used the Alert View to alert you when the Processor % Processor Time counter is more than 80 percent busy. Instead of using the Alert View, however, you decided to log the performance data and then replay it as an Alert View. In addition to the Processor Object, you are also logging the LogicalDisk and the Thread objects.

One problem with replaying the log file is that only those objects that were active at the time the log started are visible. If one of the objects is started later, you need to advance the Time Window to a time when the object was active. You can move the right and left slider tabs on the Time Window slider bar. Moving the Time Window start time past the time when the object in question started allows you to view that object's performance data.

The Time Window also enables you to limit the view of the log file to 100 points or less so that no data is lost. Remember, charts and reports of log files are limited to only 100 data points. In many cases, more than 100 points are collected. If 1,000 data points are collected, the Performance Monitor only displays every 10th point (1,000 data points/100 points). By narrowing the Time Window, you can make all the data points available.

In the Report view, you are only allowed to change the time interface and the default time interval to five seconds. This time allows you to read several values before the values change. In many cases, there is a short delay before the values appear. Dash lines instead of the actual numerical value indicate the delay. The Report view takes a snapshot of the counters at the end of two time intervals prior to displaying any data.

▨ The default value for the snapshot interval is 10 seconds.

The Performance Monitor Configuration Files

A nice feature of the Performance Monitor is the ability to save the monitoring settings in a configuration file. You select the Save Workplace menu option from the File menu. The file will have a .PMW extension, which stands for Performance Monitor Workplace. After you configure a Performance Monitor view the way you want, you can save it as a .PMW file, and when you want to use the configuration again, all you do is open the file in the Performance Monitor to see all the settings.

In addition to PMW files, you can also save individual view settings. You can save chart settings in .PMC files, Alert settings in .PMA files, Log settings in .PML files, and Report settings in .PMR files. You will see in the next section how the .PMW files are used in the Performance Monitor Service.

The Performance Monitor Service

Case Study

Users are complaining that it is taking them a long time to log in to the server in the morning. Of course, you need to collect some performance data on the server to determine what "stress" is being put on the server during login. You start the Performance Monitor and select some objects to monitor in Log view. Then, you proceed to log the system (because it is the server and you don't want users accessing the server).

You realize you have a problem. When a user logs out of NT, all the running applications stop. How do you use the Performance Monitor even if no user is logged in? You can use the Performance Monitor service.

To collect data in the background or when the user is not logged in, you use the Performance Monitor service. As with all standard Windows NT services, it runs in the background and it is configured from the Control Panel Services applet. The Performance Monitor service is available in the Windows NT Resource Kit. This service creates log files in the same format as the standard Performance Monitor. All you do is use the Performance Monitor to select the data to be collected, the collection frequency, and the name of the log file. After entering this criteria, you can start the Performance Monitor service to collect the data in the background.

Unlike the full data collection views available with the Performance Monitor, the Performance Monitor service can provide only Alert and Log views.

You establish the criteria for data logging in the Performance Monitor service by using a .PMW (or .PML file if you are logging data) file. The .PMW file contains the configuration of what objects you are going to monitor, the frequency of the logging, and the name of the log file to store the collected data.

You start the Performance Monitor service from the DATALOG.EXE program. Unlike the regular Performance Monitor, the Performance Monitor service has no direct graphical user interface. You control the service with the MONITOR.EXE utility. These two programs are available with the NT Resource Kit. You must copy both programs to the %SYSTEMROOT%\SYSTEM32 directory. You install the service by typing the following at the command prompt:

```
MONITOR \\Machinename SETUP
```

This command installs the service, although a few more things are required. As mentioned earlier, the service does not know what objects to collect and the name and location of the log file that will store the information. That is where the workspace file (.PMW) comes in. You use the Performance Monitor to select the objects to log, the sample interval, any alerts, and the log file location. Then, you save these settings to a workspace file, which has an extension of .PMW. You copy this file to the %SYSTEMROOT%\SYSTEM32 directory. To configure the service with the workspace file, you type the following at the command prompt:

```
MONITOR \\Machinename filename.pmw
```

Now, the service is configured to use the selected workspace file (and the objects, interval, and log file). To start the Monitor service, type the following:

```
MONITOR \\Machinename START
```

STANDARD LIFE

The objects being monitored are described in a workspace settings file, which is created in Performance Monitor. You use MONITOR.EXE to start, stop, and establish a particular workspace settings file describing the measurement. As an added bonus, you can execute MONITOR.EXE from a remote computer, so complete control of all your Performance Monitor services is available from any Windows NT computer on the network.

The following list shows the commands you can use in the MONITOR command line:

- **setup** sets up the Performance Monitor service Registry variables and installs the service in the Service Controller.

- **filename.pmw** establishes the file as the current workspace settings file.

- **start** starts the service.

- **stop** stops the service.

- **pause** sends a pause control to the service, and data collection is suspended.

- **continue** sends a continue control to the service, and data collection is resumed.

- **automatic** sets the service to start automatically when the computer starts.

- **manual** sets the service to require a manual start using the Control Panel Services applet or the MONITOR start command (this is the default).

- **disable** disables the service. Commands such as start are ignored. Reset this mode with automatic or manual.

You can enhance your control of the Performance Monitor service with the AT command. (For the AT command to operate, you must first start the Schedule service using the Control Panel Services applet.)

To get additional syntax information on the AT command, type AT /? from the command prompt.

Case Study

You have determined that the performance problem the users are experiencing occurs in the morning when all the users log in to the system. You want to automatically begin monitoring the system between specific times—let's say 8 and 10 a.m. when most of your users log in. Instead of manually starting the Performance Monitor logging, you can use the AT command to schedule the logging to start at 8:00 a.m. and stop at 10:00 a.m. The commands look like this:

```
AT    \\TARGET  8:00     /date:M,T,W,Th,F   "monitor START"
AT    \\TARGET  10:00    /date:M,T,W,Th,F   "monitor STOP"
```

The first command starts the Performance Monitor service (using the .PMW configuration file) at 8 a.m. and stops the service at 10 a.m. each weekday. At the end of the week, you will have a log of the week's login activity to interpret the information.

Remember that the Performance Monitor log files can become quite large, depending on the number of objects being monitored and the collection frequency. Make sure you have enough hard disk space available to store the file. Also, it is best not to create this log file on the computer being monitored. If the file is on the same computer, it can affect the data being measured.

Issues with Using the Performance Monitor

With the basics of the Performance Monitor behind us, let's look at some of the issues involved with using the Performance Monitor.

First of all, the Performance Monitor is just another application contending for processor time, and if the computer is busy, the Performance Monitor might be competing with higher priority threads for access to the processor and might not be capable of updating the counters at the interval selected. Obviously, using the Performance Monitor on the same system you want to monitor may introduce erroneous reading. This is why it is a good idea to run the Performance Monitor on another system and monitor a computer remotely.

It is also possible to start the Performance Monitor service remotely, as long as the remote system has the necessary files installed. Also, the service is forced to record the data on the drive of the machine being monitored.

It is also possible to trace a performance problem to several sources. In fact, one resource problem might be the result of problems in another resource. For instance, when memory is low, the system will begin to page more and move more data from the memory between the RAM and the physical disk. This action increases the measurement of the some of the disk counters, but it is obvious that the problem is related to a shortage of memory. This discrepancy is not really an issue with Performance Monitor per se, but an issue of how to properly interpret the data. Interpretation is covered in more detail in Chapter 4, "Determining System Performance Objectives."

As outlined earlier, many applications and vendors extend the Performance Monitor by developing extended objects. Vendors who provide extended objects (and counters) could development (and implement) them incorrectly, causing errors.

Summary

This chapter introduced the Performance Monitor. The Performance Monitor is a useful tool available with the Windows NT Server and Workstation products. This tool, as the name implies, is what you use to monitor the condition of your system. You select which component (object) of the system you want to monitor (for example, the processor) and then which instance and what counters (such as % Processor Time) to record.

To make analysis easier, you can view the data in four formats. The Chart view gives you a real-time view of the data collected as it arrives. You can examine the chart in two view: Graph and Histogram.

With the Alert view, you can have the Performance Monitor alert you when a certain condition is met. The Log view allows you to store the monitored information to a file, and you can look at the file later on any Windows NT machine. If you are just looking for numerical values, the Report view allows you to check the various counters' specific values, making it easy to compare similar counters on different machines.

Simulating System Bottlenecks

This chapter covers the following topics:

- **The Importance of Simulations.** This section stresses how simulating problem scenarios in your NT system can help with preventative troubleshooting and help you recognize when a real problem exists.

- **Hardware and Software Interaction.** To troubleshoot a problem in NT, you need to know how hardware and software interact. This section covers the components of a typical Intel-based system and the mechanics of how they work with one another.

- **Simulating Memory Shortages.** This section demonstrates how to simulate a memory bottleneck condition and how to isolate the specific memory problem.

- **Simulating CPU Activity.** This section discusses how to simulate CPU bottlenecks and how to isolate specific processor problems.

- **Simulating Disk Usage Conditions.** In an environment in which disk performance is crucial, it is important to test your hard drive system to determine how fast the drive media can transfer data.

- **Simulating Network Usage Conditions.** Windows NT in a network environment is subject to numerous sources of network traffic. This section details the types of network traffic and how to isolate specific network problems.

Whenever you have a problem to solve, you first try to understand the situation and then you try to change it. A step in the process of understanding and changing is experimentation. Of course, when you experiment, you use some type of scientific method. This means you record events, create controls, and run repeated and varying scenarios in an attempt to learn all that you can about a process, interaction, machine, being, or other curiosity. Computers are complex, and NT is no picnic to understand. On top of that, you have applications to worry about. This chapter is devoted to the subject of experimentation and the techniques of simulating loads and scenarios on Windows NT systems. Along the way, you will also receive some additional troubleshooting tips and bottleneck detection methods.

The Importance of Simulations

Simulations generally involve using techniques to create a certain situation in which you control all but one of the pieces. Creating this kind of situation and varying some parameters allow you to draw conclusions about the way NT, a service, or an application works. In addition, creating predictable simulations gives you the opportunity to zero in on the troublemaker in the system.

When you optimize an NT system, you need a way to simulate resource usage, shortage, and various other conditions. You can achieve these simulations in various ways, depending on exactly what condition you need to simulate and what results you expect. Typically, a real-world scenario could look something like the following case study.

Case Study

As a systems administrator, you must evaluate a new NT database program to be used by the corporate office. Part of your evaluation is to determine whether your current system configuration is enough to run this new program.

Beyond the usual "Do I have enough disk space to install the program?" question, you also face the question of how your system will respond with the new application running. Maybe you need more memory. Maybe you need more network bandwidth because it is a network program. The last thing you want to do is install the program and watch your network slow down to a screeching halt.

You need to run a methodical series of tests to see just how your system reacts to the new program. You will test resources individually, from memory to network, to determine the performance impact. In addition to running the test on the individual application, you also need to test the system while it is performing its normal, everyday duties.

Why more than one test? The system will usually behave differently under different circumstances. NT itself is constantly reconfiguring itself to optimize performance based on current conditions. Perhaps the application in this example works beautifully as long as the database queries don't generate results over 20KB. However, larger queries cause excessive delays in the data processing. This discrepancy might be due to the way the client side is producing the queries, the way the server database is constructed, or one of several database software parameters. Repeated trials will allow you to experiment and validate or reject each of these possibilities, or hypotheses.

This chapter examines how to simulate resource loads on the system and determine a few things: the impact the new load has on the system resources and how the resources are interrelated.

For instance, you will see how simulating a memory load could also affect the disk performance.

For many of these tests, you can use standard applications, as well as some utilities available in the Windows NT Resource Kit. To record the system response, you will use the Performance Monitor.

You might ask, "Why bother simulating resource bottlenecks?" The answer is quite simple: You cannot afford not to. You want to know how your system will react under pressure: "When I add those next 100 users, is the server going to crack, or does it still have more power left to handle the situation?" You should not wait until your NT system is in use before realizing that it will not handle the task it was implemented to perform. As a system administrator, it is your responsibility to make sure the system meets (and exceeds) the demands of your users. As this chapter discusses each resource bottleneck, you will learn about programs and techniques you can use to simulate resource bottlenecks.

Take a look at another real-life case study.

Case Study

While I was under contract with a large government organization, one of my job assignments was to determine how much load capacity the network server could handle after all 5,000 clients were using the network. The organization had built a small test environment using an NT Server and 10 NT Workstation clients. The question to answer was, "Is the NT server optimized to handle all 5,000 clients?" That is, "what is the impact on the network when all the users are logged in at the same time? What is the impact on the hard disk when users access shared files on the server? Does the server have enough disk capacity? When will we need more memory?"

These are all good and valid questions to answer. The organization did not want to go "live" without some assurances that the system would meet expectations. They wanted a realistic test drive. Without making 5,000 client connections available, how do you simulate such an environment?

The goal of this chapter is to explain how you can simulate memory bottlenecks for each resource and understand how the system responds to such problems. More important, you will also learn to use the Performance Monitor, as well as other tools, to not only track the system performance, but to also provide a different picture of what is happening in the system.

Hardware and Software Interaction

Before launching into simulations of the individual resources, let's examine briefly how a computer is divided into a series of components that work together to provide services to the user's applications. Figure 3.1 shows the layout of a typical Intel-based computer system.

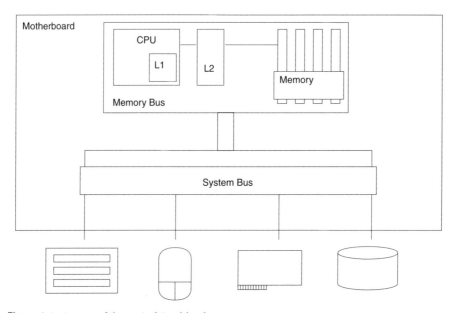

Figure 3.1 Layout of the typical Intel hardware computer system.

At the heart of the system is a central processing unit (CPU). This processor has its own Level-1 cache memory and, in addition, could have a secondary Level-2 cache. In Windows NT, the system can have more than one processor, each with its own Level-1 or Level-2 cache memory. All of the processors, however, share the same physical RAM. The RAM and the CPU communicate via a high-speed 32-bit bus.

Looking Ahead

Later in Chapter 6, "Optimizing CPU Performance," you will take a closer look at the CPU architecture. You will see how the architecture of the CPU depends on not only the manufacturer, such as Intel or AMD, but also the model. For example, the memory bus and cache structure of a Pentium Pro is different from that of a Pentium II. Also, Chapter 6 has a discussion on the newer technologies that are emerging. Technologies such as SDRAM and 100MHz memory bus systems will further enhance processor performance.

Connected to this 32-bit bus is an I/O controller that is responsible for the interface of the CPU to the attached peripherals. Possible peripherals connected in this manner include hard disks, CD-ROMs, network cards, mice, keyboards, and so on. Many of these devices are connected directly to the motherboard, but many require additional interface cards, such as a SCSI scanner device, which requires a SCSI card.

In the Intel platform architecture, the I/O bus architecture can be 8-bit, 16-bit, or 32-bit. This architecture depends on the type of I/O bus that was built in to the PC. Bus specifications include ISA, EISA, and PCI. The ISA is the oldest of the technologies and typically supports the 8-bit and 16-bit ranges. The EISA is a 32-bit functionality that isn't frequently used anymore. PCI is common and is usually built in to a system to run at 32-bit; however, the specification and technology can run at 64-bit. Examples of the interface cards that support these bus topologies are ISA, EISA, and PCI.

The CPU, memory, disks, peripherals, and I/O buses all work together to allow applications to load and run. If you look at a typical situation in which the user double-clicks an application, this is what happens:

1. The application resides on the hard disk. The mouse click informs the operating system that a click has occurred, and the OS interprets the client as a command to launch the application.

2. The application is executed. This means that the Process Manager (see Chapter 1, "Understanding Windows NT Architecture") allocates the resources necessary to run the application.

3. The Virtual Memory Manager (VMM) provides the application with up to 4GB of virtual memory to store code and data in memory. Part of the program instructions will reside in physical RAM, while the rest stay on the hard disk.

4. Parts of the program, which reside on the physical disk, are moved into memory via the I/O bus.

5. The instructions are moved from RAM to the CPU via the 32-bit bus. Instructions are stored in either the Level-1 or Level-2 cache (if present).

6. As the program executes, the VMM will return to the hard disk to load those parts not available in memory. The request will travel via the I/O controller to the hard disk device and back up to the memory.

7. The program instructions, executed by the processor, will contain instructions to do a variety of things such as draw text on the screen, write data to the network, read data from a floppy, and so on.

8. These requests will again travel through the I/O controller to the appropriate peripheral device.

The resource bottleneck can occur at any or all of these stages. The major areas that this book covers are memory, processor, disk, and network resource bottlenecks.

Keep in mind that in these eight stages, the I/O bus architecture plays an important role in system performance, especially when there is a lot of peripheral device activity. It does not matter how fast the processor is or how much memory you have. If the I/O bus speed is only 8-bit, you are effectively trying to push a lot of fast data through a slow, narrow pipe.

Recall that a component that is causing a bottleneck on a system is best defined as the component that cannot meet the demands that the rest of the system places on it. It may or may not be the slowest component on the system.

Simulating Memory Shortages

A memory shortage is probably the most common cause of performance problems. As you recall from Chapter 2, "Using the Performance Monitor," as memory resources decrease, the system begins to page more to the hard disk and the running applications have less memory to share. Recall that *paging out* is the process of moving *unused* information from physical RAM to a file on the hard drive called, appropriately enough, the pagefile. Also, *paging in*, or simply *paging* as I call it, is the process of bringing information not found in the appropriate spot in physical RAM from the pagefile or another location in RAM. Clearly, paging is an indication of a memory shortage or strain. As more applications run, the availability of memory resources is reduced. In turn, each running application gets a smaller allocation of physical memory. NT will fight to reduce the running application's allocation of memory, trimming the fat so to speak as memory runs into leaner times.

It is easy to simulate a memory bottleneck. Most of the time, you can use everyday applications such as Word or PowerPoint. Just start them all at once and watch the fireworks. Most of these applications are memory intensive, especially when they first launch, so they can work for you in a pinch if you do not have other tools available. However, they will not provide "stable" memory usage. During simulations, the name of the game is control. In any scientific methodology for testing and analysis, you must control as many of the variables as possible. Simply running an application certainly makes an effect on memory. However, for a true simulation, you want a application that can use memory in predictable blocks. Also, you want to be able to adjust the application's consumption of memory.

Some applications are better at managing memory than others. Many programs, however, have *memory leaks*, meaning they allocate memory but are not diligent at freeing memory when it is no longer used. The memory leak problem was more apparent in Windows 3.1 and Windows for Workgroups 3.11. These environments were not good at deallocating unused memory. For instance, under Windows 3.1, for an application such as Word you might notice 80 percent free resources available before starting and only 78 percent free resources available upon closing. After a while, that count gets lower and lower until you are forced to reboot the system. Windows NT, fortunately, does a pretty decent job of automatically freeing unused memory.

As an application uses more memory, other programs or the OS have less memory to use, thus creating a severe memory shortage. Other programs, although not leaking memory, are basically *fat*. They acquire and continue to use large amounts of memory while they are running but appropriately release memory when they terminate. Sometimes these memory-hungry programs can use more memory as more users start the application. This type of memory hoarding is something you want to watch.

Windows NT is efficient with memory because when an application allocates memory, the OS returns a *handle* to the memory, and NT keeps a count of how many handles have been allocated as well as the owner of each handle. If an application closes but does not free the memory it allocated, the handle to the memory becomes invalid, which means that the handle does not have a process associated with it. NT recognizes this and frees the memory in most cases. That is not to say that NT does not have programs that cause memory leaks, but they are less common than in previous versions of Microsoft operating systems.

Memory management has several other related components in the protected memory model used by NT. Applications are not permitted to interfere with other applications' memory address spaces. One of the C2 Certification rules is that all memory should be zeroed out (cleared) prior to being allocated to another application. C2 Certification is a security rating used by the U.S. government when evaluating the situations and types of data that can be kept on computer systems.

Memory Performance Monitoring Tools

Now you have an idea of the types of memory problems that might occur. You must become familiar with a few monitoring techniques to properly get a practical view of memory simulations. Several tools are reviewed here to give you a first look. Later, in Chapters 6–9, which discuss the optimization of the specific NT and computer components, you will get a more thorough description of the application of monitoring techniques.

Tracking Memory Allocation and Page Faults with PFMON

When looking at an application (or applications) that can cause memory bottlenecks or performance problems, you should be interested not only in how much memory the application utilizes, but also in how many page faults the application causes. A page fault is generated when a application asks NT for a piece of code or data out of physical RAM, but the information has been paged out to the pagefile. The system reacts to a page fault by retrieving the information from the pagefile and placing it in the location in physical RAM where the application expects to see it. There are two types of page faults:

■ **Hard page faults.** The resolution is done to the hard disk pagefile. The information sought could not be found in memory or the file system cache and thus had to be pulled from the pagefile. Disk access is clearly slower than memory access, so this process has a higher performance impact. Hard page faults are your chief concern when reviewing memory shortages.

■ **Soft page faults.** The resolution of the page is still in memory but not in the
location that the application expected. NT is constantly moving data around to
better manage the space. Prior to moving data out to the physical hard drive, the
data will pass through the file system cache. The file system cache is a section of
memory used for temporarily storing information before it goes to disk. If NT
can find the information here, it will move it to the proper location in physical
RAM where the application can use it. Also, when the data is being shared with
other applications, NT may move the information around to better optimize
memory. In either case, moving data around in physical RAM has a much lower
performance impact than pulling information from the hard drive. Most of the
discussions in this chapter do not consider soft page faults, although enormously
excessive soft page faults can still impact performance. Soft page faults are also an
indication of poor programming.

One way to look at how a particular application might cause page faults is to use
the Page Fault Monitor (PFMON) Resource Kit utility, which is a command-line
utility that accepts the arguments illustrated in Figure 3.2.

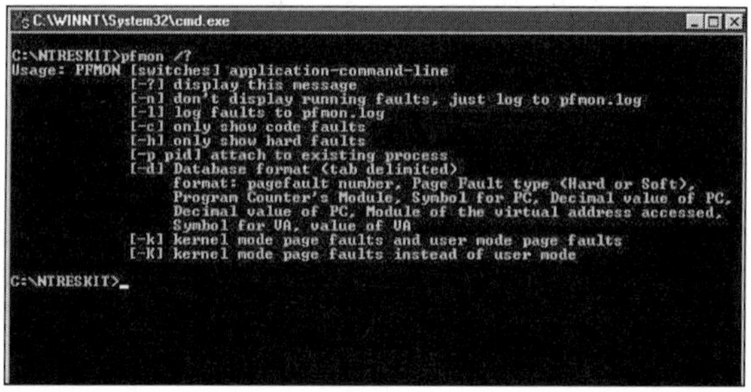

Figure 3.2 Page Fault Monitor arguments.

The following list provides some details on the PFMON command-line
arguments:

■ **-n** When PFMON is running, it displays page fault statistics and other information. This tag will suppress that information and route it to a file called
pfmon.log that is created in the directory from which you launched the
PFMON utility. Because this tool is a command-line argument that avoids
interactive displays, it is a candidate for running in the background. You can use
the NT scheduler to launch the utility when you have memory problems with
particular applications.

■ **-1** Normally, PFMON displays the information. If you want a record of what
occurred, you use this option.

- **-c** This shows only the code faults. Code faults are page faults that occur when an application makes a call to another DLL or section of code that is not loaded in physical RAM. These types of faults can give you an indication of whether the code is written poorly. Grouping disjointed functions in DLLs or segments of code can cause such behavior.

- **-h** Remember that hard page faults are the primary mark of a memory shortage. To filter the software page faults and only look at these troublesome hard page faults, use this -h argument.

- **-p [pid]** If you want to observe a running program, you can connect to it using the -p parameter. If you simply use PFMON [application], you can have PFMON launch the application for you. In this way, you get to see all the activity that the application produces. Sometimes, however, you will not want to see this activity. When an application starts, the flurry of activity that occurs is not typical of the rest of the application's behavior.

- **-d** This argument is exceptionally useful if you want to move the information into a database or spreadsheet for statistical analysis or simple charting. It will produce a tab-delimited log instead of the standard column format of the -l option.

- **-k** This argument will add kernel mode page faults and user mode page faults into the mix of statistics. You can see with more detail what sections are doing the most paging. If the user mode is doing more paging, the application's code or data is typically the issue. If the Kernel mode is producing more paging, you might have a problem with a DLL from a third party or an API call.

- **-K** This argument will focus the analysis of the PFMON utility on the Kernel mode operations that the application is executing.

One of the arguments is -p [pid]. This argument enables the utility to attach to a running process. The PID is the process ID that every running process is given. You can get a list of the PIDs for each running application by looking on the Processes tab of the Task Manager (see Figure 3.3) or by using another Resource Kit utility called TLIST (see Figure 3.4). After you have the PID for the process, you can use PFMON to monitor the page faults as well as other useful information. PFMON will list the function calls made by the program while running, display a list of the DLLs used by the program, and report a synopsis of the hard and soft page faults per DLL.

The process or application you want to monitor must be running (and have a PID) for PFMON to work. All 32-bit applications have PIDs; however, you have to watch out for those 16-bit applications. The 16-bit applications run in NTVDM.exe. The 16-bit applications do not each get a PID, but NTVDM.exe does. Thus, if you want to watch a 16-bit application, you must make sure that the application is running in its own memory space so that it is the only 16-bit application running in NTVDM.exe. This assurance is necessary for 16-bit Windows applications, but not actual DOS applications. Each DOS application will run in its own NTVDM.exe.

Figure 3.3 Examining process IDs on the Processes tab of the Task Manager.

Figure 3.4 Examining process IDs with the TLIST utility.

As an illustration of how you can use PFMON, look at an application such as Notepad and determine how many page faults it causes. The steps and figures that follow will guide you through the procedure of determining the page faults caused by Notepad.

1. Open Notepad. Notepad is available from the Accessories folder or by typing notepad from the Run command prompt (see Figure 3.5).

Figure 3.5 Opening Notepad from the Run command prompt.

2. Open a command prompt window. Type `tlist` and view the results. Record the PID value for `notepad.exe`. In this case, the PID value is 58 (see Figure 3.6).

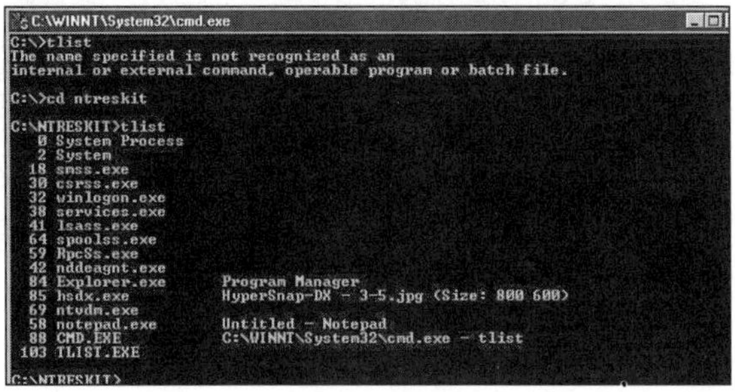

Figure 3.6 Obtaining the PID value for `notepad.exe`.

3. At the command prompt, type `PFMON -P` and use the PID number obtained in step 2. This enables PFMON to monitor the PID number for the Notepad application. You will notice some information being displayed in the command-prompt windows. This information is a real-time listing of the various function calls made to the DLLs that are loaded. The page fault types are listed next to the function calls.

4. Return to Notepad and type something (see Figure 3.7).

Figure 3.7 Generating some activity in Notepad results in various lines of code and functions being called.

5. Close Notepad, saving the information to a file on the drive. Note that PFMON will also terminate, giving you summary information, as illustrated in Figure 3.8.

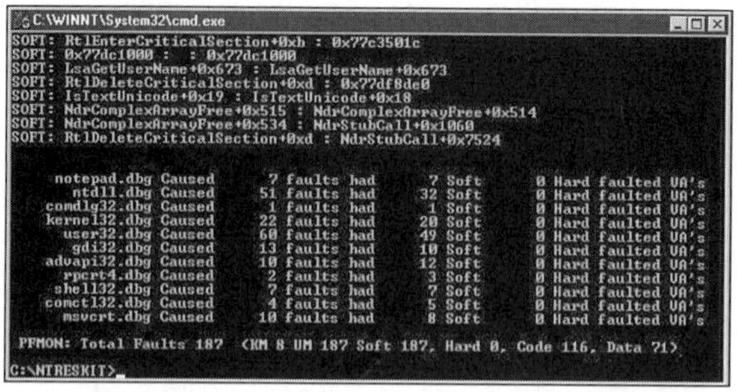

Figure 3.8 PFMON displays summary information after the application is closed. The process behind the PID ends.

Note the number of hard page faults compared to the number of soft page faults illustrated in Figure 3.8. Recall that the hard page faults are the troublesome ones. The soft page faults, although they still affect performance, are not anywhere near as detrimental as the hard page faults.

Tracking Memory Allocation and Page Faults with PMON and Task Manager

Another handy utility in the Windows NT Resource Kit is PMON. This command-line utility provides a good view of the memory allocation and page faults for all processes running (see Figure 3.9).

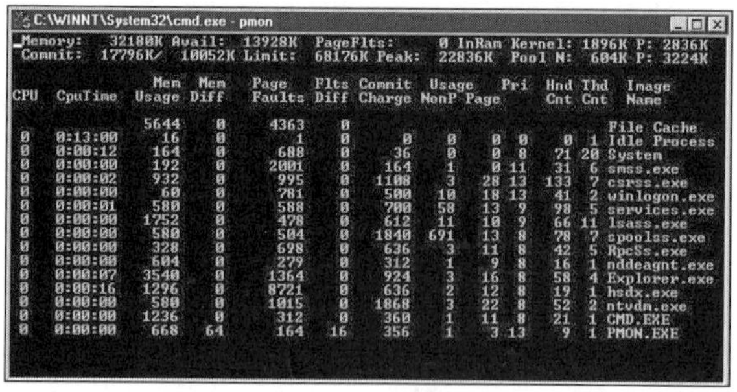

Figure 3.9 Tracking memory allocation and page faults with the PMON utility.

Notice in Figure 3.9 that the information provided is a total of the number of page faults (hard + soft) for each process, the thread count, and the amount of memory usage for both the pool-paged and the non-pool-paged memory. This tool offers the advantage of summary information for all processes on the system instead of providing the individual focus of the PFMON utility. However, it does not offer the details that PFMON does.

The same information provided by PMON is also available from the Task Manager. You can start the Task Manager in a couple of different ways—either by right-clicking the taskbar and selecting Task Manager or by pressing Ctrl+Alt+Delete and clicking the Task Manager button. Within Task Manager, select the View menu and the Select Columns option in order to select to view additional columns. Check the items you want to view (see Figure 3.10).

Figure 3.10   Tracking memory allocation and page faults with the Task Manager.

These tools are enough to get you started. Of course, the Performance Monitor is the best tool for the monitoring memory performance. That particular tool is covered in more detail throughout the book.

> I suggest that you return to this chapter to refresh your memory about how other techniques and tools you have learned might be applied to of simulating activity after reading this and the chapters on the optimization of the system components.

Now, you should be ready to begin to formulate some memory simulations.

Memory Simulation Tools and Techniques

Now that you have a couple of tools to use to watch what is going on with page faults and general memory activity, you can learn to use some other tools to actually generate the problems. In the sections that follow, you will learn about creating memory shortages, reducing programs to minimum memory allocations, and simulating a memory leak.

Each of the tools and techniques here have a specific purpose. However, be creative! Think through what a particular application or server component is doing with system resources, and combine tools and techniques to best approximate the behavior and control your experiment.

Reducing RAM to Simulate Memory Shortage

The first order of business is to create a somewhat predictable memory shortage. Several reasons you might attempt to do this are as follows:

■ You might want to see how a particular server configuration is behaving under a large memory load. You could either run a huge number of applications to create the load or actually fool NT into thinking that it does not have all the physical memory that is installed. This test is particularly useful when you want to correct your pagefile configuration.

■ You might want to see how a particular server application operates under a memory shortage. This will give you an idea of the attention that the developers of the application gave to memory consumption. Sometimes aggressive memory usage is unavoidable, but downright gluttony is an indication of potential problems. If the developers didn't deal with memory usage, you might face memory leaks.

■ You might want to reduce the size of the memory to reduce the size of the resulting memory dump generated from a blue screen. Although this is not really a simulation for memory shortage purposes, it is worth mentioning. When a blue screen error occurs and you have settings that dump the memory to a memory.dmp file, the contents of memory will be represented on disk. This arrangement is fine if you have only 32MB of RAM so that only 32MB is loaded into a pagefile and then transferred to a memory.dmp file. However, if you have 512MB of RAM, you end up needing a 512MB pagefile and an additional 512MB of space for the memory.dmp file. Telling NT that it has only 64MB of RAM will certainly alleviate the disk usage.

Okay, so how do you do it? To simulate a real shortage of memory, you'll run the program using less RAM. Instead of opening the computer case and removing RAM SIMMs, you can simulate less memory by editing the BOOT.INI file. The BOOT.INI file is a hidden, read-only file on the computer root directory of the C: drive, C:\BOOT.INI. This file controls the selections you have on the screen when you boot the system. Usually, you see Windows NT, Windows NT Base Video, and DOS. You can adjust the file and the command arguments to make NT ignore physical RAM and only use what you tell it to use. Create a new line in the BOOT.INI that is a copy of the normal NT boot. Then, add the command argument /MAXMEM= [amount of RAM] on the end of the line. Assuming your system has 64MB of RAM, reduce the RAM to only 16MB, as shown in Figure 3.11.

Figure 3.11 shows a new entry in the BOOT.INI file labeled LOWMEM OPTION, with the /MAXMEM value set to 16. Upon rebooting the system and selecting this new menu option, you will note that the amount of memory shown in the boot sequence is 16MB.

If you repeat the steps 1–5 from the previous example and compare the results, you will notice that the amount of page faults is higher. The system has less memory to work with, which forces more paging.

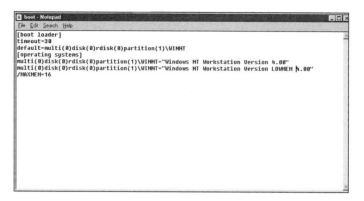

Figure 3.11 Simulating a memory shortage.

Windows NT Server 4.0 will become critically unstable if you restrict the amount of RAM to a number below 16MB. Because this is the lower limit of acceptable behavior, there is little value in testing below the 16MB boundary. On Windows NT Workstation 4.0, 12MB is possible—but you won't be happy with the performance, even for testing.

Finding the Minimum Memory Allocation

Suppose you want to find out the minimum amount of memory each application is going to take. The amount of memory that an application needs for its code and data is called the *working set*. When you push the application down to its lowest level, you get the minimum working set for the application. An NT Resource Kit utility called CLEARMEM.EXE is exceptionally adept at reducing the applications and services running on NT to their minimum working sets. You may be wondering about the value of knowing the minimum working sets for applications. Knowing the minimum working sets for applications provides you with a baseline for further analysis, subsequently enabling you to quickly identify memory-hogging applications.

Often in troubleshooting performance issues, it is difficult to tell exactly when you have a problem. You must first establish a reference point. The reference point is typically called the *baseline*. In this case, you are establishing a baseline for the applications. When you want to see how applications are responding to a memory shortage, you can compare the minimum working set size (represented in bytes) to the size of the working set in a simulation that creates a memory shortage.

If the minimum working set for a particular program is much larger than the others on the system, you might consider that program a little fat (or memory intensive). Programs can be large for several reasons, not all of them bad. Certainly, poor programming with little attention paid to memory efficiency can make a program bulky. However, in other cases, you might want more code and data loaded into memory for a specific reason.

Case Study

For example, say you are writing a piece of an application for a fuel company. The application is written for NT Server, which is interfaced with sensitive fluid pressure measurement probes. The application is built to dynamically adjust the flow of fluid through pipes to control the pressure in the pipes. The application must respond in real time to information from the probes. If the system does not respond quickly enough, the pressure in the pipes could damage the pumping equipment or even burst a pipe. In such a situation, your code must run in real-time mode or close to it. With such a single-minded task for the NT Server, you probably want to load and keep in memory the code for your application. This arrangement makes the program's minimum working set unusually large compared to normal programs; however, it also improves the performance of the application because all the components and functions are always in physical RAM.

You might also want to identify applications with memory leaks. Recall that a memory leak is a situation in which an application uses memory but fails to properly free the memory when it is done. You can find out which application has the memory leak problem by observing the minimum working set of an application when it first starts. Then, after waiting some time, you can observe the minimum working set again. If the value increases, the application has some type of memory leak. You then must evaluate whether this leak is going to present a problem for you. A user application with a memory leak is not as bothersome as a service or driver with a memory leak. A user application will terminate, and users will usually log off the workstation at some time. When this occurs, the memory for all applications in a user's process returns to the memory pool of the system.

If the memory leak is from a service or driver, the problem has more potential to disrupt operations. The services will not have the memory reset unless the system is rebooted. Thus, they continue to grow in size. It is like the movie *The Blob*; the services or drivers will simply continue to grow into a large gluttonous oozing mass of memory, sucking code until the system crashes due to a critical lack of memory. Not a pretty picture. This process can take hours or even days because memory leaks can be very small.

Determining the minimum working set actually requires two tools. You use CLEARMEM to force the applications to their minimum working sets and good old Performance Monitor to observe the value of the applications' working sets. Prior to running CLEARMEM, you need to make sure that you have a pagefile equal to the size of physical RAM at a minimum. CLEARMEM is going to force all the process's code and data out of memory, and the pagefile is the destination. The following sequence shows the steps in performing this activity.

1. Start the Performance Monitor first. CLEARMEM.exe causes a lot of activity on the system when it first starts. You won't want to start Performance Monitor while CLEARMEM.exe is forcing applications (including Performance Monitor code) out of memory.

2. In Performance Monitor, alter the type of display to a histogram view. Click Options from the drop-down menu and select Chart. Then, select Histogram and click OK (see Figure 3.12).

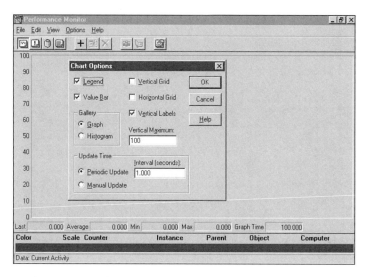

Figure 3.12 Adjusting the Performance Monitor Chart view to display a histogram view of the process' working sets.

3. Now you need to add objects and counters to the Performance Monitor to view the activity. You can press the plus sign (+) on the toolbar to add objects. Select the process object. The list of instances will appear (see Figure 3.13). If an application or service is not running at the time you add the object to the Performance Monitor, you will not see it in the list of instances. Make sure that any and all applications, services, and drivers are installed and running at the time that you do this. In the Counter box, select Working Set. In the Instance box, select all running instances. Then, click Add. Click Done.

You will notice a instance called Idle. This particular item is not really a process but a placeholder. The system runs the Idle thread on the process when nothing else is going on. CPUs always like to be busy running something. Chapter 6 covers this concept in more detail.

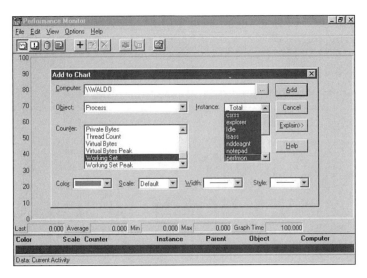

Figure 3.13 When adding the process counters and objects, you will see a list of all processes currently running on the system.

4. You are now ready to start the CLEARMEM program. Open a command prompt, and go to the directory where you have CLEARMEM installed. Now, type **CLEARMEM.exe**. When CLEARMEM.exe launches, the system will temporarily suspend other activity; this is due to CLEARMEM running several high-priority tasks. CLEARMEM will display in the DOS screen the status of the operation. As soon as it completes, run it a second time to make sure that all applications have the minimum working set in place.

5. You can then observe your findings in the Performance Monitor window. The display will look similar to Figure 3.14.

If you have the Server Services set to Maximize Throughput for Network Applications, you might need to run the CLEARMEM a third time to make sure that the services are properly reduced to the minimum working sets.

You will probably notice that the Performance Monitor has a larger working set than most of the other inactive applications. The Performance Monitor is actively attempting to collect data, so its working set is larger than programs that are primarily waiting for user input.

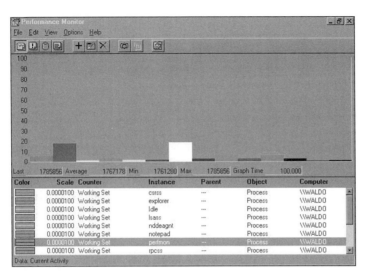

Figure 3.14   Performance Monitor displays the minimum working set sizes in a Histogram view after CLEARMEM has run twice.

Simulating the Memory Leak

You have already learned what a memory leak is. Now you will learn how to simulate a memory leak or any other slow consumption of memory. The NT Resource Kit Tool called LEAKYAPP will slowly consume memory on a system until it is almost completely used. It is like CLEARMEM in that it will reduce the applications to their minimum working sets. However, LEAKYAPP is more relentless in its memory hoarding. It will not allow other applications to retrieve the memory after LEAKYAPP has acquired it. Thus, the system must page information in and out of the pagefile. Why would you want to wreak such havoc on your system?

■ You can learn a great deal about the configuration of your system and the ability to handle critical memory shortages by creating a memory shortage using LEAKYAPP. You can see how well the system you configured interacts with the pagefiles. Then, you can tune the system for better performance under these conditions.

■ You can see what a memory leak looks like. What better way to diagnose a problem than by investigating it under controlled circumstances?

■ Because LEAKYAPP has finer control than the CLEARMEM, you can view the system behavior at various stages of memory stress. LEAKYAPP is a graphical tool that allows you to stop and start the consumption of memory. You can pause the consumption at any time. LEAKYAPP will not release the memory until the application is terminated, so the system has to run with what it has left.

To run LEAKYAPP, you first prepare the NT Performance Monitor. You also want to make sure that you have a suitable pagefile (RAM + 12MB). Then, follow the procedure that follows:

1. Open Performance Monitor to the Chart view.

2. Click the + to add counters to the Performance Monitor view. You will add the Pages/sec and Available Bytes counters from the Memory Object.

3. Click Done. Although you use the Pages/sec and Available Bytes counters just for starters, you can add other counters, depending on what you want to observe. For example, you might want to use the steps in the CLEARMEM example, where you add the working sets to view how the individual programs react to the slow reduction of memory. You might want to add the %Usage counter from the PageFile object to see how the pagefiles you set up are being utilized. You might want to look at any number of disk object counters to see how your disk subsystem is reacting to the excessive paging. The disk counters are covered in detail in Chapter 8, "Optimizing Disk Performance."

4. Start the LEAKYAPP application. You see the interface display in Figure 3.15.

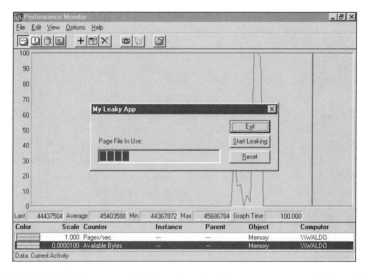

Figure 3.15 LEAKYAPP has a graphical interface that allows you to control the application's consumption of memory.

5. Click the Start Leaking button. LEAKYAPP starts using up the memory, forcing NT to push information out to the pagefile. The pagefile usage is tracked on the LEAKYAPP interface.

As the LEAKYAPP continues to use up memory, NT will continue to push information out to the pagefile. You will see the Available Memory counter in the Performance Monitor slowly degenerate. NT will deal with this reduction in memory. You will see paging increase, but perhaps not as must as you might expect (see Figure 3.16). The paging does not become a big problem until the available memory drops below 4MB, an important limit for NT.

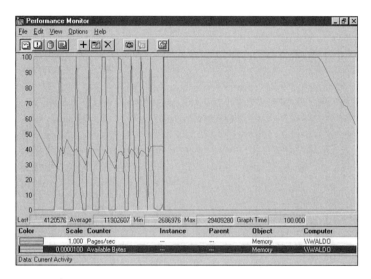

Figure 3.16   The Performance Monitor shows that NT is able to deal with the reduction in memory until it reaches 4MB.

NT attempts to maintain the 4MB of available memory for shuffling information back and forth between the various locations of file system cache, physical RAM, and pagefile. You will see NT dip into this 4MB as memory becomes very scarce. This indicates that all processes are at their minimum working sets and the file system cache has been reduced to its minimum size.

Now you are ready to simulate a multitude of memory situations on NT. Remember, you can use each of these scenarios in conjunction with the others to offer different twists on themes. Be creative when applying the simulations techniques. You are now ready to move on to CPU simulations.

Simulating CPU Activity

A CPU is the heart of the system. The main responsibilities of the CPU are executing program instructions (which can be from the OS or applications) or servicing hardware requests (interrupts). Because a CPU can only perform one instruction at a time, the performance depends on how many instructions the CPU can do in a specific amount of time. The CPU architecture plays an important role. RISC (Reduced Instruction Set Computers) processors can process more instructions per second than the CISC (Complex Instruction Set Computers) processors common to Intel-based hardware.

> With CPU architecture changing so rapidly, it is difficult to keep up. In addition, books about CPU architecture tend to delve far too deep into the realms of electronics, and CPU chip developers maintain several theories governing queue handling, cache coherency, and other concepts. At this point, you could use more information about CPU/software interrelations. A good place to look is the manufacturers' Web sites. http://www.compaq.com has my vote as one of the best sources of information. Visit the support section at that site. After you select a server, workstation, or some other technology, you will see a list of support documentation and technical white papers. A site search will always turn up some type of document. You can also find information on the Intel Web site, although it seems that Compaq has a little more information on the integration of technology with systems and software.

The CPU is responsible for executing all the instructions for each of the running applications and for the operating system. These applications come in many flavors and do many things, such as draw bitmaps on the screen, request services from the network, or request information from the hard disk.

Recall from the beginning of this chapter that the CPU has its own Level-1 cache, and, depending on the CPU type, it can have an external or additional Level-2 cache. The CPU is connected to the physical RAM using a 32-bit bus on a typical workstation. However, the memory bus speed will depend on the processor architecture. When the program executes, the program is loaded, for instance, from the hard disk into RAM (not the whole program, just a part of it) and then from RAM to the CPU, where the instructions are executed. The L1 and L2 caches store the most recently executed commands, and the cache memory is much faster than standard RAM (but also more costly).

The Windows NT applications running on a system will no doubt place some form of "stress" on the CPU. This stress comes in the form of instructions to execute. For a multithreaded operating system, the CPU is also responsible for managing the various threads of execution generated by the operating system and other multithreaded applications. A thread is a small and distinct set of instructions that the processor must respond to. The thread is the smallest particle of the programming element.

An application always has at least one thread of execution—the main schedulable thread. Remember, the process itself is not a schedulable entity. It is that initial thread of the program that is scheduled by the OS to run on the processor.

Many Windows NT applications will run many threads. You can see how many threads your NT system is handling by using the Task Manager and making sure the Thread Count option is selected in the Columns menu, as shown in Figure 3.17.

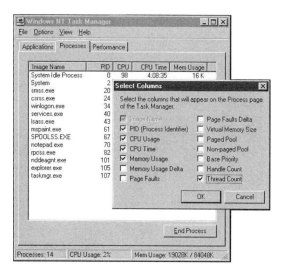

Figure 3.17 Querying the number of threads being handled by NT.

Unfortunately, many applications are not written properly and, in fact, create an excessive number of threads. If the program creates a large number of threads at the same time, the NT Microkernel component called the *scheduler* or *dispatcher* will be forced to manage them all at the same time. Think of a ball juggler juggling three balls. A good juggler can handle three balls with relative ease. Imagine someone throwing five more balls at the juggler. All of a sudden, the juggler (in this case, the scheduler) has a lot more work to do. Instead of three balls (CPU tasks) to juggle, it has eight. This jugger must truly be the best juggler of all time. At the time the additional five balls are added, the juggler becomes busier but eventually gets it under control. In other words, the work gets busy for a moment. The same thing happens when a program "launches" many threads or processes at the same time. The scheduler will get extremely busy trying to schedule the threads.

> Do not confuse the NT Microkernel thread scheduler with the Scheduler Service that runs on NT. The Microkernel scheduler controls the running of threads on the processors. The Scheduler Service is a service on NT that allows you to run programs at regular intervals, such as a backup program running every night.

Threads are more than balls in the air, however. Each thread carries with it a priority. These priorities determine which thread will get run on the processor and when. A thread of higher priority will get more chances to run on the processor than a thread of lower priority. In Chapter 6, you will be exposed to more details of this process and the theories that govern it. For now, you only need to understand the simple concept that a higher priority means more chances to run on the CPU. You will simulate the act of "throwing a lot of balls" at the CPU and see how it reacts. You can use another Resource Kit tool called CPU Stress to accomplish this. This program generates the activity needed by creating threads of a variety of priorities. You will monitor the CPU performance using the Performance Monitor. The CPU Stress program lets you create four threads for which you can select the amount of activity, as well as the priority. Using CPU Stress makes it easy to simulate thread activity, as shown in the following steps:

1. Start CPU Stress, which resides in the PerfTool\Meastool directory where the NT Resource Kit is installed. Notice that Thread 1 is already set to active (see Figure 3.18).

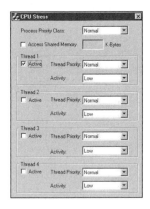

Figure 3.18 CPU Stress is a simple graphical tool with the single-minded task of generating activity for the processor.

2. Start the Performance Monitor. Select to monitor the Processor Object: % Processor Time and Interrupts/sec and System Object: System Calls/sec. Watch the activity generated (see Figure 3.19).

3. Click to activate all four threads in CPU Stress and set the activity of all the threads to busy. Note the increased activity and how the %Processor Time counter increases almost to 100 percent (see Figure 3.20). This means that the system is now CPU bound.

How can you use this information to plan your system? Although it is hard to predetermine all the applications that are going to be running on the system, you can still use these simulation tests to understand how the CPU responds to thread activity. In this process, you are also monitoring the System object's System Calls/sec and the Processor Object's Interrupts/sec. The Interrupts/sec counter relates to the number of times the CPU is interrupted by hardware devices to perform some task. System Calls/sec relates the number of calls made by the OS to the CPU. In the test scenario here, the increase in activity is caused by system calls and not a hardware device.

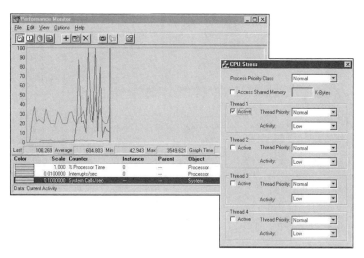

Figure 3.19 Performance Monitor is where you examine the effects of CPU Stress on the processor.

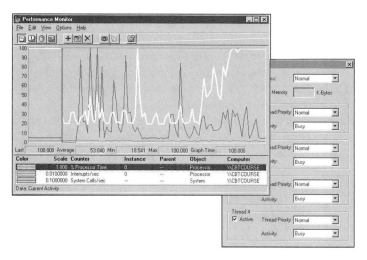

Figure 3.20 CPU Stress causes the processor to become almost 100 percent utilized.

Use the Processor: Interrupts/sec and System: System Calls/sec counters to determine whether the CPU performance problems are software- or hardware-related. This particular tactic along with some further information is presented later in the Chapter 6. In addition, the concept of a Deferred Procedure Call (DPC) is discussed. For now, think of a DPC as an interrupt whose processing is set aside until a later time.

Using the CPU Stress tool is the best way to isolate and manage the CPU performance roughly independent of the rest of the system. Now, let us move on to disk usage.

Simulating Disk Usage Conditions

In addition to the operating system, the hard disk also contains the application programs, dynamic link libraries, and data files. Poor disk performance is characterized by poor I/O performance. Figure 3.1 outlined the standard layout of a computer system with a CPU, memory, and peripheral devices. Because the disk is strictly an I/O device, you want to be able to test how fast you can read from the device and how fast you can write to the device. Obviously, the faster the reads and writes, the faster performance is overall. Good disk performance leads to faster program loads and executions.

Good disk performance has other advantages as well. First, it improves memory performance. Because the pagefile resides on the physical disk, every time the system has to page, it will obviously go to the hard disk for resolution. If the disk is slow, the paging process becomes the slower, consequently decreasing system performance.

Another benefit of good disk performance is that printing speed is faster. The spool file created by the printer is created on the hard disk. The faster the output from the disk to the printer, the faster printer output is achieved.

Keep in mind that each of these processes use the same resource—the computer's hard disk or disks. The disk systems, much like the processor, are servicing a queue. A queue in this case is a stack of requests to put and get information from the hard drive. Think of the inbox in your email program. People need you to do something; they send it to you. People need information from you; they send a request and you respond. Managing the queue can be quite a task, as anyone who gets more than 20 emails a day can tell you. Exercising how the entire disk subsystem means stressing the NT I/O manager, the disk controller, and the physical hard drive. Throughput and performance relate to how well these components work together to service the disk queue. For this reason, it is important to understand the performance of these components under specific conditions. No matter what the disk seek time might be, it depends on how fast the controller can move information to the disk.

If the system will be using the hard disk intensively—that is, many application programs are executed and issue many I/O disk requests to files—then it is important to understand the overhead associated with each I/O transaction. When you purchase a hard disk, you are given some performance numbers, such as seeks per second or data transfer rates. What are the numbers in a real-world scenario? A typical question you might ask is, "If I create a 40MB file, how many I/O operations will it take to fill the file with data and read it back?"

Is this information really important? Many people know to get the fastest disk available. For others, this information is crucial in the design of their domain system. This is especially true when the system will be used primarily as a file or print server and the hard disk will be accessed frequently. The system might serve as a database or FTP (File Transfer Protocol) server, with many users uploading hundreds of files.

Now that you have an understanding of the importance of simulating and testing disk performance, let's get a handle on how to do it.

Activating Disk Performance Objects

As with other measurements, you will use the Performance Monitor for data collection. Remember to run the diskperf utility to activate disk performance objects on the computer. To do this, open a command prompt and type **diskperf -y**, and then shut down your computer and restart. Make sure to wait a while after you reboot the system before beginning your disk drive tests. When NT starts up, many background initialization activities can interface with the measurements. If the computer you are using is connected to the network, it might be a good idea to disable the network drivers. Some drivers respond to network traffic and events even if they are not directed to your computer, creating unwanted activity.

You must be a member of the Administrators local group to run diskperf.

What exactly does diskperf do? The diskperf program installs a special device driver called the disk performance statistics driver, which gets added to the stack of drivers managed by the I/O Manager. Figure 3.21 shows where the driver is placed on the stack.

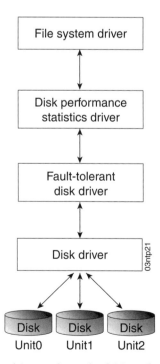

Figure 3.21 Diskperf will add a driver to the stack of drivers for the disk I/O controlled by the NT I/O Manager.

Unlike the other performance counters, the disk counters require a manual switch because they do not permanently enable performance monitoring. This decision by Microsoft was a result of the effects of monitoring the disk subsystem on an I386 machine. The 386MHz Intel processor architecture experienced a 1.5 percent performance hit when the disk counters were enabled. Microsoft felt that the user community would consider this unreasonable. It has not changed this counter, even though the performance hit on a Pentium machine is less than .05 percent. With proper disk controllers and disk caching on the controller, this value drops off into oblivion.

If you are still concerned about the performance hit on your system's disk subsystem, regardless of how small, you can turn off the disk counters. At a command prompt, type **diskperf -n**. This will disable the counters when you reboot.

If you are using a software stripe set or software strip set with parity, you need to run diskperf -ye instead of only indicating the -y argument. This will put the appropriate counter driver in place.

Now that you have activated the disk performance counters, you are prepared to begin a simulation.

Testing Hard Disk Performance with Response Probe and Performance Monitor

In this case, you will use a special tool from the Resource Kit designed to simulate all sorts of activity, the extensive Response Probe simulation tool. As discussed at the beginning of this section, you can test the performance of the disk by creating a file and determining the disk performance numbers during the file reads and writes. The Response Probe will perform this activity and many others. The tool consists of an executable and some DLLs for execution. The remainder of the tool is a combination of text files that control the execution of the simulation.

The Response Probe Simulation Tool

Before continuing, let's take a little closer look at this tool. The Response Probe attempts to simulate activity that programs or a user might create. It does this by setting up a group of processes and threads that track performance based on a bell-curve distribution you can control. The script files that Response Probe uses will determine how many times the processes and threads are executed and determine the bell curves that represent the distribution of activity performed by each thread. Each set of script files consists of the following:

- **.SCR** The main Response Probe file that outlines which process script file to run and how often.

- **.SCP** The process file that determines which thread file to run and how often.

- **.SCT** The thread file that details the bell curves in the form of standard deviation and means that govern the activity of the response probe simulation.

Of the three files, the .SCT file is the most important for simulation purposes. Look at the following diskmax.sct sample from the NT Resource Kit:

```
# Diskmax Thread Description File
#
# Description:   This script file is part of a test of maximum disk
                 throughput.
#                It creates a single threaded process that does reed
                 sequential,
#                unbuffered reads of 64K records from a 20Mb file.
#
# Format:
#              THINKTIME       Mean  SDev      (milliseconds)
#              CYCLEREADS      Mean  SDev      (number)
#              FILESEEK        Mean  SDev      (records)
#              CPUTIME         Mean  SDev      (milliseconds)
#              DATAPAGE        Mean  SDev      (page number)
#              FUNCTION        Mean  SDev      (function number 1-1000)
#              FILEACCESS      fileaccess      (file name)
#              FILEATTRIBUTE   RANDOM ¦ SEQUENTIAL
#              FILEACCESSMODE  BUFFER ¦ UNBUFFER ¦ MAPPED
#              RECORDSIZE      number_of_bytes (default - 4096 bytes)
#              FILEACTION      R ¦ W
#
#          Mean   Sdev
#
THINKTIME      0      0        No think time.
CPUTIME        0      0        No other processing time.
CYCLEREADS   100     30        Reads 100 times/cycle on average, with
                               a sdev of 30.
FILESEEK       0      0        Fileseek is ignored for sequential
                               access.
DATAPAGE       0      0        No datapage activity.
FUNCTION     500      0        Reads the middle function repeatedly to
                               simulate codepage access.
FILEACCESS          WORKFILE.DAT  Reads the 64K records from this file.
FILEATTRIBUTE       SEQUENTIAL    Reads the records sequentially.
FILEACCESSMODE      UNBUFFER      Reads directly from disk without the
                                  file system cache.
RECORDSIZE   65536              Reads 64K records.
FILEACTION   R                  Reads only (no writes).
```

This particular simulation is nicely commented. Several other examples in the Perftool\Probe\Samples directory demonstrate several features of the Response probe.

One item, THINKTIME, prompts an interesting discussion into how Response Probe works. The Response Probe is not simply copying files back and fourth; it can make an attempt to simulate various user activities. The Response Probe goes through execution in three stages:

- **Think Time (parameter THINKTIME).** This is where the system pauses. This simulates the system waiting for the user to respond to information, such as the results of a database query in an application.

- **File Access Time (parameter CYCLEREAD).** Response Probe now takes the time to access a file based on the other parameters.

- **Compute Time (parameter CPUTIME).** Response Probe will use some of the CPU's time based on this parameter.

Together, these stages outline the type of system behavior Response will simulate. Notice that each one has a mean and a standard deviation. A review of basic statistics: The mean is the average amount of time given to each process; the standard deviation describes how far off the mean the time is allowed to wander. It is much like deciding it takes 30 minutes to get to the airport, plus or minus 10 minutes. The mean is 30 minutes and the plus or minus could be considered one standard deviation. The standard deviation basically determines the maximum and minimum values to be expected. Most values (over 90 percent) will fall within three standard deviations from the mean. The example has a standard deviation of 30 with a mean of 100. Three standard deviations are 3 × 30 or 90. Thus, you can expect to spend anywhere from 10 reads/cycle to 190 reads/cycle. A cycle is determined through the speed of the processor. Now, let's get a little closer to the physical world.

Because the operating system is designed to use the file cache before going to the physical disk, you must set up the test to bypass the cache and go directly to disk. For this, you need to set the FILEACCESSMODE parameter in the Response Probe to UNBUFFER, as in the diskmax.sct example.

Applying Response Probe Disk Simulation

The Resource Kit's Response Probe is an ideal tool for testing the response of each system resource. You can also use this tool to collect baseline performance information or to determine the maximum throughput values. The ideal use for optimizing an NT system is to use Response Probe to predict how your system will handle different workloads and how changes you have made to the system have affected the overall system performance.

In this case, you want to test the disk subsystem's performance. Follow the steps outlined in the following sequence to complete this task:

1. Create a new folder and put the Response Probe programs and data in this new folder. In this case, assume the folder is called C:\DISKMAX. Copy the following files from the folder where you installed the NT Resource Kit to the folder C:\DISKMAX:

    \PerfTool\Probe\Creatfil.exe

    \PerfTool\Probe\Probeprc.exe

    \PerfTool\Probe\Probe.exe

\PerfTool\Probe\timerw32.dll

\PerfTool\Probe\statw32.dll

\PerfTool\Probe\Examples\DiskMax.scp

\PerfTool\Probe\Examples\Diskmax.scr

\PerfTool\Probe\Examples\Diskmax.sct

2. You now need to create the file. For this sample scenario, create a file that is 20MB in size. You do this with another NT Resource Kit utility called CREATEFIL. CREATEFIL creates a file of a particular size for use with Response Probe. You need to make sure that the name of the file matches the name you defined in the .SCT file with the `FILEACCESS` parameter. In the case of the DISKMAX sample, you will use the filename workfile.dat. Open a command prompt and set your directory to the C:\DISKMAX directory you created in Step 1. To create a file, begin by typing the following:

```
createfil workfile.dat 20000
```

The workfile.dat file created is a 20MB file filled with zeros. Response Probe will use this file during its simulation to create a workload for the disk.

3. Next, you use the available disk examples in the Resource Kit. They are located the RESKT\PERFTOOL\PROBE\EXAMPLES directory. The files of interest here are the three DISKMAX.* files:

DISKMAX.SCP (the thread definition file)

DISKMAX.SCT (the thread description file)

DISKMAX.SCR (the process file)

You copied these files to the C:\DISKMAX directory in step 1.

4. You also need to use the Performance Monitor to monitor the disk activity. For this, you'll monitor the LogicalDisk object illustrated in Figure 3.22.

Figure 3.22 Adding the LogicalDisk object to the log file for monitoring purposes.

Instead of using the Chart view, you will log the data. Logging the data will give you the opportunity to examine it later. The specific counters you want for the LogicalDisk object follow:

- **Avg. Disk Bytes/Read.** The average number of bytes transferred from the disk during read operations.

- **Avg. Disk sec/Read.** The average time (in seconds) it takes to read data from the disk.

- **Disk Read Bytes/sec.** The rate at which bytes are transferred from the disk during read operations.

- **Disk Reads/sec.** The rate of read operations on the disk.

Set the Performance Monitor to log the information to a file at an interval of 15 seconds in the Periodic Update box, as shown in Figure 3.23.

Figure 3.23 Setting the Performance Monitor logging interval.

5. You are now ready to start the simulation. Use the Probe.exe program to process the script file. The syntax follows:

```
Probe diskmax.scr 600 diskout.out
```

You'll use `diskmax.scr` as the name of the Response Probe script file. The `600` refers to the total test time in seconds, and `diskout.out` is the name of the output file. This output file name is optional. The default output filename is the same as the process script file with the .OUT suffix.

The Response Probe does not actually begin the test immediately. It waits about one half of the test time before measuring any values. The simulation has this delay while the system quiets down. Resource Probe is the same as other applications in this regard; the resource usage during startup is not exemplary of the system usage during regular runtime.

Figure 3.24 shows the collection taking place while the Response Probe is processing the script file.

Figure 3.24 Data collection activity occurs while the Response Probe is running and the Performance Monitor is logging information.

After the Response Probe completes its operation, you will have a Performance Monitor log that contains information from the entire simulation. Using any one of the Performance Monitor views (such as Chart or Report), you can load this log file and review the information.

Figure 3.25 shows the LogicalDisk counters using the Performance Monitor report format. To view information from a Performance Monitor log, access the Chart, Alert, or Report views and click Options from the drop-down menu. Then, select the Data From option. You will be prompted for the location of a file. Figure 3.25 shows the disk throughput denoted by the Disk Read Bytes/sec value.

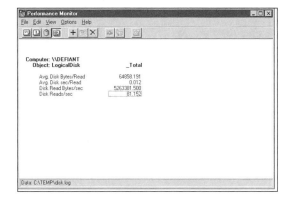

Figure 3.25 Using the Performance Monitor Report view, you can see the information collected during the simulation.

This sample simulation indicates that the disk throughput is 5263381 bytes/sec. Whether this is good depends on the disk subsystem architecture, the seek time on the disk, and the controller. For an ISA EIDE drive of decent power, this number is excellent. For a SCSI device on an ISA controller, it is good. For a SCSI device on a PCI controller with plenty of RAM on the controller, you might need to wonder what is wrong. More details about how the architecture affects throughout is available in Chapter 8.

Take a look at the other parameters. The Disk Reads/sec tells you how many times the disk was read to satisfy the requests for information. A decent I/O system is capable of about 40 I/Os per second. This report shows an impressive 80 I/Os per second, indicating a good controller. The Avg Disk secs/Read is a value that you compare to the seek time the manufacturer reported for the drive. Under the best conditions, the values should be close.

Using the Response Probe, you can simulate other types of activity. For disk activity, reporting that this one trial is a complete reflection of disk performance would be a mistake. The disk subsystem is servicing a queue, so it is subject to changes in how data is placed in the queue. The disk is also susceptible to changes in the size of the file reads. When the reads match the sector size, life is good. When they don't, life gets a little harder for the disk. In the example, the files were read sequentially. If you modify the test to use random reads, the performance of the disk will drop. Random reads mean the disk must spend more time moving the reader arm around on the physical disk platen, which takes time.

Simulating Network Usage Conditions

In an NT domain, the network could be considered the "veins" of the system. Information is carried to and from the network, providing a conduit for network traffic, such as logon validations, resolution of NetBIOS names, handling of DHCP requests, file transfers, downloading of Internet pages, and directory replication. As with the blood in your veins, you take the actions of the network for granted. You know the network is functioning; you just don't see what is being sent across it. Like your veins, the network can get clogged when all of a sudden, the data is not being pumped as fast as it used to be.

You can create a stress load on the network in several different ways. If you really want to simulate the effects of a SAM database replication between the PDC and the BDC, for example, you need to capture that event. The best tool to use is a network sniffer, such as the Microsoft Network Monitor. The Network Monitor and its usage are covered in detail in Chapter 9, "Optimizing Network Interface Performance."

If you want an easy way to determine how the network handles network traffic, however, it can be as simple as creating a large file and transferring it across the network. This methodology may be a bit crude, but it does do what you want: put a load on the network. If you need to replicate a 1MB file from one machine to the next every hour, you could create a 1MB file and copy it manually while looking at your network performance.

In this case, you do not necessarily need to use the Network Monitor. You can use the Performance Monitor, provided the Network Monitor's extended objects are installed. You can install them by installing the NT Server version of the Network Monitor tools. From the Network icon in the Control Panel, select the Services tab. Then, click the Add button and select the Network Monitor Tools. Install, and, when prompted, reboot. You will need the NT distribution CD-ROM to complete this operation.

When you reboot and you start the Performance Monitor, you see an additional object called the Network Segment. This object contains numerous counters, including % Network Utilization, which is what you will use for testing purposes in this section.

Now you need a large file to test. You can use the CREATEFIL utility from the Resource Kit. Create a 10MB file:

```
C:\TEMPDIR\createfil testfile.tst 10000
```

To make it easy, create a recursive batch file that copies this file to another computer, deletes it from the current machine, copies it back to the computer, and deletes it from the remove computer. The batch file would look like this:

```
REM NWLOAD.BAT
Copy c:\tempdir\testfile.tst \\remote\c$\testfile.tst
Del testfile.tst
Copy \\remote\c$\testfile.txt c:\tempdir\testfile.tst
Del \\remove\c$\testfile.txt
Call nwload.bat
```

The sole purpose of this batch file is to create network traffic by copying this large 10MB file back and forth across the network.

Now, open the Performance Monitor and look at the % Network Utilization counter of the Network Segment and the Current Bandwidth of the Network Interface object. From a command prompt, start the special batch file that you just created. You should see the Network Utilization counter increase but the Current Bandwidth counter remain constant, in this case, at around 10. Why? You are using a 10BaseT network with a maximum bandwidth of 10 megabits per second.

Assume that the % Network Utilization counter is at a constant 85%. This generally indicates that the network bandwidth is being fully utilized. Consider the following crude but illustrative calculation:

Network speed: 10Megabits/sec

Convert to Megabytes:

10 Megabits/sec × 1 Megabytes/8 Megabits = 1.25 Megabytes/Sec

Transfer Time for the File:

10MB file ÷ 1.25MB/sec = 8 seconds

This calculation tells you that for eight seconds, the file transfer will use 100 percent of what the network has to offer. However, the value that was displayed in the Performance Monitor was only 85 percent. A network can't really reach the 100 percent mark. The network will become saturated, and the transmission of additional new packets of data will be inhibited due to collisions and retransmissions on the network.

Summary

You can use the techniques in this chapter to apply a resource load to the system and simulate a bottleneck. These techniques will also help you understand what happens when the tested resources are in short supply and high demand.

More importantly, you now know the various Performance Monitor counters that you can use to understand how the system is affected by the simulated workloads. Revisit the case study presented at the beginning of the chapter.

Case Study

As a systems administrator, you must evaluate a new NT database program to be used by the corporate office. Part of your evaluation is to determine whether your current system configuration will be enough to run this new program.

Beyond the usual "Do I have enough disk space to install the program?" question, you also face the issue of how your system will respond with the new application running. Maybe you need more memory. Maybe you need more network bandwidth because it is a network program. The last thing you want to do is to install the program and watch your network slow down to a screeching halt.

In this case, you need to determine the impact of this new program on the system with relation to the memory, for instance. The steps you could take follow:

1. Determine how many page faults the new program generates. Use the Resource Kit PFMON utility as demonstrated earlier in the chapter.

2. Run this application along with the Performance Monitor to determine whether your application is CPU intensive by monitoring the % Processor Time counter.

3. You can determine if the normal operation consumes excessive network bandwidth by monitoring the % Network Utilization counter.

4. You can determine the impact on the disk resource by monitoring the LogicalDisk object.

4

Determining System Performance Objectives

This chapter covers the following topics:

- **Determining System Performance Objects.** What does optimization in Windows NT mean? What are the system resources you need to monitor? This section describes optimization and capacity planning.

- **The Memory Resource.** This section describes the memory resource and how it can affect the Windows NT performance.

- **The CPU Resource.** This section describes the CPU and what role it plays in the NT architecture.

- **The Disk Resource.** Application programs as well as the pagefile are stored on the disk. This section explains how the disk performance can affect the memory performance and the different disk configuration options.

- **The Network Resource.** Optimizing the network is complex because there are many components to the NT architecture. This section describes how NT implements networking and how the networking layer affects performance.

- **Determining System Baseline Performance.** With an understanding of the resources and how they relate to NT, this section describes what counters you need to monitor for each resource object.

This chapter deals with specific information on how to begin the process of optimizing your NT system. Optimization and bottleneck detection is basically the same thing. What is improving performance? It's getting your system to work as efficiently as possible. If the art of bottleneck detection involves finding out which of the system resources is experiencing the highest demand, then optimization is the art of reducing the number of bottlenecks.

For an analogy, consider the simple act of moving dirt from one location to the next. The first thing you do is use a wheelbarrow. This wheelbarrow has a specific size and can carry a limited load amount. Also, the larger the load, the more work it is to move it. You fill the wheelbarrow with dirt, and you take it from location A to location B. You time how long it takes you to get there and how much work it took. In an ideal work situation, the trip takes you a specific amount of time with any work stress. Unfortunately, this is different in the real world. Many things (some within and out of your control) can affect the time (and the amount of work) it takes you to perform that task. As you carry more loads, the work of lifting and moving the wheelbarrow is getting harder, taking more time and adding more work on your part. Perhaps you need another person to help you (like adding a CPU) or perhaps you hire someone stronger than you (like upgrading the processor) to do the work. Maybe you want to carry more dirt per trip, so you need to increase the size of the wheelbarrow (like adding more memory or hard disk space). Perhaps the route you take has too many problems that slow you down, and you need to find another path (like getting a faster network).

What happens after you feel you have the work trip highly optimized? Then, you need to ask yourself some questions such as "What would happen if I take a break every hour? How would that affect my performance? How much faster will the work go if I add another processor? How will that affect my performance?" To answer these questions effectively, you need to collect daily information on the trips. Managing these problems and knowing what to do is the key to optimization. Knowing how well the currently implemented system will work with your system growth is referred to as *capacity planning*.

Tuning a Windows NT system follows the same methodology as the simple act of moving dirt. The areas that can cause system bottlenecks are the memory, processor, disk, and network. Understanding which resource is experiencing the greatest demand is the key to resolving bottlenecks. What you are trying to accomplish is relieving the demand on each resource while maximizing the throughput and ensuring that any resource can service the demands placed on it.

Let's suppose the processor is experiencing 100 percent utilization. You have several options. You can upgrade the processor or add another processor. In many cases, it is not always possible to upgrade or add a processor. Your job then is to see how else you can alleviate the problem. Something is causing the processor to work at 100 percent capacity. The task is to find out what that is.

To perform this optimization, you need to look at each resource individually. More important, you need to understand what the computer is doing and what resources it uses heavily to support its responsibilities. Take, for instance, an NT server installed as a file and print server. Which resources do you think are the most used? After you can answer that question, you can begin to look at ways to improve the system performance at those components.

The sections that follow cover system resources and how they affect system performance. A solid understanding of these resources and the problems and issues that can creep up in each will enable you to formulate an intuitive strategy for combating system bottlenecks and optimizing performance.

The Memory Resource

Most of the performance problems in Windows NT systems have to do with a short-age of physical memory (see Figure 4.1).

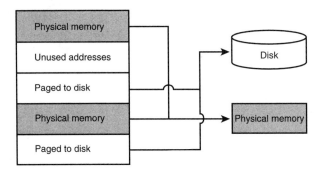

Figure 4.1 Memory shortage in Windows NT systems.

When the memory is low, the system has to page to the PAGEFILE.SYS file. The PAGEFILE.SYS file (or paging file) is a reserved block of disk space that is used to back up committed memory that can be contiguous or fragmented. *Committed memory* refers to memory that has been allocated for a given process. By default, the paging file is set to the size of physical memory plus 12MB, but this can be changed. Increasing the size of the paging file often resolves virtual memory shortages.

Increasing the pagefile can also mask problems instead of correcting them.

The more paging that occurs, the worse the performance will be. To make matters worse, remember that the PAGEFILE.SYS file is located on the hard drive, so the speed of the disk also affects your memory performance. The Virtual Memory Manager (VMM) manages memory in fixed length (4KB) units called *pages*. Pages can be copied between pagefiles and physical memory efficiently because all pages are the same size. Any available space in physical memory or the pagefile can accommodate a page transferred from the other.

When pages are copied from physical memory to a pagefile, the address translation tables used to access the pages are marked to indicate that the pages are not in physical memory, but in the pagefile instead, as illustrated in Figure 4.2.

Pages residing in the pagefile affect performance because now, instead of the operation happening completely in RAM (which is fast), the hard disk is involved (which is slower than RAM). Now that the hard disk is involved, you must take into account the disk performance.

When an application attempts to access a page that is not in physical memory, a fault occurs, as demonstrated in Figure 4.3.

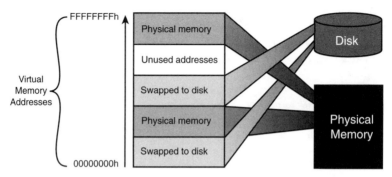

Figure 4.2 Memory pages residing in the pagefile.

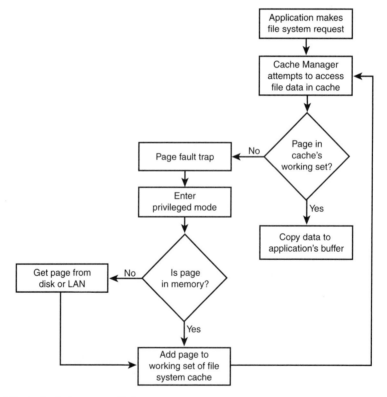

Figure 4.3 A physical memory fault.

In response, the Virtual Memory Manager copies the required page from a paging file to an available page of physical memory. The Virtual Memory Manager then updates the address translation tables to indicate where the page is located in physical memory. After the address translation tables are updated, the application can access the page. If the VMM has to get the data it needs from the physical disk, that is called a hard page fault. If the VMM finds the data in another location in memory, that is called a soft page fault. Hard page faults are case performance issues more often because they involve going out to the hard disk.

In Windows NT, paging is a way of life. When an application executes, the operating system takes the executable from the storage media and places it in RAM. However, only a portion, not the entire program, is placed in RAM. The Virtual Memory Manager is responsible for allocating and maintaining the virtual memory needed by the application, which is 4GB for 32-bit applications.

Another important memory concept is the memory pool. Windows NT uses memory pools that contain the objects created and used by the applications and even the operating system. These memory pools reside in the kernel layer and are only accessible in privileged mode (or the kernel mode discussed in Chapter 1, "Understanding Windows NT Architecture"). The two types of memory pools follow:

- **Paged pools** hold objects that can be paged to disk.
- **Nonpaged pools** hold objects that are never paged to disk. The Microkernel is one of those components that is never paged to disk.

Initially, the size of the memory pools is based on the amount of RAM in the system. After that, the size is adjusted, depending upon the applications and services that are running. This adjustment is dynamic; however, when you first install Windows NT, a setting in the Registry "hard-codes" the memory available for the memory pool. If you add more memory after the initial installation of NT, you might need to change this Registry value to accommodate the new increase.

Under Windows NT 4.0, all virtual memory in Windows NT is reserved, committed, or available. *Reserved memory* refers to memory targeted for a process but not yet used. Memory is *committed* when the VMM saves space for it in the paging file. *Committed memory* (memory allocated for a given process) is limited by the size of the paging file. The *commit limit* is the amount of memory that can be committed without expanding the paging file. If disk space is available, the paging file can expand, and the commit limit is increased. The act of expanding the paging file dynamically indicates that there is a potential memory problem because there is not enough RAM to support the running application. *Available memory* refers to that memory that is neither reserved nor committed. To put it in terms of the virtual memory allocation for an application, the virtual memory = reserved memory + committed memory + available memory.

Something to look for when optimizing memory is how much the system has to page. Specifically, you should be concerned with the number of hard page faults, which force the VMM to go to the hard drive to retrieve data, resulting in a system bottleneck. When using the Performance Monitor, you can select to monitor the Memory object and the Pages/sec counter. This counter gives you the total number of page faults (both hard and soft). The counter's Input Pages/sec value gives you the hard page fault information.

Some programs in NT enable you to look at these memory values. In the Administrative Tools folder is the WinMSD program that includes a Memory property sheet (see Figure 4.4). This property sheet displays not only the amount of physical RAM, but also the number of committed bytes and the number of bytes in the paged and nonpaged memory pool.

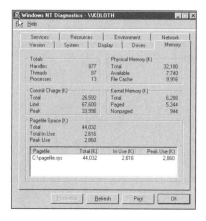

Figure 4.4 Analyzing memory properties on the Memory property sheet of the Windows NT Diagnostics utility.

The CPU Resource

The CPU or processor resource refers to the actual processor technology and how it executes instructions. When applications are executed, they are placed in memory and the processor executes the instructions. The basic premise is that a CPU can execute one instruction at a time. The CPU services two major components. The CPU services applications and operating system functions. When calls are made to the Windows NT operating system in support of operating system functions, they are called system calls. The second component the CPU supports is the hardware interrupt, which is when a particular hardware device (or interface controller) requires the CPU for its operations. These are called interrupt calls. The more the hardware interrupts the CPU, the busier the CPU will be, consequently restricting the time it has to perform its other duties.

As discussed in Chapter 1, the processor has to operate within the concept of the user mode and the kernel (or privileged) mode. While in the user mode, the processor services mainly applications because they run in user mode. When the processor is servicing functions in the kernel area, this is called privileged time. You can monitor this distinction using the Performance Monitor. In the Process object are two counters that provide information about how much time the processor spends servicing user mode and kernel mode. The counters are % User Time and % Privileged Time. If most of the processor time is spent in kernel mode, you immediately know that the processor is busy servicing kernel-mode–related functions.

You should also look at the processor in the context of Windows NT being a multithreading operating system. On a single CPU system, NT is not really handling more than one instruction at one time. Instead, NT switches from one thread to the next (at a very high speed), giving the illusion that it is running several threads at the same time. When the system has more than one processor, each processor can execute a separate thread for a truly multithreading environment.

The top portion of Figure 4.5 shows a system with one processor, executing four task units over a period of time. The bottom portion of Figure 4.5 shows the same system with three processors. Notice that with more processors, the system can complete the four task units in a shorter amount of time.

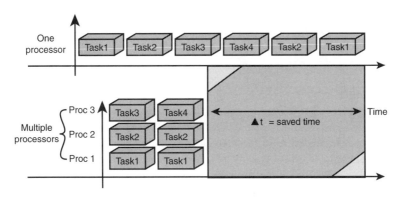

Figure 4.5 Threads in Windows NT.

Let's consider the scenario outlined at the beginning of this chapter. As the load of dirt being carried becomes heavier, more stress is placed on the person moving the dirt. Adding another person to help with the load will result in the load being evenly distributed. This is exactly what adding another processor does for an NT system. It allows the operating system to evenly distribute the workload.

More to the point, Windows NT is a symmetrical operating system. This means that all the processors share equally in the workload, executing both application threads and operating system (kernel) threads as shown in Figure 4.6. Asymmetric operating systems usually reserve one processor for running kernel threads and the other processor for running the application threads.

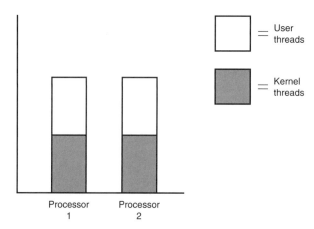

Figure 4.6 Processors in Windows NT share the workload.

> The term task here is used to express a unit of execution. In Windows NT, this is a *thread*. A thread is a schedulable unit of execution, and every process has at least one thread of execution. Windows NT Workstation supports up to two processors and NT Server supports up to four processors.

The Disk Resource

Disk performance typically refers to the disk speed and the amount of time it takes for the data to be transferred from the disk to memory (and back). There are a few more things to consider, however. First, remember that the paging file resides on the physical disk. Therefore, the disk performance affects the memory performance and vice versa. If the operating system has to page, the potential bottleneck is the disk if the disk has a low transfer rate. Having a fast disk also reduces the time it takes an application to load (from disk to memory) and also improves printing speed because the spool file also resides on the disk.

Many other things affect disk performance. The disk technology is important because some disks are faster than others. Some of the options of disk architecture include IDE and SCSI. The hard disk controller also comes into play. Disk controllers can be programmed I/O—that is, they rely on the CPU for data transfer operations. In this case, the speed of the CPU also affects the disk transfer rate.

In addition to fast transfer disks, you should also look at disks with fast disk-seek times. Many times, the operation spends more time looking for the data than actually transferring it. Disk output is affected by other important factors:

- **Whether the files are read randomly or sequentially** If the disk is read randomly, it creates large disk queues, which take longer to process.

- **Disk and file fragmentation** Fragmented files slow down performance because the OS has to look for portions of the file in different disk locations.

The selection of disk formatting options is also important. Windows NT provides the option of installing FAT (File Allocation Table) and the new NT-native NTFS (NT File System). Chapter 7, "Optimizing CPU Performance," covers the impact of each disk formatting option.

The Network Resource

With the network resource, you need to examine it in the context of the architecture model. Windows NT follows a client/server model. As a client, NT can connect to other servers to access their resources. As a server, NT allows other clients to connect to it. The Windows NT built-in networking software includes the SMB server message block) protocol, which is essentially a peer-to-peer network server. More important, NT can use other network servers in addition to the built-in protocol.

The OSI Seven-Layer Networking Model

As with many other operating systems, Microsoft implemented the Open Systems Interconnectivity (OSI) seven-layer networking model, as illustrated in Figure 4.7.

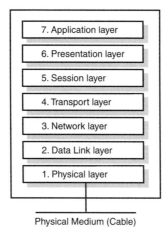

Figure 4.7 The OSI seven-layer networking model.

One of the features of the OSI model is the communication scheme between the layers on the machines. Each layer assumes it is talking with the same layer on the other end. For instance, the application layer on computer A assumes it is talking with the application layer in computer B. In essence, it does, but the transmission is sent down the layers until it reaches the physical layer (the network card) and moves across the wire, through the other machine's physical layer, and up to the application layer (see Figure 4.8).

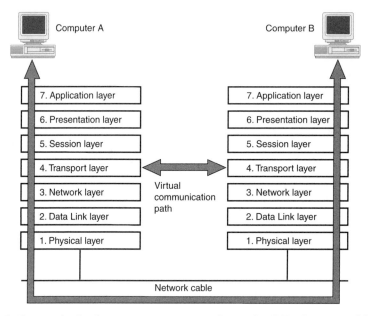

Figure 4.8 Communication between computers according to the OSI reference model.

Although the scope of this book does not include NT networking, a basic understanding of each OSI layer and what it does is important. The following sections describe the functionality of each of the seven layers in the OSI reference model. You will see later in this chapter that not all the layers are important when it comes to optimization. We concentrate only on the application, transport, and physical layers.

The Application Layer (Layer 7)

The application layer handles the transfer of information between network applications. Examples of application layer services that operate at this layer are email packages and file transfer programs. Many Windows NT system services operate at this layer, and their configuration can affect NT network performance.

Some examples of application layer services include mail programs, the NT Workstation and Service services, and Replicator services.

The Presentation Layer (Layer 6)

The presentation layer handles formatting data. The presentation layer also manages network security issues by providing services such as data encryption. This layer provides rules for data transfer and provides data compression to reduce the number of bits that need to be transmitted.

The Session Layer (Layer 5)

The session layer is responsible for the establishment of a session between two computers wanting to communicate with each other.

The Transport Layer (Layer 4)

The transport layer is responsible for converting a network message into packets or frames and making sure they are received in the correct order. The choice of transport protocol affects network performance.

Windows NT supports several protocols, including TCP/IP, NWLink (Microsoft's IPX/SPX Novell-compatible stack), and NetBEUI.

The Network Layer (Layer 3)

The network layer is responsible for message addressing. This layer determines which path the data should take, based on network conditions, priority of service, and other factors. The network layer also manages traffic problems on the network, such as switching, routing, and controlling the congestion of data packets.

The Data Link Layer (Layer 2)

The data link layer provides the error-free transfer of the frames to the physical layer. Windows NT implements this layer using NDIS drivers. This is the layer that also allows NT to support multiple network cards and multiple protocols per card.

The Physical Layer (Layer 1)

The physical layer relates to the actual physical components, including the network card and cable. The type of network topology and network card can affect system performance.

As we discussed, for NT performance improvement issues, you should only be concerned with the physical, transport, and application layers. The sections that follow look at each of these layers individually and outline what you can do to improve NT performance.

Performance at the Physical Layer

This physical layer relates to the actual physical components of the network, including the cable and the network card. You can immediately do several things with the physical layer to get more from the network.

Use a 32-bit adapter (PCI) if the motherboard supports it. A 32-bit board is faster than older 8- or 16-bit boards because it can transfer more data at one time. Older boards are sometimes programmed I/O devices, which means they rely on the CPU for data transfer assistance.

You should also look at the actual cable topology. A 10-BaseT Ethernet connection has a data throughput of 10 Mb/sec, whereas a 100-BaseT connection has a data throughput of 100Mb/sec.

Performance at the Transport Layer

As mentioned previously, Windows NT supports multiple protocols and multiple network cards per system.

According to Microsoft, NDIS 3.0 allows an unlimited number of network adapter cards in a computer and an unlimited number of protocols bound to a single adapter card.

During the installation of NT, you can select which protocols you want to install. When installing applications, you might be tempted to install all the options. When it comes to network protocols, selecting all the transports is *not* recommended. When an NT machine acting as a client and a connection to a server computer needs to be established, the client will send the session request across all the loaded protocols (and all the network cards). If the specific request needs to go out via TCP/IP, and TCP/IP happens to be the last protocol on the stack, the request is sent to all the other loaded protocols first. This, of course, has a major performance implication.

Luckily, you can set the binding order for the protocols. That is, you should place the most widely used protocol on the top of the stack so that when the session request is made, it finds the correct transport protocol right away. Figure 4.9 shows the Bindings property sheet from the Network applet in the Control Panel. Select the protocol used the most, and place it on the top of the list.

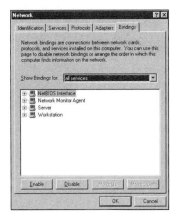

Figure 4.9 Analyzing network binding properties in the Bindings property sheet.

The transport protocol installation options for NT are NetBEUI (NetBIOS Extended User Interface), TCP/IP, and NWLink (IPX/SPX-compatible protocol). The following sections address some issues to consider when choosing one of the three NT transport protocol installation options.

The NetBEUI Transport Protocol Installation Option

In earlier implementations of Microsoft operating systems, the NetBIOS Extended User Interface (NetBEUI) protocol was an interface layer that sits on top of Microsoft's NetBIOS (Network Basic Input/Output System), in essence, extending the NetBIOS interface. In Windows NT 4.0, Microsoft has changed things quite a bit. NetBEUI 3.0, instead of extending the NetBIOS interface, is an upper-level interface that follows the transport driver interface (TDI). To support previous versions of Windows, NetBEUI does use the NetBIOS Frame format (NBF) protocol. Network applications that want to implement the NetBEUI 3.0 protocol must now use the TDI commands instead of the NetBIOS commands. This means that Microsoft has separated the programming interface from the transport protocol, making it a truly layered architecture.

Despite Microsoft's efforts to improve the flexibility of this protocol, it is not the best protocol to implement. First of all, NetBEUI is a broadcast-intensive protocol, which means that when a network connection request is made, the protocol broadcasts the request to all the connected machines. Perhaps in small LAN environments (10 machines or less), this may not be a problem, but for large network environments, this broadcasting definitely causes performance problems.

All these broadcast messages generate excessive network traffic, using valuable network bandwidth. NetBEUI is not a routable protocol, making it viable for LANs, but not for WANs or for use over routers. The positive side is that NetBEUI is easy to implement and configure.

The NWLink Transport Protocol Installation Option

NWLink is Microsoft's Novell IPX/SPX-compatible protocol and provides for connection to Novell servers. You do not, however, need to have a Novell server or other Novell machines to use NWLink. You can use this protocol in all Microsoft network configurations. NWLink is fast and easy to configure, and it is routable, so it can be used for LANs as well as WANs.

There are several advantages to using NWLink. First, it is not as broadcast-intensive as NetBEUI, making it ideal for small networks. NWLink is also a routable protocol, so you can use it over routers. NWLink is also fast and easy to configure. Unlike with TCP/IP, there is no need to assign IP addresses with NWLink.

NWLink is ideal when implementing a proxy server. A proxy server is how you connect the network to the outside world (such as the Internet) but protect the internal network from damage. Using the Microsoft Proxy Server product, for instance, you can install the proxy server on a Windows NT server with two network cards. You configure one of the cards to use the TCP/IP protocol to connect to the Internet. You configure the other card to use NWLink, which is connected to your internal network. This configuration adds security; the outside world cannot "see" your internal network because there are no IP addresses assigned to the computers.

The TCP/IP Transport Protocol Installation Option

TCP/IP is the protocol used primarily to communicate with the Internet, although you can use TCP/IP for your everyday network use. It is ideal for both LAN and WAN use. The drawback is that TCP/IP is complex to configure, requiring knowledge of IP addressing, subnet masks, and Domain Name Service (DNS) servers.

If you are using one protocol, you do not need to be concerned with the binding order. However, if you are using more than one, from the client-connection point of view, the binding order of your network protocols will play a role in the system performance.

Case Study

While working at a client site, I noticed that network performance was a bit slow compared to the performance a few months before. When asked what had changed in their network configuration, the employees told me that a few months before, they connected all the computers to the Internet using the Microsoft Proxy Server.

Originally, their network was configured using NetBEUI, but because they wanted to connect all the computers to the Internet, they were required (so they thought) to install TCP/IP on all the machines.

First of all, they had a large user base (about 300 machines), so using NetBEUI was causing a lot of unnecessary network broadcast traffic. Second, when they installed TCP/IP, they neglected to change the binding order for the client machines to place TCP/IP on the top of the list. (Most of the client machines were primarily using TCP/IP.)

My recommendation was first to remove NetBEUI and replace it with NWLink, which alleviated the excessive network traffic. I also told them to remove TCP/IP from all the client machines. Because they were using a proxy server, they could configure the proxy machine with two network cards. One card was configured with TCP/IP, which connected to the Internet, whereas the second card was configured with NWLink to support the client connections. Several problems are solved. They no longer had to worry about the complex TCP/IP configuration of client machines because the Microsoft Proxy Server supports IPX/SPX clients. Also, the network traffic was reduced significantly because the removal of NetBEUI eliminated the broadcast chatter.

Performance at the Application Layer

The application layer is the top layer in the OSI architecture, as illustrated earlier in Figure 4.7. In addition to the application-level interfaces such as email and database access, it also serves as the level where many of the NT support applications operate. An NT architecture environment has a lot of background network communication between NT machines.

Windows NT operates in a client/server architecture, which means that NT systems can act as clients, connected to a resource on a server machine, and also act as a server, supporting client requests. You can use several NT services that are user configurable to increase the overall performance. The NT application layer services that you should examine when optimizing Windows NT include:

- Netlogon
- Server
- Workstation
- Replicator

The important feature to consider with all these services is that they are Windows NT services and, as such, they operate regardless of whether a user is logged in. The following sections discuss what each one of these services does and how they affect network performance.

The Netlogon Service

The Netlogon service is an important component of the user login validation mechanism, specifically for domain logins. The functions of the Netlogon service follow:

- Search for an available domain controller
- Establish a secure channel between the domain controller and the workstation
- Provide for passthrough authentication of user login requests
- Synchronize the Security Accounts Manager (SAM) database between the primary domain controller and the backup domain controllers

The Server Service

The Windows NT Server service's responsibility is to establish sessions with remote stations and receive server message block (SMB) request messages from those stations. These SMB requests are typically used to request the Server service to perform I/O operations such as open, read, or write on a device or file located on the Windows NT Server station.

The Workstation Service

The Workstation service enables a computer to access resources on the network, including the capability to log in to a domain (which is also done in conjunction with the Netlogon service), connect to shared directories and printers, and use client/server applications over the network.

All user mode requests go through the Workstation service. The two main components to the Workstation service are the user-mode interface and the redirector. An example of the user-mode interface component is the Explorer interface or the use of the "Net use" commands. The redirector component provides print and file translation services to access remote drives and printers.

> If you want to connect your NT machine to a Novell server, you need a special redirector service that understands how to communicate with the Novell server operating system. Under the Workstation product, this is the Client Service for NetWare. Under the NT Server, this is the Gateway Services for NetWare.

The Replicator Service

The Replicator service for Windows NT provides for automatic replication, or duplication of information between multiple computers. The replication is done without user intervention. Replication requires the existence of an export server and one or more import servers. The import server establishes an SMB connection with the export server. The export server uses an export directory that contains the information (files and login scripts) duplicated on the import machines.

Determining System Baseline Performance

Now that you understand the key components of the NT operating system and what areas could be problems, you need to be able to determine the baseline performance of your system.

First of all, what is a baseline? Do you remember the example of using the wheelbarrow to carry the dirt from one location to the next at the beginning of the chapter? The act of moving the wheelbarrow without the load and taking some measurements is the act of determining how the cart will operate under nominal conditions. Then, you apply a load (move the cart with dirt in it) and take another measurement. This new value is your reference on how well the cart works when it is actually doing its task.

The same analogy applies to the computer system. The baseline is how your system functions under nominal conditions. Then, you apply a load to the system (transferring files, running programs, and so on) and take the same measurements again. What are the resources that you should monitor to get the initial baseline? The answer returns to those four main system resources: memory, processor, disk, and network.

The Performance Monitor is the main tool that you use for measuring the baseline performance of a system. Table 4.1 shows the basic system component objects and the primary counters to monitor.

Table 4.1 **System Component Objects and Primary Counters**

Resource Object	Primary Counter	Description
Processor	% Processor Time	Percentage of the elapsed time that the processor is busy executing a thread
Memory	Page/sec	The number of pages read or written to the disk to resolve memory references to pages not in memory at the time of the reference
LogicalDisk	Avg. Disk Queue Length	Average number of read and write requests queued for the disk
Network Segment	% Network Utilization	The percentage of network bandwidth in use for this segment

Case Study

Looking at Table 4.1, you can collect data from a system and get a pretty good picture of how a system is operating.

A client of mine called me because she was concerned that her NT SQL Server system was operating a bit slow. She wanted an accurate explanation of why all of a sudden, her system was not performing as well as before.

Luckily, I had made some baseline measurements about six months prior, using the standard memory, processor, logical disk, and network objects for my baseline. The numbers were as follows:

% Processor Time: 10%

Page/sec: 4

Avg. Disk Queue Length: 1

% Network Utilization: 12%

These values represent her system working under nominal conditions. When I took the latest measurements of the same objects and the same counters, the values changed to:

% Processor Time: 60%

Page/sec: 8

Avg. Disk Queue Length: 2

% Network Utilization: 90%

As you can see, there was a significant increase in both the processor time and the network utilization. Unfortunately, I do not yet have enough information to determine the exact cause of the problem, but at least I have a place to start.

To prepare for measuring baseline performance, you should be familiar with all the available counters for the main resource objects and what information they provide. Remember that there are many counters available for each resource object. The counters outlined in the following sections should get you started and give you enough detailed system information to determine how your system is operating.

Please note that these next sections just discuss the various counters and what they mean. They do not address what could be the cause for the problem. Causes are addressed in detail in Chapter 6, "Guide to Changing Performance Settings."

Memory Performance Counters

The following list covers the typical memory performance counters you should monitor:

- **Pages/sec.** This value represents the number of times the VMM has to page to disk to resolve a memory reference. Remember that the more paging occurs, the worse system performance is. You should consider that when this value is at or above 10, there is a definite problem. The typical way to solve this problem is to add more memory. You should also look at the size of the paging file to make sure it is set correctly.

- **Available Bytes.** This refers to the amount of free (unused) bytes of the virtual memory. If this value is consistently under 4MB, you should add more RAM. Remember that regardless of how much RAM you have, at least 4MB is reserved for use by the VMM. If your system has only 12MB (the Microsoft recommended minimum for NT Workstation), this means that effectively, you only have 8MB to work with.

- **Committed Bytes.** This refers to the size of the virtual memory that has been committed (as opposed to just reserved). Committed memory must have either hard disk storage to back it up, or it must be assured never to have to go to disk. If the value of Committed Bytes exceeds the available bytes, the memory resource is overextended.

Processor Performance Counters

The main concern when it comes to processors is finding out how busy they are. If the processor is always busy, it could be because the CPU is handling many software tasks at the same time or because the processor is busy servicing hardware or system interrupts. The following list describes the counters to measure to determine processor performance:

- **% Processor Time.** Refers to the percentage of the elapsed time that the processor is busy executing a thread. If this value is at or near 100 percent, your processor is the bottleneck.

- **Interrupts/sec.** This counter points to the number of device interrupts the processor is experiencing. When the processor is interrupted, normal thread execution is suspended. If this value is greater than 1,000, look for some I/O device that is perhaps generating interrupts.

- **System Calls/sec.** This counter is actually in the System object. This refers to the frequency that Windows NT makes calls to NT system routines. If the Interrupts/sec is more than System Calls/sec, there is a hardware device generating excessive interrupts.

Disk Performance Counters

When using the Performance Monitor to collect information on the disk, you need to activate the Performance Monitor counters. Enter the command `diskperf -y` and reboot the computer.

> The counters are disabled by default. In previous hardware configurations using the Intel 486 processor, activating these counters affected overall system performance considerably. This is no longer true with the newer processors such as the Pentium. If you have a stripe set configuration, the command to activate the disk monitor counters is `diskperf -ye`. To deactivate the counters, use the `diskperf -n` command.

The following list covers the counters you should measure to determine disk performance:

- **% Disk Time.** This counter returns the percentage of elapsed time the disk is busy servicing read or write request. If this value is above 67 percent, the disk could be the bottleneck.

- **Current Disk Queue Length.** This counter returns the number of outstanding requests. If the returned value is more than 2, the disk could be congested.

- **Avg. Disk Bytes/Read.** counter This counter returns the average value of bytes read.

- **Avg. Disk Sec/Read.** This counter determines how long it takes to retrieve the data.

■ **Disk Read Bytes/sec.** This counter indicates how many bytes are read each second.

■ **Disk Reads/sec.** This counter indicates how many reads occur per second.

Even though you are looking at the disk resource, make sure to consider some of the other resources as well. For example, check whether the processor is excessively busy when accessing the hard drive. If the processor is excessively busy, it could point to a problem with the hard disk controller or a device that uses the CPU for data transfer.

Network Performance Counters

Other tools such as the Network Monitor are more capable of collecting network traffic data. In any case, you can use some objects in the Performance Monitor to gain a good understanding of what is happening with the network. The following list covers the counters you should measure to determine network performance:

■ **% Network Utilization.** This counter returns the percentage of network bandwidth in use on that particular network segment. If this value is over 50 percent, the network could be a bottleneck.

■ **% Broadcast Frames.** This counter returns the percentage of network bandwidth that is made up of broadcast messages. Remember that some network protocols broadcast more than others, consequently generating excessive traffic on the network.

These counters are available in the Network Segment object. The Network Segment object is an extended object, and it is installed when you install the Network Monitor Agent service. You install this service from the Network applet of the Control Panel.

Defining an "Ideal" System

The definition of an ideal system varies, depending on what you expect the system to do. No matter how much you optimize, you'll always encounter a bottleneck. This bottleneck does not have to be a bad thing, but it is a bottleneck, nevertheless. No system resource will work at 100 percent efficiency.

You can go round and round optimizing one resource after the next and never be done. As soon as you finish optimizing the network, the memory could exhibit other problems and become the bottleneck. So you add more memory to correct the problem, but then, the CPU becomes the bottleneck. And so on and on. There comes a point when you say, "I've done enough optimizing. This is as good as it gets."

Performance is also a personal perception. Some people consider waiting two minutes to get their user accounts validated at the domain server satisfactory, whereas some users would think that is an eternity. Is more than two minutes a real problem? That is up to you and what your clients have to say about it.

In any case, you need to start from a baseline and then see how the NT system operates under stress. If it performs well, you have done your job correctly. If the system does not perform well, you need to determine which resource is causing the bottleneck and start looking at possible solutions to the problems.

## 5

Understanding Network Traffic

This chapter covers the following topics:

- **Network Capacity Planning.** This section takes the concept of capacity planning one step further; the addition of the network component.

- **Gathering Network Traffic with the Network Monitor.** The Network Monitor is a powerful tool what can be used to gather useful network traffic information for in-depth analysis.

- **Understanding and Predicting Network Traffic.** Once the network traffic has been gathered, this section will discuss how to disseminate and understand the data. It is important in a network environment to estimate the amount of the generated network traffic. This section discusses the various types of network traffic and how to predict the traffic bandwidth.

Network Capacity Planning

What is network capacity planning? Let's take a look at a possible real-life scenario:

Case Study

Your company was previously using static IP addresses for all of the 500 client machines. You are asked to determine if this is the best configuration. Your company recently announced a merge with another company and therefore, will be adding a new domain to the current network. This new domain will have a primary domain controller and four backup domain controllers. In addition, this domain has 800 client machines. You decide that perhaps you should implement a DHCP server to centrally manage the use of IP addresses. The default lease life will be seven days.

The questions you need to answer are:

- How much additional traffic will DHCP add?
- How much increased traffic is generated by the new domain?
- If you establish a trust relationship between your existing domain and the new domain, what is the increased traffic then?
- How much network traffic is generated by the replication of the SAM database between the PDC and the BDCs, and can this be controlled?
- Should I be concerned with WINS replication?
- What are the demographics of the machine being added? Are they laptops, desktops, servers, or printers?
- What resources will this new domain need to access?

Probably one of the main goals of network planning is to make sure there is adequate bandwidth to support network users and their daily usage. This encompasses users logging on, accessing network files and printers, and so on. Client access is not the only cause of network traffic generation. The NT system itself will generate network traffic to support its various functions. For instance, as soon as a BDC is added to the domain, there will be an increased amount of traffic generated to support the BDC functions.

To begin looking at network traffic, we need to determine a goal. In some cases, the goal is to reduce overall traffic; however, in many cases the goal is to reduce traffic during a particular event, such as users logging on in the morning. Taking for example, the case study previously presented. There will be undoubtedly increased network traffic due to the increase of client machines logging on in the morning.

Therefore, the key is to capture and analyse the traffic that we are interested in. For instance, capture the data when users log on in the morning. With this capture, we can see specifically the types of network traffic generated. With this information, we can determine if we can further optimize that specific function.

In many cases, we will have to "predict" how each of the network functions that generate network traffic will affect the overall network traffic. The network topology will play an important rule in our calculations. For instance, the addition of the new domain will no doubt add network traffic, but if the connection was over a slow WAN link, could the new network accommodate the extra bandwidth?

The following list constitutes the types of generated network traffic. Our goal is to analyse each one and find ways to optimize their impact as much as possible:

- DHCP
- WINS client to server
- User logon validation

- Browsing
- User file session activity
- Directory services database synchronization
- Trust relationships
- Directory replication
- WINS server to server

Gathering Network Traffic with the Network Monitor

For the capture and analysis of network traffic, you are going to use Microsoft's Network Monitor. The Network Monitor is a software-based network protocol analyzer available with the NT Server product. This version, however, has limited capabilities. This limited edition version can be used to monitor frames destined only to the computer it is running on. Also, you can install the NT Server version from the Network icon in the Control Panel. Select the Services tab and click on the Add Services button. Select Network Monitor Tools and Agent and click OK (see Figure 5.1). You will need to have the NT Server CD-ROM available.

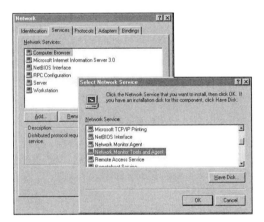

Figure 5.1 Installing the Network Monitor.

A more powerful version of the Network Monitor is included as part of Microsoft Systems Management Server (SMS) product. This version of Network Monitor can be installed and used separately from SMS. This enhanced version of the Network Monitor does not require any special hardware, but it does require a network adapter card that supports being placed into promiscuous mode. A card in promiscuous mode means that the card can collect network traffic that is not destined to that specific machine running the Network Monitor.

There are many other third-party network sniffing tools, some are software-only solutions and some are hardware solutions. Only the Microsoft Network Monitor is discussed here because the limited-edition version is already included in the NT Server product. Each product has its own set of strengths and weaknesses such as features, ease of use, and price.

The Network Monitor is essentially a packet sniffer. Network traffic consists of network packets or frames. These frames contain information as to who the packet is for and where the packet came from. This information is contained in the "Address From" and the "Address To" frame header. When the card is placed in promiscuous mode, the Network Monitor can look at data even if it is not destined for that computer (see Figure 5.2).

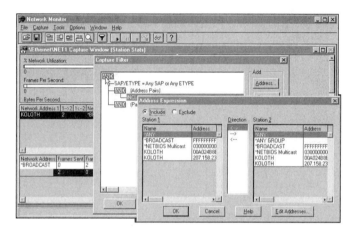

Figure 5.2 Using the Network Monitor as a packet sniffer.

If the card cannot be placed in promiscuous mode, then that computer can only look at packets destined for that computer. For right now, let's look at the Network Monitor user interface and what it all means.

A list of Network Monitor tested and supported network adapters included in the Release Notes for Systems Management Server and at Microsoft's Web page.

The Network Monitor Interface

Upon starting the Network Monitor, you will see the user interface shown in Figure 5.3. The default interface is called the Capture window.

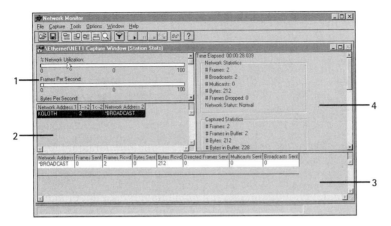

Figure 5.3 The Network Monitor interface.

The Network Monitor is comprised of four different window panes, each one providing different information as covered in the list that follows.

- **Graph pane (1).** Located in the upper-left hand corner, the Graph pane displays the current activity as a set of bar charts indicating the % of Network Utilization, the Frames Per Second, Bytes Per Second, Broadcasts Per Second, and Multicasts Per Second during the capture process. Use this pane to see a quick snapshot of the type of activity on the network. When a thin line appears on the bar graphs that indicates the maximum value for that session for each bar.

- **Session Statistics pane (2).** Located in the middle left, the Session Statistics pane, which displays the summary of the conversations between two hosts, as well as which host is initiating broadcasts and multicasts.

- **Station Statistics pane (3).** Located across the bottom of the window, the Station Statistics pane displays a summary of the total number of frames initiated by a host, the number of frames and bytes sent and received, as well as the number of broadcast and multicast frames initiated.

- **Total Statistics pane (4).** Located in the upper-right corner, the Total Statistics pane displays statistics for the traffic detected on the network as a whole. These statistics include the frames captured, per second utilization statistics, and network adapter card statistics.

Monitoring and Collecting Network Traffic Data

Monitoring and collecting data with the Network Monitor is very easy. After starting the Network Monitor, you simply click the Start Capture button on the toolbar, select Start from the Capture menu (see Figure 5.4), or press the F10 key.

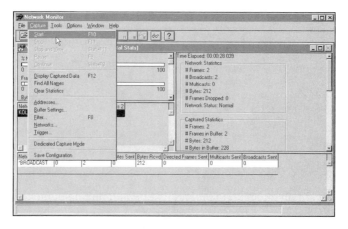

Figure 5.4 Starting a network capture session.

This begins the data collection and you should see some activity taking place on the network. Once you have captured enough data, you can stop the data collection by clicking the Stop Capture button on the toolbar or choosing Stop from the Capture menu (see Figure 5.5), or press the F10 key.

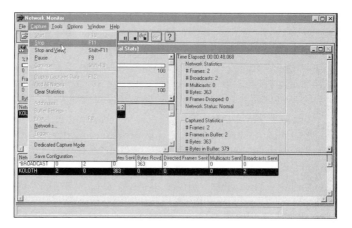

Figure 5.5 Stopping network data collection.

The data collected by the Network Monitor are placed in a special reserved memory buffer area. The size of this buffer area can be adjusted from the Buffer Settings option on the Capture menu (see Figure 5.6).

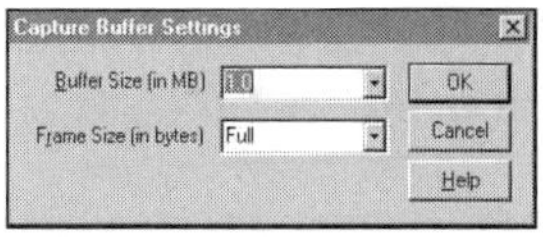

Figure 5.6 Setting memory buffer size.

From this dialog box, you can also change the Frame Size. This value is used to specify the number of bytes you want the Network Monitor to capture from each frame.

> The Buffer Size should not exceed the amount of physical memory on the system. If it does, frames are dropped because of memory swapping. Also be aware that dedicating more memory to this buffer will deprive other systems of this resource.

In addition, in the Capture menu, you can set up capture filters. These filters enable you to configure the Network Monitor to capture only specific information. For instance, it may be desirable to only collect FTP transmissions or only data going to and from Machine A to Machine B. By default, the Network Monitor collects all information (assuming of course the SMS version of Network Monitor is running and the network card supports the promiscuous mode). There are several reasons why you should use a capture filter. Not only is it useful in reducing the buffer size, it is ideal for only capturing the protocol packets we want, and discard all other extraneous data.

Let's take the scenario that we want to collect only Netware 802.2 data. This can be accomplished as follows:

1. Select the Filter menu option from the Capture menu (see Figure 5.7) or press F8.

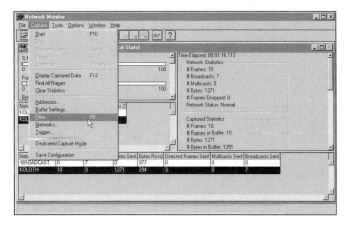

Figure 5.7 Selecting a capture filter.

2. Highlight the SAS/ETYPE line and select the Edit Line button (see Figure 5.8). This will allow you to edit the selection.

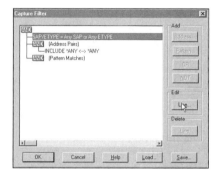

Figure 5.8 Editing a capture filter selection.

3. Click the Disable All button and select the Netware 802.2 from the Disabled Protocols list and hit Enable (see Figure 5.9). Now the only enabled protocol should be the Netware protocol. Click the OK button.

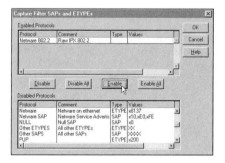

Figure 5.9 Setting the filter to collect specific protocol information.

4. Click the OK button again. Now you will only capture Netware 802.2 packets (see Figure 5.10).

Saving and Viewing Collected Network Data

Once the data is collected, you can save the data to a file or you can view the data. To save the captured data to a file, select the Save As command from the File menu. Within this dialog box (Figure 5.11), you can save the data as a CAP file.

Figure 5.10 Selecting specific packets for capture.

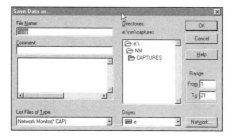

Figure 5.11 Saving captured network data to a file.

To view the data, select the Display Captured Data toolbar button (the glasses icon), select the Display Captured Data option from the Capture menu, or press F12. You will notice the display window changes for what is called the Frame window (see Figure 5.12). With the Network Monitor, you cannot view the data at the same time that you are collecting it. You want network collections to occur with optimal efficiency so that you do not lose any packets of interest. Thus, the user is not allowed to interfere with the data during collection. So, when you click on View it is actually "Stop and View."

By default, the Frame window displays a summary of all of the data (frames) captures. This window also has three panes: the Summary pane, the Detail pane, and the Hex pane as illustrated from top to bottom in Figure 5.13. You can invoke the three frames by double-clicking any displayed frame.

The Summary pane (top) lists all of the frames that were captured. If a frame is highlighted in this pane, the Network Monitor will display that frame's contents in the Detail and Hex panes. The Detail pane in the middle displays protocol information of the frame currently highlighted.

The frame could contain several protocol layers and in this case, the Detail pane displays information on each layer in detail. If the protocol displayed has a plus sign

(+) next to it, it means that additional information can be displayed by clicking on the protocol and expanding the line to expose additional lines beneath it as shown in Figure 5.14.

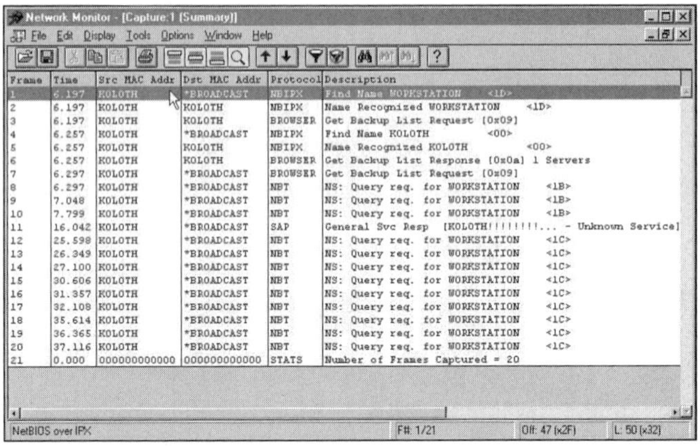

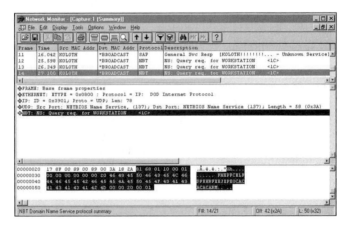

Figure 5.12 Viewing captured network data in the Frame window.

Figure 5.13 The Summary pane, Detail pane, and Hex pane of the Frame window.

To view detailed information on the information in the Detail pane, use the bottom pane called the Hex pane. The Hex pane provides specific information such as the data being sent or what call was being used in a particular transaction. For instance, the Figure 5.15 shows the Hex pane with information from the Browser protocol on getting the list of backup browsers.

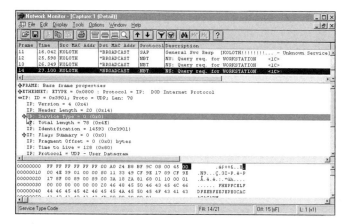

Figure 5.14 Exposing additional information about a protocol.

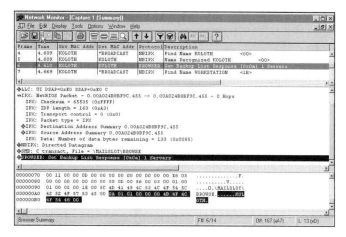

Figure 5.15 Viewing detailed information in the Hex pane.

Customizing Collected Network Data for Analysis

You can also customize what we see in this Frame window. Just like the customizations we can make in the Capture window, we can use the Display filter to display only specific protocols or only frames from one machine to another. In cases where you have collected a lot of network traffic, sometimes looking for a particular protocol transaction becomes a paramount task. The Display Filter is invoked by selecting the Filter command from the Display menu or by pressing the F8 key (see Figure 5.16).

> The Display Filter will not cause the lose of any data already collected. It will only temporarily hide data that you are not interested in.

As you can see in Figure 5.16, we have a small sample of collected data. If we were only interested in SAP protocol (Netware Service Addressing Protocol) we would want to filter this from all of the other data. The steps for accomplishing this are as follows:

1. Selecting the Filter command from the Display menu (see Figure 5.16) to show the Display Filter dialog box.

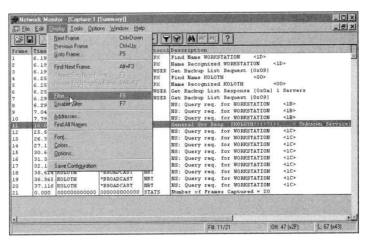

Figure 5.16 Selecting a filter from the Display menu of the Network Monitor.

2. Highlight the line Protocol==Any and click the Edit Expression button (see Figure 5.17). You will notice that all of the protocols are enabled. The idea is to only enable the SAP protocol so we begin by disabling all of them and then only enabling SAP.

Figure 5.17 Enabling/disabling protocols for network data analysis.

3. Click on the Disable All button, find the SAP protocol in the list and select Enable (see Figure 5.18). Now only the SAP protocol should be visible in the Enabled Protocol list.

4. Click on OK twice to return to the Frame viewer window. You should see now only the frames associated with the SAP protocol (see Figure 5.19).

You also have the option of changing the colors of a particular protocol. For instance, you can change the color for all NBT frames to red, making it easier to find all of the NBT frames in the captured buffer. This can be done by selecting the Color option on the Display menu selection as shown in Figure 5.20.

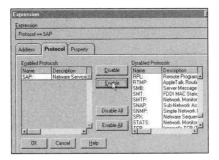

Figure 5.18 Enabling/disabling protocols for network data analysis.

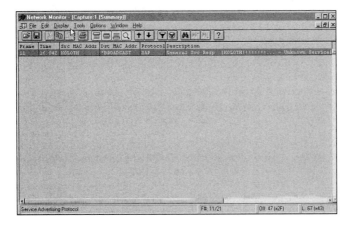

Figure 5.19 Viewing the enabled protocol for network analysis in the Frame window of the Network Monitor.

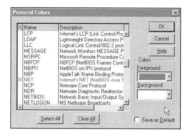

Figure 5.20 Marking protocols by color in the the Frame window.

Understanding and Predicting Network Traffic

Now that you understand a little bit about how to collect network data and statistics, it's time to see what information you can gain from it. The amount of network traffic generated will depend on what protocol is used. When installing NT, you have the option of installing TCP/IP (the default), NWLink, and/or NetBEUI. Some protocols are more efficient than others. NetBEUI, for instance relies on using broadcast while TCP/IP is more frames-oriented. Broadcast on a network can have severe impact, especially if these broadcasts are forwarded by routers. If your network has routers and you install only NetBEUI, many broadcast requests will not travel past the routers.

Of all of the network protocol choices available, the most popular is TCP/IP. This protocol is an ideal choice for WAN as well as LAN setups, plus it provides the advantage of providing Internet access. Regardless of which protocol you choose to implement, the network analysis procedure will be the same. Network analysis takes time. Ensure accurate data collection and analysis by adhering to the following steps:

1. **Isolate the network.** This means determine what component of the network traffic you want to collect and turn off all other network traffic (if possible).

2. **Use the Network Monitor to capture the data.** Determine what type of data you wish to collect. In the case scenario outlined at the beginning of the chapter, we may want to collect the frames to analyze logon traffic. You do this by simply logging off and on at the client machine.

3. **Once the sequence of whatever you are collecting is completed, stop the capture.** Using the Frame window, identify each frame to make sure the traffic generated came from the function you wanted to capture and not from some other event.

4. **The final step is the analysis.** Using the Frame Viewer window, find the protocol traffic of interest and chick on the appropriate frame. This will expand the frame and then it is possible to see detailed information on the information contained in each data packet.

Another useful Network Monitor feature is to retransmit captured data back across the network. This feature is particularly handy when you need to generate network traffic over and over again while looking for a particular problem. However, it should be used with caution as re-transmitting packets onto a production network can cause problems on machines. It is often best to construct a test network for such exercises. You can choose to send the data one of as many times as you would like, as shown in Figure 5.21.

So what specific network traffic are we most likely to be concerned with? In our case scenario above, we are interested mainly in logon validation (which included DHCP, WINS, logon sequence, and logon script processing), and the SAM database replication traffic. In essence, we are interested in the following:

- DHCP traffic
- WINS name resolution and database replication
- Logon sequence
- Network browsing
- Directory/database replication
- Domain trust relationships

Figure 5.21 Setting times to transmit frames.

Because the systems administrator in our case scenario is planning to move from static IP addresses to using a DHCP server, let's see what impact that has on our network traffic. Let's analyze the DHCP traffic first.

Looking at DHCP Traffic

In a TCP/IP environment, every workstation must have a valid IP address and subnet mask. If a DHCP server is not used, then the settings must be configured locally and manually at the client workstation Interestingly enough, using a DHCP server does not add a significant amount of network traffic. This is because the assignment of the IP addresses is done during the IP address lease and the IP address renewal sequence.

When a DHCP client initializes, the first thing it has to do is to acquire an IP address. The first frame the client sends out is a broadcast, called a DHCP Discover packet. This is the packet sent to attempt to locate a DHCP server. This broadcast is necessary, because the client has no idea if there are any DHCP servers available. If the network contains routers, the broadcasts will travel across the routers provided they are BOOTP enabled.

> A DHCP server can provide IP addresses to clients in multiple subnets if the router that connects the subnets is an RFC 1542-compliant router. RFC 1542 specifies the DHCP/BOOTP relay agent.
>
> A *relay agent* is a program used to pass specific types of IP packets between subnets. A DHCP/BOOTP relay agent is either hardware or a software program that can pass DHCP/BOOTP packets between subnets.

Once the DHCP server has received this Discover packet, it determines if it can accommodate the client request. The client request of course is for the DHCP server to provide an IP address. The DHCP responds with a DHCP Offer message that contains the IP address the client can use. The client will then select an offer (since there could be more than one DHCP server responding to the client request) and respond back to the DHCP server with a DHCP Request frame. This Request frame informs that it is accepting the offer.

The DHCP server then responds to the client with a DHCK ACK messageAnd other information as well, such as Domain Name Service (DNS) server addresses and Windows Internet Name Service (WINS) server addresses. The DHCP server can be used to configure what options that are parsed out to the client. In summary, the handshake is as follows (see Figure 5.22):

1. DHCP Client issues a DHCP Discover packet (342 bytes).
2. DHCP Server issues a DHCP Offer packet (342 bytes).
3. DHCP Client issues a DHCP Request packet (342 bytes).
4. DHCP Server issues a DHCP ACK packet (342 bytes).

These four packets take up around 1,368 bytes of network traffic, but again, it only happens once, when the client first logs on to the system.

If the DHCP client reboots the machine, the IP address must be renewed. This transaction is much simpler, consisting of only two packets. The client will request a renewal of its IP address with a DHCP Request packet and if successful, the DHCP server will respond with a DHCP ACK packet. Also, note that the "conversation" between the client and the server for a renewal transaction is not broadcast-based. That is, the conversation occurs directly from machine to machine. DHCP clients also get to renew their IP address at least at one half of the Time-to-Live (TTL) value. This value is configured at the DHCP server. To summarize, the IP renewal process is as follows (see Figure 5.23 on page 110):

1. DHCP Client issues a DHCP Request packet.
2. DHCP Server issues a DHCP ACK packet.

These two frames will take up around 684 bytes.

This book assumes some familiarity and knowledge of TCP/IP.

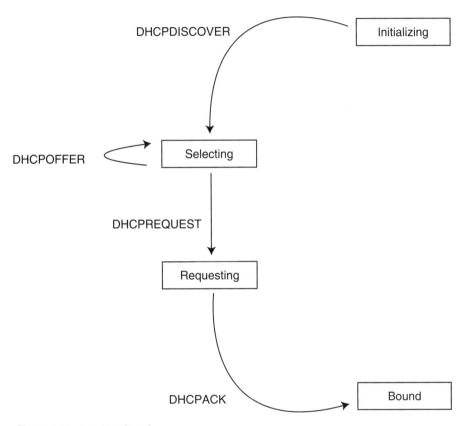

Figure 5.22 DHCP Client lease sequence.

Using the DHCP Manager(in this case the Microsoft DHCP Manager) as shown in Figure 5.24, you can adjust the lease duration in the Scope Properties dialog box. Increasing the lease life from the default of three days to, say 30 days would reduce the frequency of renewals by the DHCP clients on the network.

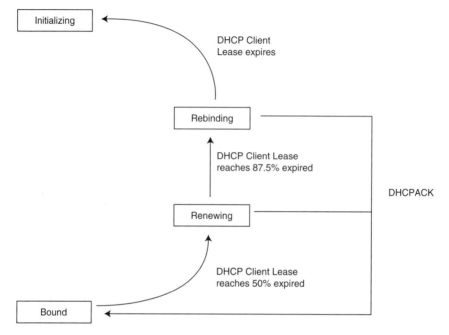

Figure 5.23 DHCP Client renewal sequence.

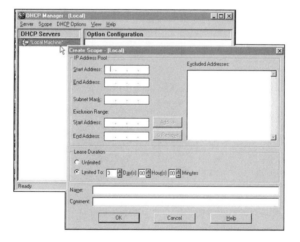

Figure 5.24 Adjusting the lease duration for DHCP clients.

If the number of DHCP clients is close to the number of IP addresses available in the DHCP server, then use a short lease life. This is because it takes less network traffic to renew an IP address than it takes to establish a new one. However, if the number of DHCP available IP addresses is much larger than the number of DHCP clients, then longer lease periods is better.

If you have several subnets in your domain and your routers are BOOTP enabled, these routers will forward the DHCP Discover messages to all other subnets to which the router is connected.

Many routers can be configured to vary the number of retries that must occur before the router forwards the local request to other subnets. This means that if the local DHCP server is busy, and does not answer the request immediately, configuring this parameter would allow a certain number of tries for DCHP resolution before forwarding the request to other subnets. Microsoft's implementation in NT allows the setting of "Seconds threshold" and "number of hops."

Looking at WINS and NetBIOS Name Resolution

After the successful DHCP transaction and the client has an IP address, the next thing needed is to register the NetBIOS name. The NetBIOS (Network Basic Input Output System) name is essentially the computer name. The NetBIOS name is a 16-byte character name. The first 15 bytes are the name itself and the last byte is reserved for a special "information" byte to represent the role of that computer in the domain.

When naming the machines in your domain, the maximum name length is 15 characters. It is best not to use spaces in the name, since some of the name resolution techniques do not know how to interpret spaces in the name. That is, do not create a computer name like WARP SPEED but instead call it WARP-SPEED or WARP_SPEED.

When a WINS client registers its name with the WINS server, it generates 214 bytes of network traffic. Once a name is registered, the WINS server responds with a success message that includes a TTL value (much like the TTL lease value for DHCP). This TTL indicates when the client will be required to refresh the name. The default WINS configuration is to assign a TTL value of 345,600 seconds or four days. The WINS renewal will occur at one half the TTL value or every two days. These values can be modified by using the WINS Manager as shown in Figure 5.25.

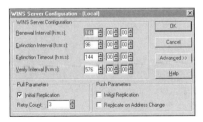

Figure 5.25 WINS Server Configuration Settings dialog box.

WINS (Windows Internet Name Service) is essentially a NetBIOS Name Server. If a WINS server is not available, one of the ways the system will resolve the NetBIOS name is by broadcasting.

Broadcasting for name resolution is essentially "shouting" across the network to determine if a particular machine is available and what its address is. For instance, Computer A wishes to communicate with Machine B and to do this, needs to know the IP address of the machine (NetBIOS over TCP/IP name service functions use UDP Port 137). Computer A, not knowing if Computer B is there, will broadcast a message to all of the machines on the domain asking essentially "is Machine B out there and what is your IP address?" Because it is a broadcast, it will be heard by all of the machines on the domain, essentially creating excessive traffic. A WINS server on the other hand, is dynamic NetBIOS name resolution server. So instead of Machine A broadcasting to find Machine B, it simply will ask the WINS server for Machine B's IP address. If Machine B has registered itself with the WINS server and the server has its IP address, the information is forwarded to Machine A.

Another problem is not that a broadcast creates excessive traffic, but that it will cause CPU interrupts on all machines that receive the broadcast. In general, systems that rely on broadcasts get clogged due to the amount of rebroadcasting that happens when a client does not get a response.

The resolution follows these steps:

1. Client sends a Name Query Request to the WINS Server.

2. WINS server responds with a Name Query Response frame.

The client request contains the name of the name to be resolved. The server response contains the IP of the name requested by the client. This two frame conversation requires about 200 bytes of traffic. If the requested name is not in the database, the WINS server responds with a "Requested name does not exist" message and the client will then use a broadcast request to resolve the name. Figure 5.26 illustrates the client WINS process and replication between WINS servers.

It is possible to have more than one WINS server. While Microsoft documents that a single WINS server can support 10,000 WINS clients, it is perhaps a good idea to have a backup server. Having multiple WINS servers requires these servers to replicate or share their databases with each other. Because the databases can be shared, each WINS server will be able to provide name resolution to other WINS clients that have registered with its WINS partners.

Using the WINS Manager program, you can configure a replication partner (see Figure 5.27).

The amount of traffic generated during the configuration of a replication partner will vary. However, replication partners can be configured to either push the information or pull the information to the partners. Push partners send announcements to their configured partners when a specific number of entries have changes. Pull partners, on the other hand, request updates when notified by the push partner.

Configuring the push notifications informs the pull partner that there are updated records. You can configure push partners to initiate the push notification after a specific number of record changes have been accumulated (the default is 20). Increasing this number will reduce the frequency of the WINS replication.

Domain Logon Validation Sequence

Windows NT 4.0 uses domain controllers to provide logon validation. An NT domain must contain one primary domain controller (PDC) and one or more backup domain controllers (BDCs).

> Windows NT 5.0 Server will no longer implement the concepts of the PDC and BDC, as it is known in NT 4.0. See Chapter 8 for what will be new in NT 5.0.

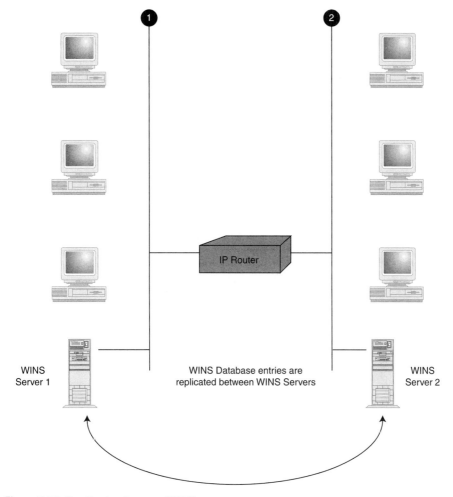

Figure 5.26 Replication between WINS servers.

A client, in order to logon to the domain, requires first finding a domain controller. One method is to query the WINS server for all registered domain controllers and the other is to broadcast a request using the NetLogon service. When logging on to the domain, the user provides not only his/her name and password, but also provides which domain to log on to from the logon screen. This domain name is used as the destination NetBIOS name with a <00> in the sixteenth position. If, for instance, the user tries to log on to a domain called "MAINOFFICE" then a request is sent to "MANOFFICE <00>" with spaces padded to fill the 15 characters, then <00>. This frame size will be around 300 bytes, but depends on the computer name. Each registered domain server, also running the NetLogon service, will respond to the client. This response includes the IP address and the name of the domain logon server. This frame will be about 240 bytes, but also depends on the computer name.

If a WINS server is used to find a logon server, the client will query the WINS server for the domain name but with a <1C> appended as the sixteenth character, making the standard query a size of 92 bytes. The WINS server in turn returns a frame that includes the name of all registered domain controllers. The size of this frame will vary, depending on the number of domain controllers registered in the database. Once the WINS server responds with the names of the domain controllers, the client will send a message to each domain server for a logon request validation.

Figure 5.27 Configuring WINS server replication partners.

> On a completely Windows NT 5.0 network, WINS will not be needed in native environments. In mixed environments with Windows NT 4.0 and NT 5.0, it should remain the same as previously described. Most of this has to do with NetBIOS name resolution which is being eliminated in NT 5.0. NT 5.0 will be using more of a X.500 scheme that looks much like the standard Internet addresses (such as `mydomain.mycompany.com`). WINS will be part of DNS which in turn will be renamed to dynamic DNS.

The domain that responds to the client logon request will then resolve the server's NetBIOS name by querying the WINS server or by broadcasting. Then a TCP session is established and a secure SMB (Server Message Block) connection is made to `\\logonserver\IPC$`. This IPC (Interprocess Communication) connection is used to provide secure transmissions between the client and the logon server. This process generates about 1,370 bytes of data.

At this point, the client has not yet "logged" to the domain. A series of API (Application Programming Interface) calls are made and the server responds with a success or failure message. This handshake generates about 5,000 bytes of traffic, including the following:

- About 2,000 bytes to retrieve the list of trusted domains.

- 1,400 bytes to establish the secure NetLogon channel. It is here that the computer is validated to make sure it is a member of the domain.

- 900 for the actual validation. An additional 700 bytes is generated only if this is the first logon.

Additional network traffic is generated from logon scripts, user profiles, and system policies. Once the user is logged on, the connection to the IPC$ is disconnected and the NetBIOS and TCP sessions are terminated. This takes up about 360 bytes of traffic. The entire sequence is summarized as follows:

1. Broadcasting to NetLogon. Used to find the name of the domain. Frame size is 300 for a Windows NT system (260 for Windows 95).

2. Each domain controller in the domain will respond to the request (provided the NetLogon service is running) and will respond with a message indicating that it can service the logon request. The Frame size is about 270 bytes.

3. If a WINS service is used, the WINS client sends a query to the WINS server for the domain name. This standard query is 92 bytes.

4. The WINS responds with about 75 bytes for domain controller address.

5. The session establishment generates about 1,370 bytes of traffic. This provides for the NetBIOS name resolution, establishment of a NetBIOS session with the logon server and the Server Message Block (SMB) protocol negotiation.

6. Nearly 5,000 bytes for the actual logging on to the system.

7. Additional traffic for logon scripts and downloading of user profiles.

8. When the session is terminated, an additional 360 bytes total for session breakdown.

A Look at Browser Traffic

The concept of the browser service has been around since Microsoft introduced Windows for Workgroups. The idea is that once a user is connected to the network, the most likely next step is to access whatever network resources are available. In Microsoft terms, this is function is called the Browser service. Unfortunately, browsing is based mainly on using broadcast packets, which means that every computer on the domain will hear a browser service request. Generally, browser frames are about 300 bytes in size.

Windows NT uses what is known as a Master Browser and a Backup Browser. Master Browsers maintain a list of all of the computers and the Backup Browsers keep (as you might expect) a copy of the list. Backup Browsers receive updated browse lists from the Master Browser to make sure they are up to date. A client, wishing to "browse" the list, will request the list from either the Master Browser or the Backup Browser.

When a computer joins the domain, it will announce itself to the browser every 12 minutes and generates about 243 bytes of traffic. After the client has announced itself, the client may need to connect to a shared resource (like a folder) and to do this, it needs to get a list of available resources. To find the local Master Browser, the client sends a "Get Backup List Request" message to the domain. This request generates about 215 bytes. In turn, the local Master Browser responds with a "Get Backup List Response" message with the list of available Backup Browsers. This response will vary in size. When the client connects to the Backup Browser, it retrieves the browse list. This is what you would see in the Network Neighborhood. This entire process generates over 2,150 bytes of network traffic. The sequence for browser traffic is summarized as follows:

1. Any computer that shares its resources will announce themselves to the network every 12 minutes. This takes approximately 243 bytes. This announcement actually occurs even if the computer does not have any shared resources.

2. The computer then needs to get a list of Backup Browsers. The issuance of the "get backup list" generates about 215 bytes.

3. The local Master Browser responds with a variable frame size. If there are two servers for instance, the size might be around 230 bytes.

4. An election might be forced if the local Master Browser does not respond. In this case, the client sends an Election frame of 225 bytes.

5. The client then generates over 2,150 bytes to connect to one of the browsers in the list once it receives the list of Backup Browsers.

There are many types of browser messages. For instance, computers with Server service components running announce themselves to the Master Browser for their local domain. The purpose of this announcement is to identify itself as a member of the network that may be providing resources, such as shared folders. Once a browser computer has initialized, it must determine who is the Master Browser for its domain.

If a Master Browser cannot be found, the computer that detects the absence of the Master Browser will force an election to establish a new Master Browser. When an election is performed, the host that initiated the election sends an Election frame, indicating it is forcing an election, along with its election criteria. All browser computers receive this election frame, and if a host has a higher election criteria, it responds with an election packet with its criteria. Eventually, the computer with the highest criteria wins the election, and assumes the role of the Master Browser. Once a Master Browser has been elected, it must announce itself as the Master Browser for the domain.

If a client needs to access resources on other subnets, each domain elects a Master Browser on each subnet. These Master Browsers all exchange browse lists with the domain Master Browser every 15 minutes. This update of browse information is then provided to the client computers through Backup Browsers.

When a user attempts to display a list of network resources (via the Network Neigborhood icon), a Backup Browser is used to get that list. In order to find a

Backup Browser, the client must first send a "Get Backup List Request" message to the Master Browser of their subnet. The Master Browser responds with a list of Backup Browsers. Finally, the client selects a Backup Browser from the list, and establishes a session to retrieve the current browse list.

Looking at Account Synchronization Traffic

As we discussed earlier, an NT 4.0 domain environment can contain more than one backup domain controller. Client connections can get their accounts validated at either the primary or backup domain controller. Each BDC must contain an exact copy of the Security Accounts Manager (SAM) database. This means that the databases must be synchronized. This is done via the NetLogon service. The SAM database synchronization can be performed manually by using the Server Manager as shown in Figure 5.28. Because the BDCs will always need the updated database, however, this process occurs automatically.

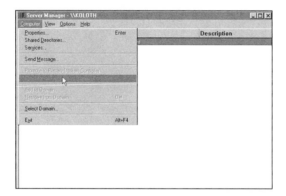

Figure 5.28 Synchronizing the SAM database with the Server Manager.

If you remember from our case scenario, the following question was asked: "How much network traffic is generated by the replication of the SAM database between the PDC and the BDCs and can this be controlled?"

To answer these questions, refer to when the SAM database is replicated:

- When a BDC is installed or restarted
- By manual command in the Server Manager
- Automatically and periodically, based on Registry settings

In each one of these cases, The BDC must query for the primary controller. The PDC responds to the request with a "Response to Primary Query" frame and includes the name of the PDC as well as the domain name. The total number of bytes needed to discover the name of the PDC is 545 bytes of traffic. The next step is to verify the version of the SAM database. To verify the database, NT must establish a session and prepare for verification of the database. This generates 1,200 bytes of traffic. Once this process is completed, a secure channel is established, generating 1,500 bytes. The verification of the database takes place by several request frames that are sent numerous times. A minimum of three frames are sent and are used to tell the PDC the serial number of each of the databases at the BDC. This generates 1,344 bytes of data.

The PDC by default will verify its databases every five minutes. When a change is noticed, it will "pulse" the BDC(s) that need notification. This indicates to them that an update has been made to the database. Since the PDC maintains a list of all of the BDCs in the domain, it can check to see if a BDC has an up-to-date database and if so, it is not notified of the update (see Figure 5.29).

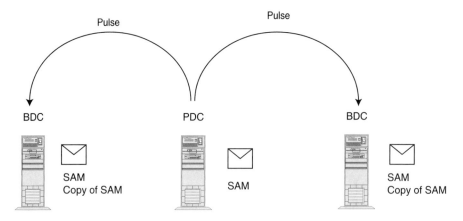

Figure 5.29 PDC sending a pulse to BDCs to determine if their SAM databases need updating.

To better understand the database update, let's go through the scenario where a user is added to the SAM database:

1. A new account is added to the SAM database.

2. The PDC detects the change.

3. The PDC announces the change to the BDC's (as needed).

4. The BDC establishes a connection to the PDC using the IPC$ channel.

5. The BDC then establishes a secure channel to the PDC using the NetLocon service.

6. Depending on the size of the update, the BDC will use either SMB or RPC (Remote Procedure Calls) to transfer the new data.

Depending on the number of updates, the network traffic generated by this process will vary. The size of the frame will also be affected by the information on each new update including full name, comments or group membership information. As a test example, it may take about 4,459 bytes to update a SAM database with four accounts.

The SAM database synchronization takes on average about 1KB per change. Take note if the synchronization is going to happen over a slow WAN. There are some Registry settings we can modify to help relieve the network traffic. They are as follows:

- **HKEY_LOCAL_MACHINE\SYSTEM\CurrentControlSet\Services\Netlogon\ Parameters\ReplicationGovernor.** Controls the percentage of network bandwidth the NetLogon service may use at any one instance while performing directory services synchronization. The default value for this parameter is 100 percent.

- **HKEY_LOCAL_MACHINE\SYSTEM\CurrentControlSet\Services\Netlogon\ Parameters\Pulse.** Controls how often the primary domain controller looks for changes to its directory services database, and sends synchronization messages to the backup domain controllers that need updating. The default value is five minutes, and can be increased to a maximum of 60 minutes.

- **HKEY_LOCAL_MACHINE\SYSTEM\CurrentControlSet\Services\Netlogon\ Parameters\PulseMaximum.** Controls how often the primary domain controller will send a pulse message to each backup domain controller, even if its directory services database is up to date. The default value is every two hours, and can be increased to every 24 hours.

- **HKEY_LOCAL_MACHINE\SYSTEM\CurrentControlSet\Services\Netlogon\ Parameters\ChangeLogSize.** Controls the number of changes to the directory services database before a full synchronization event occurs. The default value is 64KB.

Looking at Trust Traffic

In a multiple domain environment, it is often necessary to establish trust relationships between the domains. This allows a user from one domain to have access to resources in another domain. Establishing these trusts does generate network traffic.

Trust relationships by default are one-way only and are not transitive. That means that if Domain A trusts Domain B and Domain B trusts Domain C, it does not mean that Domain A trusts Domain C.

Here is a summary of the traffic generated by establishing a trust relationship:

- Over 15,000 bytes of traffic is generated when a trusted domain permits a trusting domain to trust its accounts and the trusting domain accepts the offer.

- Over 24,000 bytes of traffic is generated when a trusting domain imports the accounts from the trusted domain.

- Around 3,700 bytes of traffic is generated when a user in the trusted domain attempts to access a resource in the trusting domain.

Predicting Network Traffic

Remember the case study at the beginning of this chapter? Here it is again:

> ## Case Study
>
> Your company was previously using static IP addresses for all of the 500 client machines. You are asked to determine if this is the best configuration. Your company has announced a merge with another company and therefore, will be adding a new domain to the current network. This new domain will have a primary domain controller and four backup domain controllers. In addition, this domain has 800 client machines. You decide that perhaps you should implement a DHCP server to centrally manage the use of IP addresses. The default lease life will be seven days.

With the information provided regarding the traffic generated by the various network services and components, you can begin to predicting how much network bandwidth will be generated. In this case scenario, we are going to use DHCP for the management of our IP addresses. Lets take how much traffic is generated by using DHCP.

First of all, the impact of using DHCP is minimal, since it is only used during logon. For a network with 1,300 machines (the original 500 plus the new 800 clients), however, the traffic generated by DHCP would be:

1,300 clients×1,368 bytes=1,778,400 bytes

Again, other factors will affect this value. For instance, not all clients will most likely be logging on at the same time. Also, if the lease TTL has expired, the DHCP manager will renew the lease. But if you use this number as the "worse" case value, it will provide you with a good place to start. After this, your use determines the other types of traffic generates (WINS, browser, and so forth) and performs the same calculations.

Summary

Network traffic optimization should be done very carefully. Making too many changes at one time can prove to be very dangerous. Predicting the affect of the implementation of adding a service such as a DHCP or WINS server becomes an easier job if we analyze each component individually. It is best to adhere to the following recommendations:

- Identify and analyze the traffic associated with a specific function.
- Identify which additional service you wish to implement on the network and determine the impact of adding such a service. For instance, if you want to analyze the affect of implementing DHCP, you will need to know how many DHCP servers will be installed, how many DHCP clients will be used, and how long the lease duration is.

6

Optimizing CPU Performance

This chapter covers the following topics:

- **Hardware: CPU Architecture.** This chapter begins with a discussion of the foundation for system performance, the hardware. This section discusses some of the basics of the CPU and its interaction with the rest of the system. This section will also look at a couple of the current CPU technologies in the marketplace.

- **CPU and the Operating System.** Once you understand how CPU hardware works, you will see how NT tries to utilize as much of the processor at all times. This section discusses a little queuing theory and talks about how NT manages threads. This section also looks at how NT takes advantage of mulitple processors.

- **Monitoring CPU Activity.** With all of the basics out of the way, you can begin some serious analysis of Windows NT and the applications that are running on it. By the time you're done, you will know our processor backward and forward. With this knowledge you will be able to make the changes on your systems to improve performance.

Hardware: CPU Architecture

What better place to start than with the hardware. The CPU, that small square sitting on a maze of metal snaking around the green field of the motherboard, powers the computer. A wafer of little more than sand performs millions of transactions per second, manages hardware requests, balances system resources, and performs a variety of other small miracles. To understand system performance, you must first understand this small dark obelisk and components that it interacts with. This section looks at how this unobtrusive emperor commands memory, cache, disk, and controller through the communication channels of the system and memory buses. You will learn the strengths and weaknesses of the CPU which will set the stage for examining how the operating system manipulates the CPUs kingdom to get work done.

General PC System Layout

The processor is the key component for marking the speed of a system. The only resource perhaps more affecting performance is memory. The processor is nonetheless the key to the system performance and often the user's ego. The general layout of the system board can be thought of as a series of channels on a board connecting components that rely on each other to complete the task of computing. Figure 6.1 depicts the relationship between some of the various components of a computer system.

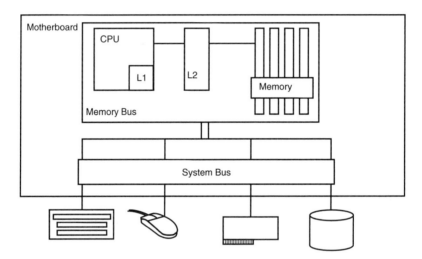

Figure 6.1 System Board Layout.

The disk, network, and keyboard communicate with the system using the system bus. Chapter 8, "Optimizing Disk Performance" covers the system bus in more detail. The system bus is slower than the memory bus, which connects the memory, cache system, and processor together. The memory bus is a high-speed bus meant to move the information between these components quickly. Currently, the memory bus can operate at about 66MHz, which, while not much compared to the processor, is a significant increase to the system bus. New architectures are allowing the memory bus to operate at a speed of 100MHz. This architecture should offer an additional 20% performance increase to the current Pentium processor systems.

Already we have learned some insight into performance monitoring and tuning. The system is only as fast as its slowest component. If you have a really fast processor, but don't buy high-speed RAM or the faster memory bus, you won't get the performance you could be getting with a little more of an investment.

This little review of the system layout focused some attention on the communication between the processor and the memory. The following section takes a closer look at this memory and the importance of this interaction.

The Processor/Cache Relationship

Processors must move information from the memory (RAM) in order to be able to execute instructions that run programs and respond to hardware interrupts. For this information to get to the processor, it must pass from the RAM, to the L2-Cache, and finally to the L1-Cache. The cache is not an imposition on the system, but an enhancement. The processor basically is a beast that needs to be fed information constantly. The RAM simply cannot feed the processor fast enough to keep performance up. The cache and the cache controller attempt to anticipate the information that the processor is going to needby implementing several types of caching algorithms that vary with the vendor of the cache. More importantly, the cache is trying to anticipate the processor's needs and feed it the right stuff.

The more often the cache anticipates correctly (cache hit), the less often the processor is waiting for the right information. Of course, when the cache does not anticipate the processor correctly (a cache miss), the processor ends up waiting for information that it needs to complete the transaction. With this in mind, you can see that the larger the cache, the better the chance that the information needed will be present. The physical RAM is where the information is being pulled from. The better the L2-Cache size to RAM size is, the better the chances for the L2-Cache to have the information that the processor needs, resulting in a better performing system. Granted there is more to the system and algorithms, but this gives you the general idea.

The Level 1 (L1-) Cache typically is integrated onto the processor chip. It wasn't to long ago when this cache was about 8KB. Nowadays, some of the chips have as much as 32KB of L1-Cache. This allows the processor to keep more information "closer" to the processor. This statistically allows the processor to get at the information that it needs when it needs it, making the whole process quicker.

The L2-Cache is the next step away from the processor. The L2-Cache generally comes in sizes of 256KB up to around 1MB. This memory is used to basically "map" the information from the physical RAM into the processor. It is the staging area for information while it is on its way to L1-Cache where the processor can directly consume the information. Chapter 7, "Optimizing Memory Performance," discusses the various innovations that have occurred in memory and cache technology, for now let us return our focus to a couple of current processor architectures.

Workstations and servers are distinctly different. Although the concepts presented here are the same for both, servers will tend to be more of the high end. When you purchase a server, the cost isn't simply for the sake of a bigger box, it typically has a more complex internal bus structure that pushes performance higher. The more advanced technology and complex components contribute to the price.

Intel Pentium II

The Intel PII processor is primarily useful in workstations. The chip has exceptional speed performance, managing speeds in 300MHz range to date, but is currently not scalable past two processors. In addition, the configuration of the system, while allowing the processor to run faster, prevents the system from supporting more than 128MB of RAM. The processor does have an extended L1-Cache, 32Kb, which assists in the transfer of data, but the limited L2-Cache again prevents the system from supporting more than 128MB of RAM. Lastly, the L2-Cache speed is in the 66MHz range.

While this information may be applicable to machines purchased just six months prior to the release of this book, we all know how fast hardware architectures and strategies can change. Excellent sources for information on the CPU technology are Intel, the chip makers, and Compaq. Compaq often posts white papers on its web site describing the technology and the implementation of that technology into servers and workstations.

> You can find information on chip technologies that are emerging at `http://www.compaq.com`—the Compaq computer web site and `http://www.intel.com`—the Intel web site. Compaq is exceptionally good at posting up to date white papers on the application of Intel chip technologies in server and workstation products.

Intel Pentium Pro

The Intel Pentium Pro is the more likely candidate for higher power servers. While the current processor speed is slower than that of the Pentium II, 133MHz, the memory access and the ability to scale to four processors is often the deciding factor. The memory access is faster with the L2-Cache running at the same clock speed. The L1-Cache is 16KB, so it is not quite as prominent as the Pentium II there, but the L2-Cache can extend to 1MB making putting 1 Gigabit of memory on a server a possibility without a sacrifice of speed.

CPU and the Operating System

This section reviews how the operating system schedules threads on the processor as well as some information on how tasks are generally handled. This will lead to a little theory-discussion that you will have to wade through, but nonetheless, it is a discussion that will help you in determining the behavior of the operating system and applications.

Understanding Thread Scheduling

So NT is multithreaded, big deal. What is that supposed to mean anyway. Well, here is where we are going to find out. This section takes a microscopic look at these little threads that make up the fabric of Windows NT application performance. Just like our busy schedules at work, NT has tasks to complete. NT needs to prioritize each task, assign an appropriate amount of time to each, and distribute the tasks as appropriate to each worker (or CPU in this case). Sometimes we have emergencies or new higher-priority tasks interrupting the normal work flow. Just as much as you have to deal with the marketing department's urgent need for a demo product, NT must deal with a new tasks need to get addressed if it really has a higher priority. Too bad you can't do something about the marketing guys' priority.

Threads

Threads are the same pieces of re-entrant code that run on a processor. They are the minute little activities that are conducted in an order governed by a program. Think of the threads like strands of fiber that are intertwined to make a cloth. The cloth is the program that contains patterns, shapes and colors as defined by its creator—the programmer. While collectively threads are similar to one another, each thread is very distinct. Threads vary in length, color, and purpose. Each thread runs independent of the other, yet they are intertwined in a specific pattern to produce a vivid cloth with pleasing patterns. Sounding a little too 60s isn't it. I am sure you get the idea. Each thread exists within a specific process. The process is described as containing multiple threads as well as security information, memory pools, data, code, and identifying information about itself and the threads running within it. The process also contains a process priority class. The priority class ranges from Idle to Real-time. Each priority class covers a range of priorities. These priorities are used with threads as well.

Thread Priority

Threads are given priorities to operate in. The term *preemptive* refers to when one thread is running on the processor and another thread comes along that needs time on the processor and has a greater priority. The thread with the greater priority will pre-empt the thread on the processor. Thread priorities generally float around in the process' priority class. The thread priority numbers from 0 to 31 as seen in Table 6.1.

Table 6.1   Process/thread priorities

Base	Priority Class	Thread Priority
31	Real-time	Time critical
26	Real-time	Highest
25	Real-time	Above normal
24	Real-time	Normal
23	Real-time	Below normal
22	Real-time	Lowest
16	Real-time	Idle
15	Idle, Normal, or High	Time critical

continues

Table 6.1 continued

Base	Priority Class	Thread Priority
15	High	Highest
14	High	Above normal
13	High	Normal
12	High	Below normal
11	High	Lowest
10	Normal	Highest
9	Normal	Above normal
8	Normal	Normal
7	Normal	Below normal
6	Norma	Lowest
6	Idle	Highest
5	Idle	Above Normal
4	Idle	Normal
3	Idle	Below normal
2	Idle	Lowest
1	Idle, Normal, or High	Idle

When a process is created, it is assigned a priority class. When a thread is created within the process, the thread is assigned a thread priority (column 3 of Table 6.1) that is within the process's priority class (column 2 of Table 6.1). These all correspond to the base priority numbers 1–31 (column 1 of Table 6.1). As you can see in column 3, the thread priority can fluctuate in the process's priority class. Thus, when a thread might need a little boost to get the job done, it will change thread priorities from a normal to an above normal priority within a process's priority class. In general, the thread is permitted to fluctuate its base priority +/− 2 points.

From Table 6.1, you can see that the idle and the real-time priorities are the exception. Most of the user applications and processes will operate below a level of 16. After 16, the processes are typically Kernel mode operations. You can, of course, up the priority of a process to any level. Doing so, however, could jeopardize the operation the entire system.

Thread States/Scheduling

A thread goes through a series of thread states in its lifetime. There are 6 of these states, several of those being very transitory. Thus, we stick with the three major operating states: Ready, Running, and Waiting.

The Ready state is one in which the thread is prepared to execute on the processor and simply waiting for its turn. Once the thread has the opportunity to run on the processor its state switches to the Running state.

In the Running state, the thread any execute any of a variety of commands to get its work done. Some of these actions may require it to make requests to other portions of the system like the disk, network, or the keyboard. Any such requests result in the thread being moved from the processor and into a Waiting state until the hardware device responds with the information. The processor's time is assumed to be in high demand, so allowing a thread to sit on the processor waiting for a slower hardware component to respond to a request would be a neglect of the urgency with which tasks must be executed.

The thread, if not requesting information from other pieces of hardware, will run on the processor until the end of its turn. Again, since the processor's time is so important, it must be divided up among all of the waiting (Ready) threads. Each thread will get a slice of processor time. The time slice is called a *quantum*. All quantums are not created equal however. The Kernel mode thread quantum is longer than the User mode thread's quantum. This makes sense, since in most cases we would prefer the Kernel operations, which supply all of the resources and service our requests, to complete as soon as possible.

The Waiting state occurs when the thread is waiting from a response from some other piece of hardware. When the response is received, the thread will often get a +2 boost in its priority from the scheduler in order to make sure that the received information is processed in a timely fashion.

To summarize, a thread will be scheduled on the processor by a component called the dispatcher or scheduler (part of the NT Microkernel—see Chapter 1, "Understanding Windows NT Architecture"). The thread will run on the processor until one of three conditions is met:

- The thread finishes its time slice (quantum).
- The thread is preempted by a thread of higher priority.
- The thread, in the course of operation, requests information from another piece of hardware and becomes "I/O Bound."

Now that you understand the basics of how threads work, you need to become familiar with how the queuing of tasks works.

Queuing Theory

When tasks are stored in a queue for a mechanism to service, there are a general set of rules or observations that can be made about the queue and the completion of the tasks in the queue. This is seen in everyday life at the grocery store, at stop lights, in lines at Disneyland. We are the threads in the queue and the cashier is the processor. Take a look at a couple of simple examples.

Assume that we all have gone to the store to get a gallon of milk. We each have a $5 bill for which the cashier must make change. She can make change in 10 seconds, not bad for the kind of cashiers I have seen at 11:30 at night. Suppose that we all don't arrive at the same time but get in line just as the other person is finished. Assuming we have our $5 in our hand as we walk up, the cashier will be able to handle six customers every minute, 1 customer/ 10 sec x 60 sec/minute. This would be the cashier's peak performance. There would be no line since we are arriving every 10 seconds just as the customer ahead of us has finished. Also, she would constantly be busy. She would be 100% utilized, yet not have a queue. No one is waiting, so there is no bottleneck at the cashier's register.

Now instead, say just the first guy has a $20 bill instead of a $5 bill. It takes the cashier 15 seconds to handle a twenty. Some people still have a five. What happens now if we are still arriving at regular 10 second intervals? A queue would build and build quickly. Let's say that the first person gets there with a twenty. In 10 seconds another person arrives with a five, but he must wait nine seconds before the person, the one with the twenty, already in line is done. A queue of one is now present. In another 10 seconds another person arrives, but the first guy with five just got to the register after waiting for the cashier to provide $20 to the very first customer. So we see that it might take the cashier 10 seconds for one person and 25 seconds for another depending on the type of bill presented. The cashier will still be 100% busy since they are always working, but will also have a queue of something just below one person on the average. This indicates that performance is slipping.

What if people start arriving at different intervals with different types of bills. Thus, each transaction takes a different amount of time and the transactions arrive at different time intervals, meaning that the cashier is sometimes not doing anything. During some time intervals, the cashier will have a long queue of several people (darn those coupons!). Other times, she won't have anyone in line. Thus, the cashier won't be 100% busy, but there is still a queue, on the average. In fact, the queue could be large enough that another register has to be opened to handle the load.

So, what have we learned? Always carry exact change? No. We have learned some basic queuing theory. When dealing with queues of tasks that must be completed, the resource servicing the request:

- Can be 100% utilized (like 100% processor time) and still not have a queue and thus not be a bottleneck.

- Can be a bottleneck, have a queue of more than two tasks waiting, and still not be 100% utilized.

Thus, while you examine resources like the processor and later the disk you must keep in mind that the percentage of utilization in these cases does not completely ensure that the device is a bottleneck.

Systems Calls Versus Interrupts

The processor is usually thought to be servicing the whims of the person at the keyboard. However, software is not all that the processor must deal with. The processor must keep all of the background services and hardware communicating and running in synchronization. Thus, whenever we think of the processor we must think of both software and hardware.

System Calls (Software)

When observing the processor it is good to keep and eye on the Server: System Calls/sec counter. System calls are calls other programs make to the Windows NT System services, primarily Executive services. Recall that applications for the most part don't do much accept ask the Executive services to perform actions on their behalf. Tracking the system calls will come in handy when you are trying to determine what is causing the processor performance to suffer. One thing to bare in mind is that the system calls counter will represent the calls the Windows NT system receives to perform actions. This will exclude the video calls. Thus, we could run into situations where the System Calls/sec counter seems to be okay, yet the processor is still running at near 100%.

Interrupts (Hardware)

Interrupts are the way for hardware to get the system's attention. When an interrupt is executed it "interrupts" the processor to get is attention. The operating system then is responsible for identifying the interrupt and handling the interrupt. The identification of an interrupt is done through a table of interrupt request levels (IRQLs). When a driver is started on Windows NT, it basically puts an entry in the IRQL table so that NT can identify the urgency or priority of the task and where to send information for further processing. This is a shared duty between some of the components of Windows NT, primarily the Microkernel and Hardware Abstraction Layer (HAL). In general, the value of the Interrupts/sec counter will roughly mimic the behavior of the System Calls/sec counter. In situations where hardware drivers are misconfigured, hardware is malfunctioning, or hardware is excessively interrupting the CPU, the value for the System Calls/sec counter will become excessive.

> Generally, if you see the interrupts/sec very much dominating the system, it is usually a decent next stop to pop the cover on the system. If the system is older or has just been moved, the adapter cards may have partially popped out of the slots. Pressing them firmly back in may fix the problem. Also, heavy buildups of dust can cause some real grief on some systems. A little spring cleaning now and again is a good preventative maintenance idea. One more situation I have experienced is when you get a power surge, like a close lightening strike. It may not have been enough to short the breaker or surge suppressor, but it might have been enough to pop a card out of its slot.

Deferred Procedure Calls (DPCs)

DPCs are related to interrupts in that they can interrupt the processor; however, they have lower IRQLs. Also, the system may create DPCs after receiving information on a standard interrupt. The processor takes care of the immediate needs dictated by the interrupt and then defers further processes and a lower interrupt level. DPCs are often associated with network connectivity.

Monitoring CPU Activity

As previously noted, the CPU is a very valuable resource on the system. It is also perhaps a little too generous. Being the good king of the land o' the PC, the CPU likes to do as much work as possible. However, this can lead to poor performance if someone doesn't watch out for the overgenerous CPU. The sections that follow walk through the steps to good analysis of CPU performance. This knowledge will then be applied—along with that favorite tool, the Performance Monitor—to sniff out the abusers of the CPU's generosity. As you recall the CPU has two demands on its time, software and hardware. It's kind of like work and family, you have to balance the two in your life. You will first need to isolate each type of problem. Then, you will learn the potential resolutions. Onward brave souls!

Steps to Analyzing CPU Performance

The analysis of a processor problem will begin with the analysis of the entire system. Before you perform any type of troubleshooting on NT, you will always have an overall look at the operating system's performance. Again, you need to turn to the Performance Monitor to observe the four basic food groups of overall system performance: Disk, CPU, Memory, and Network. These four objects and the relevant counters associated with them in Table 6.2 will enable you to make a quick determination about the overall health of the system and where to continue the search for the bottleneck.

Table 6.2   Primary counters

Object	Counter	Value to watch for
Processor	%Processor Time	> 80%
Physical Disk	%Disk Time	> 80%
Memory	Pages/sec	> 12
Network Segment	%Utilization	>60%

The next step is to follow a basic troubleshooting methodology that will help you no matter what resource is causing the bottleneck. The basic steps are as follows:

1. Establish baselines—an activity that should have preceded the troubles.

2. Observe overall activity.

3. Eliminate other sources of performance degradation.

4. Identify generally overwhelmed resource or faulty application/hardware.

5. Zero in on the cause.

Of course step 1 was to have done a little baseline development to begin with, which involves establishing a point of reference where you would expect performance to be during normal operation of the system. Step 2, again was to look at the counters listed in Table 6.2 and get a handle on the overall system behavior. This is when you will rely on how well you know your system architecture. If you can visualize how the various components are interacting with one another, you will be able to tell which one might be masking a problem with the other.

Observing the Processor

When observing the processor, you first want to make sure that you actually have a processor problem. Remember the queuing theory rules: it may be at 100%, but still not be a bottleneck. So, first you need to look at some counters to identify if you do, indeed, have a processor problem. Then, once you have identified the processor problem, you will want to determine if it is primarily hardware- or software-related.

General Counters in Performance Monitor

In order to measure how busy the cashier was in the example earlier, you needed to know what percentage of the cashier's time was being spent actually dealing with customers and how often customers were waiting in the queue. The following list outlines the processor counters that will help you to identify the processor problems:

- **Processor Object : % Processor Time.** This counter provides a measure of how much time the processor actually spends working on productive threads and how often it was busy servicing requests. This counter actually provides a measurement of how often the system is doing nothing subtracted from 100%. This is a simpler calculation for the processor to make. The processor can never be sitting idle waiting to the next task, unlike our cashier. The CPU must always have something to do. It's like when you turn on the computer, the CPU is a piece of wire that electric current is always running through, thus it must always be doing something. NT give the CPU something to do when there is nothing else waiting in the queue. This is called the idle thread. The system can easily measure how often the idle thread is running as opposed to having to tally the runtime of each of the other process threads. Then , the counter simply subtracts the percentage from 100%.

- **System Object: Processor Queue Length.** Oddly enough, this processor counter shows up under the System object, but not without good reason. There is only 1 queue for tasks that need to go to the processor, even if there is more than one CPU. Thus, counter provides a measure of the instantaneous size of the queue for all processors at the moment that the measurement was taken. The resulting value is a measure of how many threads are in the Ready state waiting to be processed.

- **Processor: % User Time.** The value of this counter helps to determine the kind of processing that is affecting the system. Of course the resulting value is the total amount of non-idle time that was spent on User mode operations. This generally means application code.

■ **Processor: % Privileged Time.** This counter indicates how much time is spent running Kernel mode services.

A busy processor is not necessarily a bad processor. The processor enjoys its work and will happily push it limits. However, the processor illustrated in Figure 6.2 is certainly having a problem.

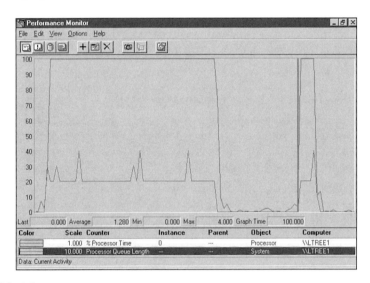

Figure 6.2 A busy processor.

As you can see, the %Processor Time counter is well into the 80% to 90% range and does not appear to be coming down. Still, this by itself is no indication that a problem exists. Turn your attention to the Processor Queue Length counter which indicates a queue of about three to four transactions. These two pieces of information make it pretty clear that the processor is having a problem keeping up with amount of work it is being requested to do. Finally, you can see that most of the operation appears to be in the Kernel mode. Although these results aren't a strong enough indication to make any conclusions, they lean toward a driver or hardware problem.

A processor must always have something to do. Thus, Windows NT, like many other operating systems, creates an Idle thread. The Idle thread is a way of telling the processor to basically twiddle its thumbs for a moment while more work is shipped its way. Remember in our efforts here NOT to include the Idle thread in our analysis, it is only a placeholder and does not contribute to performance degradation in any way.

Separating Hardware from Software

When observing the processor you have to remember to keep in mind that the processor is servicing two very different clients, hardware and software. When presented with a problem, you must identify which of these two clients is causing the problem and then continue with your analysis to find the exact cause as we begin to do in Figure 6.3. So, here you must separate the problem down to software or hardware.

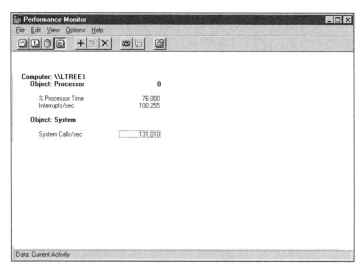

Figure 6.3 Comparing software/hardware.

Figure 6.3 uses the Performance Monitor's Report view to compare some values and get an idea where you should go next to get a solution to the problem. In this case, you are comparing a couple of counters:

- **Processor : Interrupts/sec.** The numbers of interrupts the processor was asked to respond to.

- **System : System Calls/sec.** This is the number of system calls that were processed on the average. This again excludes the video calls. This is important since you may see situations were the processor's usage and queue indicate it is busy yet the interrupts and the system calls indicate no issues.

From Figure 6.3, the System Calls/sec counter values appear to be the most significant, although they are in general close. Most hardware issues will present themselves with an excessive amount of hardware interrupts.

Examining Software Issues

Once you have identified the problem as being most likely software, you will then want to find out if it is a general software problem or it is a specific piece of software that is causing the issue.

Counters for Analyzing Software-Related Problems

If you want to figure out what is doing all of the processing on the system, you will have to examine each process individually. This is actually not too bad of a task using the Performance Monitor. Here are some of the counters that you will want to look at for each process:

- **Process Object : % Processor Time.** This counter is a natural choice that will give use the amount of time that this particular process spends using the processor resource. There are also % Privilege Time and % User Time counters for this object that will help to identify what the program is spending most of its time doing.

- **Thread Object : % Processor Time.** This counter takes the analysis to the next level. Typically, this counter would be for programmers, but occasionally there is a more global use for it. For example, if you are trying to examine the actions of a 16-bit process. The 16-bit application will actually be running as a thread in the NTVDM process. If you wish to see the processor usage by the 16-bit without obscuring it with the processing of the NTVDM and WOWEXEC.exe, you will want to examine the individual thread. BackOffice applications tend to have very distinct multiple threads that sometimes are worth examining individually as opposed to in a group. Often the threads of more sophisticated applications can be configured independently from the entire process.

- **Process Object : Process ID.** Each process on Windows NT gets a process ID that identifies it as a unique process on the system. You can reference the Process ID counter to gain information about the process through API calls. The Process ID is guaranteed to remain unique to the particular process during the entire time that it is running. But, the process is *not* guaranteed to have the same Process ID each time that it is run.

A Word About Monitoring Processes

When looking at process information either interactively or in a logged file in Performance Monitor, there are a couple of issues that you should be aware of. You should always monitor the Process ID when you are monitoring a process. If the process stops and restarts during the course of monitoring, the Performance Monitor can display erroneous results. There will be spikes in the data. If you are monitoring the Process ID, you will see the value of the Process ID counter drop to 0 for as long as the process was not present on the system.

When viewing information from logged data, the Performance Monitor may not display all of the process instances in the Add Objects dialog box. The dialog box will look at the starting point of the Time windows in the Performance Monitor and check to see which processes are running and display those in the list of available processes. This makes it important to have the start point of the Time windows at a point of interest prior to selecting which process instances to monitor. The best way to do this is through the use of Performance Monitor alerts, as illustrated in Figure 6.4.

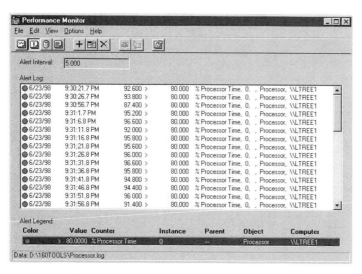

Figure 6.4 Creating an alert for the processor.

You create an alert so that the times when the processor is over 80% busy are displayed as points in the Alert view of the Performance Monitor. You should then make a note of a couple of the points down to the tenth of a second. Next, you need to adjust the Time window so that the start of the window is at the exact time of one of the alerts as we have done in Figure 6.5.

It is at the alert point where you are guaranteed that the application causing the degradation in processor performance is going to be running. Thus, when you display the list of processes in Performance Monitor, you will have the one you are looking for among the innocent bystander processes.

Zeroing in on the Culprit of the Software-Related Problem

At this point we have adjusted the time window to ensure that if there is a single program abusing the CPU and taking up all of its time, it will certainly be visible in the Performance Monitor. So the listing of processes in the Performance Monitor has now turned into a police line-up of suspects. To zero in on the real culprit application, you need to chart the Process Object:%Processor Time counter for each instance. In this case an instance will be a process. For example, if Microsoft Excel were running we could chart the Process : %Processor Time counter for the Excel process instance. This would show us the amount of time the Excel program was using the processor over all other programs on the system. We also want to observe the Processor Object: %Processor Time which is a total of all the processes' usage of the CPU. We look for the process whose line closely approximates the Processor Object's line as in Figure 6.6.

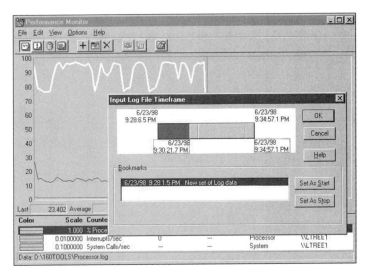

Figure 6.5 Logged data adjusted to ensure bad process is running.

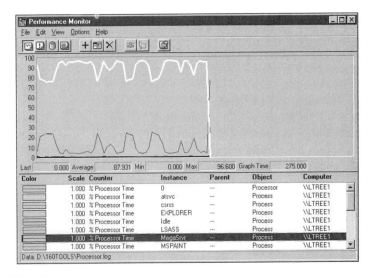

Figure 6.6 Finding the errant process.

From Figure 6.6, you can see that the process MegaSrvr is taking all of the processor time. Figure 6.6 also reveals that there is a line that seems to be the inversion of the %Processor Time counter. This line is, of course, the idle thread's %Processor Time. As the %Processor Time increases, the mark of a busy processor, the idle time would decrease.

General System Overloads

On occasion, you will look at the graph as displayed in Figure 6.6 and not see a particular application that is taking all of the CPU time. This will be seen more as a general overload of the system as illustrated in Figure 6.7. You are simply running more applications than the processor can handle. There is another option. You may have more than one poorly performing or poorly written application.

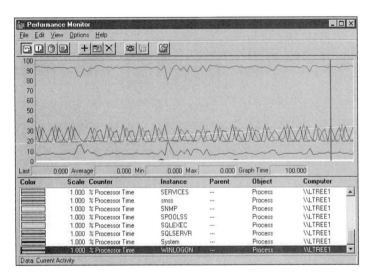

Figure 6.7 General system overload.

Steps for Resolving Software-Related Processor Problems

Now that you know the source of the problem, what do you do? Well, the first solution sounds like the old doctor joke—"If it hurts, stop doing it." If you find a particular application taking up all of the processor time, you would of course like to see if you could reconfigure it first. Often, server-oriented applications can have configuration options all the way down to controlling how many threads it will run. Also, you may wish to contact the vendor and report your findings, especially if you are running with the hardware specified as being acceptable for their software. To be honest, there are a lot of people writing software out there and they don't all pay attention to application performance. A lot of time and worry is spent on feature sets, bells and whistles, as opposed to simply making sure the application runs well using as few resources as necessary to achieve the performance goals of the application.

If you have a general system overload, you may wish to make sure that you need to run all of the applications and services that you are running on that particular server. If this is an application server, you may wish to consider buying a second processor for the system. Generally, application servers benefit from multiple processors better than from faster processors.

Lastly, if a general system overload occurs on what is felt to be a suitable system, you may wish to check on the L2-Cache/RAM ratio. If you add RAM to the system, a suitable amount of L2-Cache should be added as well.

Possible Causes of Hardware–Related Problems

If hardware is the problem, you need to check a couple of items. The CPU is servicing the hardware, but abundant hardware requests can have several sources, including the following:

- Errant driver
- Poorly configured hardware (irq/dma conflicts)
- Disk activity or old controller (PIO Device)
- Network activity

Counters for Analyzing Hardware–Related Problems

When you believe that the hardware might be the issue, you must revisit a couple of pieces of hardware that may actually be causing the processor overhead—the disk and the network card. You will want to look at the following counters:

- **Processor : %Processor Time.** Amount of time the CPU was actually bust with software or hardware service requests.
- **Processor : %Privilege Time.** This is the amount of time the processor was busy with Kernel mode operations. This is routinely hardware interrupts, but of course includes any of the Executive Services.
- **Processor : %User Time.** This is the time spent on User mode operations. This is often the graphical manipulation of windows and text.
- **Processor : Interrupts/sec.** Reports how often the processor was interrupted with a hardware request.
- **Processor : %Interrupt Time.** This is the amount of CPU time that was spent on hardware requests.
- **Processor: %DPC Time.** Much like the other values this counter shows the amount of time that the processor spends servicing DPC requests. DPC requests are more often than not associated with the network interface.

■ **Physical Disk: %Disk Time.** This counter is an indication of how often the disk is busy.

Zeroing in on the Culprit of the Hardware-Related Problem

Monitoring high the aforementioned counters will provide you with good idea of what the processor is spending of all its time on. If you see that the % interrupt time is high along with the %Processor Time being high (around 80%), you should recognize this as a potential hardware problem. You would then want to check and see what hardware is causing the problem. Let's say that you also notice that the disk is really busy. This would actually point to the disk controller and subsystem potentially being a PIO.

PIO devices can take as much as 40% of the CPU's time. Thus, you will want to be well aware of any potential PIO devices in our machines. Typically, we are concerned with the disk controller and the network card. IDE/EIDE controllers use a technology that utilizes the CPU. Older ISA-IDE cards were exceptionally dependent on the CPU to move data, which is where our quoted 40% usage of CPU comes from. Chapter 8, "Optimizing Disk Performance," discusses these devices in greater detail. Network cards are a little faster on their feet, but can often have many more interactions with the CPU. These will be of special concern on systems that have heavy network traffic, like a web server. These devices will examined in Chapter 9, "Optimizing Network Interface Performance."

Steps for Resolving Hardware-Related Processor Problems

To resolve hardware issues, you typically start out by insuring that the hardware that you have implemented is on the Hardware Compatibility List (HCL). The most current copy of this list can be found on the Microsoft Web site, (http://www.microsoft.com). Once you've established hardware compatibility, you may want to get an updated driver for the hardware if there are no resource conflicts. Resource conflicts, as well as showing up as unusually high interrupt rates, often show up in the NT Event Viewer/System log.

The CPU and disk activity just described point to an outdated disk subsystem. In such cases it is simply time to consider spending the money to get an updated component or replacing the machine with something that better fits the performance requirements that you have set.

The network interface card and the DPCs involve some special concerns, particularly when you are running IIS on NT. If the number of hits on the Web site is growing rapidly or past the estimation that you used to configure your server, you may notice that the system's processor performance is dropping a little faster than expected. Excessive DPCs resulting from network interface cards (NICs) will often cause this. When a NIC is added to the system, it is by default tied to a particular processor for processing of DPCs by the NDIS driver. If you have a dual-processor system, the driver will send the interrupts to one processor, which will then forward the DPCs to the other processor. This is known as DPC distribution. There are different ways of distributing the DPCs among the processors, symmetrical and asymmetrical.

DPC Distribution

DPC handling is another one of those areas where hardware vendors are encroaching on what software was used to handling. Again the Compaq Web site proves to be a good source of information on the topic. However, Microsoft Technet/knowledgebase articles also address the various situations and techniques for DPC handling. This is most likely due to the affect on Internet Information Server (IIS), which relies heavily on the network interface.

The easiest way to find out which method of DPC handling that the your system is using is to look at the processor with the highest number. The processors are numbered Processor 0, Processor 1, ... Processor x. Go to the highest numbered processor and check the Processor : %Processor Time and Processor: %DPC Time counters

In most cases, if the value for the %Processor Time counter is very high and the value for the %DPC Time counter is around or above 50% for that particular processor, then the system is using asymmetrical distribution. The way to correct the issue is to add NICs into the system such that there is one per processor. This will force each NIC to be associated with a processor and thus process all of its DPCs in the same processor that handles its interrupts.

If the system is using is symmetrical distribution of DPCs, the easiest way is to adjust the following Registry setting:

```
HKEY_LOCAL_MACHINE\System\CurrentControlSet\Services\NDIS\Parameters
ProcessorAffinityMask = 0
```

Prior to actually setting this value, it would be wise to save the value out to a .reg file using RegEdit. There is not a lot of clear documentation currently for this key, so returning it to the old value if necessary may be difficult if you don't save the value first. Better safe than sorry, right?

Summary

We have come a long way in the chapter in really understanding how the system operates. We have a solid view of the CPU and its role in system performance and operation. We recognize that we are going to have to rely on other components to feed the processor the information it needs to get the jobs done. We noted that the CPU is involved in a couple of different job types, software (System Calls) and hardware (Interrupts). We have learned to distinguish between the two situations and make determinations about the origins of CPU usage. We also learned how to alter best to alter the hardware/software to correct for performance dips.

On Your Own

Hey, the only way to get used to all of this stuff is to use it. So start the Performance Monitor and have a look at a few of your busy servers. See if you don't just have a processor problem that you weren't even aware of. Got a spare machine? Configure a network card to conflict with another piece of hardare and see what this does to processor performance. Have an older system sitting around? Look at the CPU performance of an older system, paying close attention to the Interrupts. Compare this with a newer system, and see if you can explain the results based on information in the text.

Optimizing Memory
Performance

This chapter covers the following topics:

■ **Hardware: Memory Architecture.** This section discusses some of the technology surrounding the memory chips used in computers today. This section investigates how these various architectures affect the performance of your machine. This should offer you a good basis for looking at the operating system as well as figure what is a worthy price for some of the memory that you may want to add to your PCs.

■ **Operating System.** Once you have a good understanding of how the memory chips fit into the PC, you need to know how the operating system takes advantage of memory. As you will see, you can never have enough memory and will need to understand how the operating system attempts to compensate for the lack of memory and the speed of the system bus.

■ **Monitoring Memory Activity.** With these strong foundations, you will then be ready to first identify the types of problems that you might have regarding memory on a PC. This section will then explore the techniques to deduce which of the issues you have and how best to correct the problems.

Memory is perhaps the most valuable resource on a PC. Applications crave it, processors usurp it, interface cards steal pieces like scavengers in the night. Amidst all this is the operating system. It too feeds off the memory resource, but also serves as the supply chief. The operating system guards the resource and balances the needs of the other services requesting it, rationing when resources are tight and freely distributing it when resources are abundant. There are, however, those services and applications in this world that would subvert the system. They steal the memory and hide it away in a mattress and return claiming they need more. This chapter teaches you to fine-tune the balancing act that the operating system must perform and detect the usurpers in the PC kingdom that steal memory without concern for other systems or applications.

Hardware: Memory Architecture

Memory is used by the computer system to store information on its way to the processor or to I/O devices like the disk or network card. Application code as well as data is stored in the memory. Managing the memory resources against memory demands is the key to the performance of the machine. Of course, the speed with which the system can access the memory is very important as well.

Recall that the processor must move information from memory to the closer cache locations, where it can be moved onto the CPU where it can be processed. The L2 Cache serves as a step into the processor realm. Also recall that the L2 Cache is used to essentially "map" the RAM so that the processor can address and access the memory locations needed.

Memory has evolved to faster and cheaper chips. Even so, the communication and the speed of memory has not kept pace with the advances of the processor industry. In addition, memory buses and the systems for accessing the memory have changed in order to improve the capability of the processor to move information to and from the physical memory. For more information, check out Chapter 6, "Optimizing CPU Performance."

There are several memory types in use today for the standard personal computer. These types have their various improvements and advances. In addition, they will appear in 32-pin or 72-pin types with gold or tin as the metal for the main conductor. The memory types include the following:

- **DRAM (Dynamic RAM).** This is the most common physical RAM that was used in PCs just a year ago. As memory chip makers continued to attempt to improve throughput, they began to try to utilize other chip strategies.

- **EDO (Extended Data Out).** EDO memory was used to try to improve the system's performance and reduce the reliance on L2-Cache SRAM, which was more expensive. However, like DRAM, EDO was unable to improve on the communication speeds between the CPU and the memory.

- **SDRAM (Synchronized DRAM).** This is the emerging technology that is targeted to deal with the faster CPU speeds of the processors. SDRAM uses a timing clock, the same clock the CPU uses to keep its timing. Because of this and some other technical advances, the memory is capable of communicating at speeds of 100Mhz. This is a marked improvement over the DRAM and EDO speeds of 66Mhz. The architecture is more complex, but is expected to improve even current 200Mhz Pentium systems' performance by at least another 20 percent.

The switch from tin to gold presents a special problem. The Gold interface that the new chips are using provides better conductivity and allows for faster error-free rates. However, in short it also melts easier. So, if you have an older PC, check to see what type of bus you have; the color is a sure giveaway—tin/silver, gold/gold. While this has not been a specific problem with all machines, it is something to be aware of.

When buying memory chips, the speed of the chip used to be an issue. Many older chips were 80NS. Most modern chips permit 60NS or 70NS The lower the number, the better the chip. Many chips nowadays will run at 60NS or 70NS. If you happen to be adding memory, you will want to see if you have any slower 70NS SIMMs (Single Inline Memory Modules). All the memory will run at the same speed, which is the speed of the slowest SIMMs in the set.

In addition to the speed issues are the issues of communication channels. The older technology was using 32-pin Single Inline Memory Modules (SIMMs). The current SDRAM is using 72-pin Dual Inline Memory Modules (DIMMs). In the near future, the memory will become more compact and the interface will be a 168-pin Dual Inline Memory Module. The move to put more memory on a single chip will further reduce the communication interfaces that have to be crossed to move information back and forth to the memory chips.

The reason the number of pins is being increased is that each of the pins represents a channel into the chips. The more channels, the more traffic that can theoretically be moved. It's just like a freeway—more lanes is better. The increased number of pins also allows memory manufacturers to put more memory on a set (DIMM).

Operating System

Now you should have a foundation of how the chips operate and perhaps are a little wiser about what to buy. Now you must look at the great compromiser—no this isn't a history lesson about President Polk. This section discusses the operating system and how it keeps every application's memory needs fulfilled and tries to prevent the greedy from stealing what it doesn't need.

Memory Usage (Short Refresher)

The Windows NT operating system attempts to provide each application with 4GB of memory. Of course, most of use don't have hundreds of GB of RAM, so NT must supply *virtual memory* to the applications. The virtual memory is mapped to physical memory by an NT Executive Service called the Virtual Memory Manager. The Virtual Memory Manager (VMM) provides virtual address ranges to the applications and then performs a slight of hand trick in the background to make sure that information is in the right place at the right time (see Figure 7.1).

When an application requests an address to retrieve data or to load further code, the VMM responds with the correct information. Behind the scenes, the VMM is mapping to a physical address space. The physical address space certainly does not match the 4 gigabits per process. Thus, VMM uses a process of shuffling information in and out of physical RAM called paging.

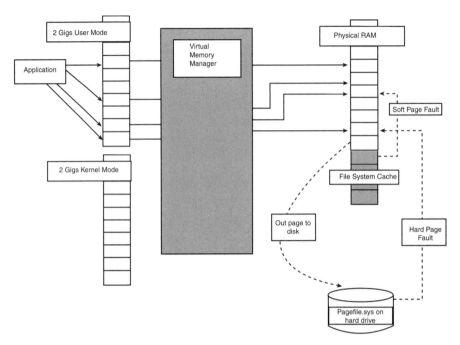

Figure 7.1 Virtual Memory Manager.

Paging

The VMM attempts to keep the memory as clear of unused or unneeded information as possible. Only information that is actively being used is allowed to stay in memory. It is sort of a "use it or lose it" policy. Paging is the process of either moving the information out to disk or retrieving it from the disk.

> When you are paging, your are either moving information out or in to memory. The outpaging, while important is typically not a performance concern. If an application does not need the data, then it is not important if and when it is moved out. Inpaging, however, is more critical. Inpaging results from an application or service requesting something that it is expected to be in memory. Thus, it must wait while the VMM retrieves the information. This may be on the order of milliseconds, but when you consider the processor is running at nanoseconds, this is a long time to wait. So, whenever paging is referenced in this chapter, it is generally referring to inpage operations.

Once information is moved out of its original location in the physical RAM, it can reside in one of two places: the file system cache or the pagefile. The file system cache, or system cache, is a location in memory that is reserved for information that has just recently been sent to disk, or for information that has been anticipated to be request-ed. The VMM provides the file system cache, and the I/O Manager uses what the VMM has provided. When the VMM is asked to retrieve a piece of information that is not in the proper memory location, it will produce what is know as a page fault. The page fault can take on two forms, hard page faults and soft page faults.

> The I/O Manager actually has a thread called the Cache Manager that is specifically servicing the file sys-tem cache. The file system cache is thus considered part of the I/O Managers *working set*. Working sets are covered in more detail later. Suffice it to say that the working set comprises all the active code and data that a running application requires to get its work done. The Cache Manager services the cache, but is not in charge of how big or small it is. As a piece of code, it is permitted to request more memory resource only from the VMM like any other application.
>
> The Cache Manager does have a slight edge in that there are methods to favor the file system cache growth over the growth of the memory for other applications. The exact size of the system cache cannot be adjusted through any interface or Registry entirely. This adjustment is entirely up to the discretion of the VMM.

A soft page fault occurs when the sought after piece of information is found in another location in memory, most likely the system cache. The information is then moved from its location in the system cache into the physical RAM location for the requesting application. This will satisfy the request for the information and do it much faster than if the information had to be retrieved from the pagefile on the physical disk. A hard page fault is one that requires the information to be retrieved from the physical hard drive. This would be from the `pagefile.sys` file. This information is com-paratively much more time-consuming to retrieve.

From this information, you can see that there will be a good deal of memory per-formance that will be dependent on the page file and the disk subsystem. The issues directly related to the disk subsystem will be addressed in Chapter 8, "Optimizing Disk Performance." Chapter 8 looks at how to configure your disk to optimize the reads and writes to the pagefiles. Chapter 8 also looks at how to optimize disk performance for other BackOffice applications.

Now that you have an idea of how the information moves about in memory, the next couple of sections examine a little more about how the memory is divided up.

Memory Pools

The memory pools are nonpageable and pageable, as illustrated in Figure 7.2.

Nonpageable memory is memory that has been quarantined from being moved out to the pagefile. Nonpageable memory is necessary for part of the kernel and some other critical drivers in the operating system. The pageable memory pool is then divided up among the programs that are requesting memory. A section of the remain-ing available memory is then allocated to the file system cache. This part of the mem-ory is again used to cache or stage information that has been recently requested or written to the hard drive.

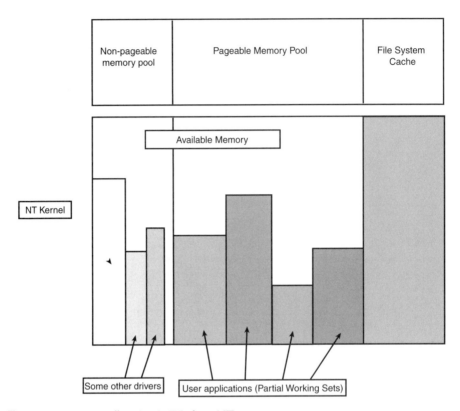

Figure 7.2   Memory allocation in Windows NT.

When an application starts, it requests a certain amount of memory called a *working set*, which is needed by the application as it runs. Initially, the working set of an application is larger than it needs after it gets started. Once an application loads the necessary modules and data such as splash screens and initialization programs have closed, the application will be running with its normal working set. Whenever you request a new module, more information is added to the application's working set.

For example, if you open Microsoft Word and start to type, the application's working set will become fairly stable. When you stop and run the spell checker, however, the disk will run, and the new component will be loaded into memory, increasing the application's working set for a time. When you don't use the spell checker for a little while after that, the system will consider paging the information out to disk and again reducing the working set of the application. The minimum amount of memory that the application requires for it to still be able to run is called the *minimum working set*. Techniques used to reduce applications to the minimum working sets help to identify problems with specific applications and poor memory utilization.

File System Cache

The file system cache is dynamically adjusted by NT. From the moment the system starts and you start that first service or application, NT is reevaluating the application's use of memory and the size of the system cache. In general, the file system cache and working sets from other sources are not permitted to exceed a size that would leave the system with less than 4MB of available memory. This allows Windows NT a little time to cope with large applications or heavy requests for memory. The file system cache will be adjusted when the system is undergoing heavy file transfers. The disk drive is often the slowest piece of hardware on the system. When you transfer a large file over the network, the system is receiving the data a lot faster than the disk can routinely handle. To compensate for this delay, the system will store information in memory, the file system cache. Memory is of course much faster than disk. Then, when the system has a little more time, it will move the data to the hard drive. On Windows NT, the system cache size cannot be adjusted manually. Issues with the size of the file system cache are generally due to a lack of memory. Poorly written applications, however, can result in system cache issues that will in turn affect the overall performance of the system. In general, cache problems do not occur on workstations unless highly complex multimedia or CAD software is being utilized. Servers, however, can have issues with cache consumption from applications that are not smart in the method of requesting information. Database applications have such potential.

At this point, you should be familiar with how the operating system uses memory. During the course of this examination, you should have discovered several issues that might have an affect on the performance of the operating system and the applications that it is supporting. The sections that follow will investigate the various potential problems including the following:

- Memory utilization
- Memory bottlenecks
- Paging/disk issues
- System cache issues

Monitoring Memory Activity

When monitoring memory issues, you need to examine the issues from a broad perspective in order to consider the whole system working together. This will enable you to make a determination as to whether you really have a memory problem, a disk problem, or a system cache issue. Then, you must analyze the specifics of what is causing the problem and finally resolve it. This chapter specifically addresses the issues of memory and cache.

You should always keep in mind that a bottleneck is partially perception. For example, when you go to a nice sit-down restaurant, you expect a good meal. You are typically willing to wait 20 minutes while the chef prepares your roast pheasant. However, when you pull into the drive-thru of the local burger joint, anything over 5 minutes is a painful drain on your time. There are couple points to be made in such an example:

■ Manage user perception

■ Understand your system's role

Managing user perception cannot be stressed enough in any part of the computer or services industry. We have all run into those users who have had their perceptions twisted one way or another—some into believing the impossible and others into accepting the abominable. Thus, you might have the user who believes transmitting 500MB of data should be as fast as 500KB. Another user may have been lulled into a sense of complacency. I have seen situations where it was generally accepted by the users to start their email program and then walk off to get a cup of coffee while it downloaded messages. If they stopped to talk to coworkers, the program might actually be done when they returned to their desk. Someone had these folks under an evil spell that led them to believe that this was the best that technology today could offer. As administrator, consultant, advisor, and friend, it is your job as the informed and trained professional to combat this evil of evils and not let your users' perceptions stray into the extreme.

The second important item is understanding the system's role. Running into the fancy restaurant to get a quick burger and fries would probably leave you a little disappointed at speed of delivery, as well as the cost of the meal. So we must know what our system is to be used for in order to tune it correctly. Knowing how the system is being used will also assist with the diagnosis of problems. An application server will use resources differently than say a file server, as illustrated in Table 7.1.

Table 7.1   Server resource usage

Server Type	Memory	Processor	Disk	Network
Application	Heavy	Heavy	Light	Light
File/Print	Light	Light	Heavy	Medium
PDC/BDC	Medium	Light	Light	Medium

Table 7.1, of course, is not a hard-and-fast rule, but more of a general sense of how the systems resource consumption will be weighted. In addition, you might often utilize a system in more than one role. Thus, you often are concerned with contention for various resources. Mixing a PDC with an application server could be bad news since they both will be trying to use a lot of memory.

Okay, so now you've spent 15 minutes in the drive-thru. There is something wrong with the system somewhere. Your perception that 15 minutes is a long time in the fast food drive-thru is valid since they advertise 5 minutes or less. How are you going to figure it out? Easy, step out of the car and peek in the window. You'll do the same with NT. The window is created via a tool called the Performance Monitor.

Observing Memory Performance

Observing performance starts with a set of rules, some of which some you are already familiar from other chapters. With memory the ultimate rule is always find out what is using memory and why. Resist temptation to go for the quick fix. Adding memory will always appear to fix the problem, at least initially. But, if you have one of those thief-in-the-night applications whose thirst for memory will never be quenched, the problem will present itself again. You will have only delayed the inevitable and used company funds to do it. So your pursuit of the truth must take on a relentless take-no-prisoners attitude. At the same time, you cannot forsake the scientific methods of recording information and making changes to the system in a controlled manner to isolate the problem. You are the secret agent looking to capture the bad guys and shut down their operation. The bad guys are applications and services that erroneously devour memory or cause imbalance in the memory optimization. Your weapon of choice is the Windows NT Performance Monitor. If you are to be successful you must understand the bad guy and the weapon that you will be using to catch him. So far, the focus in this chapter has been learning how the memory resource can be subverted. Now, you must have a look at several Performance Monitor counters. The counters for memory performance will enable you to analyze the clues to track down the source of problems, determine their origins, and alter their configuration to operate in a more memory-friendly manner.

General Counters in Performance Monitor

You first need to familiarize yourself with the Performance Monitor counters related to memory and exactly what you might be able to retrieve from them. In general, you mark the performance of memory usage by the amount of paging that the system must do to meet the needs for physical memory that the applications are requesting. Thus, many of the memory counters have to do with paging. The relevant counters for analyzing memory performance are as follows:

- **Page Faults/sec.** This counter gives a general idea of how many times information being requested is not where the application (and VMM) expects it to be. The information must either be retrieved from another location in memory or from the pagefile. Recall that while a sustained value may indicate trouble here, you should be more concerned with hard page faults that represent actual reads or writes to the disk. Remember that the disk access is much slower than RAM.

- **Pages Input/sec.** Use this counter in comparison with the Page Faults/sec counter to determine the percentage of the page faults that are hard page faults. Thus, Pages Input/sec / Page Faults/sec = % Hard Page Faults. Sustained values surpassing 40% are generally indicative of memory shortages of some kind. While you might know at this point that there is memory shortage of some kind on the system, this is not necessarily an indication that the system is in need of an immediate memory upgrade.

■ **Pages Output/sec.** Recall that as memory becomes more in demand, you can expect to see that the amount of information being removed from memory is increasing. This may even begin to occur prior to the hard page faults becoming a problem. As memory begins to run short, the system will attempt to first start reducing the applications to their minimum working set. This means moving more information out to the pagefiles and disk. Thus, if your system is on the verge of being truly strained for memory, you may begin to see this value climb. Often the first pages to be removed from memory are data pages. The code pages experience more repetitive reuse.

■ **Pages/sec.** This value is often confused with Page Faults/sec. The Pages/sec counter is a combination of Pages Input/sec and Pages Output/sec counters. Recall that Page Faults/sec is a combination of hard page faults and soft page faults. This counter, however, is a general indicator of how often the system is using the hard drive to store or retrieve memory associated data.

■ **Page Reads/sec.** This counter is probably the best indicator of a memory shortage because it indicates how often the system is reading from disk because of hard page faults. The system is always using the pagefile even if there is enough RAM to support all of the applications. Thus, some number of page reads will always be encountered. However, a sustained value over 5 Page Reads/sec is often a strong indicator of a memory shortage. You must be careful about viewing these counters to understand what they are telling you. This counter again indicates the number of reads from the disk that were done to satisfy page faults. The amount of pages read each time the system went to the disk may indeed vary. This will be a function of the application and the proximity of the data on the hard drive. Irrelevant of these facts, a sustained value of over five is still a strong indicator of a memory problem. Remember the importance of "sustained." System operations often fluctuate, sometimes widely. So, just because the system has a Page Reads/sec of 24 for a couple of seconds does not mean you have a memory shortage.

■ **Page Writes/sec.** Much like the Page Reads/sec, this counter indicates how many times the disk was written to in an effort to clear unused items out of memory. Again, the numbers of pages per read may change. Increasing values in this counter often indicate a building tension in the battle for memory resources.

Other counters directly indicate the current status of the memory and how it is being allocated:

■ **Available Memory.** This counter indicates the amount of memory that is left after nonpaged pool allocations, paged pool allocations, process' working sets, and the file system cache have all taken their piece. In general, NT attempts to keep this value around 4MB. Should it drop below this for a sustained period, on the order of minutes at a time, there may be a memory shortage. Of course, you must always keep an eye out for those times when you are simply attempting to perform memory intensive tasks or large file transfers.

- **Nonpageable memory pool bytes.** This counter provides an indication of how NT has divided up the physical memory resource. An uncontrolled increase in this value would be indicative of a memory leak in a kernel-level service or driver.

- **Pageable memory pool bytes.** An uncontrolled increase in this counter, with the corresponding decrease in the available memory, would be indicative of a process taking more memory than it should and not giving it back.

- **Committed Bytes.** This counter indicates the total amount of memory that has been committed for the exclusive use of any of the services or processes on Windows NT. Should this value approach the committed limit, you will be facing a memory shortage of unknown cause, but of certain severe consequence.

Other counters will be useful later throughout the chapter, but these will do nicely for now. Now you have the knowledge and the tools to be able to track down the members of chaos that are disrupting the optimization of memory.

> When you are adding counters to the Performance Monitor, you may notice an Explain button to the right on the dialog box. Pressing this button will display helpful information at the bottom of the Add Counter's dialog box. Most of the time you will see information that helps describe the counter's value and use. Sometimes, it is a simple message that doesn't give much insight. Note also, that the help messages will not be available for viewing when you are viewing information from a Performance Monitor Log as opposed to getting the data from real-time collection. NT 5.0 corrects the issue of not being able to view the help information.

Identifying Memory Issues

We begin our investigation with a look at what might be outward indications of a memory problem. Memory is directly tied to paging and thus the disk so let's look at a few scenarios.

Case Study

An NT Workstation user is experiencing a general slowdown in his system. In this case, the applications that he is running are stored on a network server. The applications are loaded over the network and run in local RAM. It is primarily the loading of the network applications that is slow. The user has been complaining to the network group for a couple of weeks now and is awfully frustrated with the response. The network support group has reviewed the network settings for the machine as well as for the network node (routers) in the area. The network seems fine. The user simply cannot accept the answer.

You visit the user tying to help with the diagnosis. You are first drawn to review the network settings. In troubleshooting, no matter how good the other troubleshooters are, you will usually want to verify their findings before continuing down another path. While at the user's workstation, you load the network application. The application loads slowly and the disk seems to be very busy. You ask the user if this is normal, and he says that this is what has been happening. The disk activity, while normal for an application that is installed locally, is not common for an application that is starting over the network. Thus, we can conclude that since the memory is tied to disk performance that we may actually have a memory issue. We're done, right? Of course you're not. To identify the memory issue is simply the first step. Hunting down the cause can be much more complex and sometimes time consuming. We could, of course, just add more memory. This may solve the problem—it may not. Adding more memory may simply mask the problem temporarily. I have learned in the course of my career of troubleshooting and bottleneck detecting that it takes a certain amount of obsessive tendencies to want to be able to find the problem before trying to find the solution.

Memory issues are identified when the system has excessive paging. Nonetheless, you must keep in mind that when you are monitoring the system, the first step is always to gain a general overall impression of what is going on. Notice that in the preceding case study, the initial troubleshooters and even the user failed to observe the system operation as a whole. When you do not know the nature of a problem, every operation and behavior of the system must be treated with speculation and reflection. You must think through what the machine is attempting to do and what components are involved.

As you can see, architecture information *is* important. To review, the four basic objects that you need to examine include Memory, Disk, CPU, and Network. In general, each object can in some ways affect the other. You use the corresponding default counters in Performance Monitor to examine these four objects. While you can expect increased disk activity when memory is becoming scarce, paging still remains a stronger indication of memory problems than disk problems. Chapter 9 distinguishes between these two problems more succinctly. Figure 7.3 provides an example of what short memory might look like when observing the general counters in Performance Monitor.

Notice that the excessive paging has increased the disk queues and is straining the disk's total throughput. Of course, this could have many different sources. Consider just a few as follows:

- The memory could generally be in demand. This of course would cause the effect.

- The disk could already be under the demand of another application, which would cause disk activity to be unusually high. In addition, the memory paging may end up waiting in the line behind the disk writes and reads that have nothing to do with paging. In this case, the memory is not really short on supply. The problem is that NT is trying to do normal paging, but is having to wait in line for other disk activity.

- The disk could be physically damaged, consequently creating problems with duplicate writes as bad sectors are detected.

- The disk controller could be improperly configured or not properly installed on the motherboard. This scenario may also appear as increased processor drains as well as a reduction of disk and memory performance.

- The paging file could be configured incorrectly. If the paging file is smaller than is required for the size of the task and the amount of data that needs to be moved, a lot of time could be spent on growing the pagefile while the system is attempting to page out data. This could have the effect of doubling or tripling the normal amount of reads/writes it takes to move pages of data back and forth to the disk.

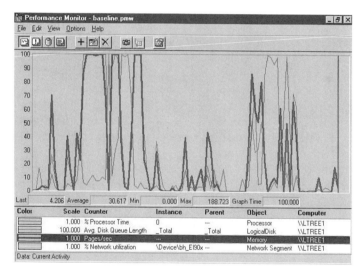

Figure 7.3 General look of a memory issue.

Needless to say, you've got your work cut out for you. You will take the tools that you have and attempt to diagnose which of these problems is causing the memory performance drain (or if it's another problem altogether). Table 7.2 provides some counter values that point to some general indications that memory is becoming a problem on NT.

Table 7.2 **General guidelines for memory**

Counter	Nominal Danger Value	Indications
Page Reads/sec	> 5	High paging and disk activity
Pages/sec	> 12	High disk activity
Page File Size	> RAM+12	Growing pagefile
Available bytes	Consistently below 4MB	Memory performance generally slow
Committed bytes	> RAM or approaching committed limit	Extremely slow system

Every system will experience peaks and valleys in demand for system resources. It is a busy world inside a computer. When monitoring any counter value, you must keep in mind that sustained values are true indications of problems.

The first counter to consider is the Page Reads/sec counter, which again indicates how many times the disk had to be read to satisfy page faults. The next counter to examine is the Pages/sec counter, which will include not only the reads but also the writes to disk. As the demand for memory resources increases, the amount of information being pushed out to disk will be increased. You can also see this demand increase as you open applications. If the system cannot allow allotting an application an abundant amount of memory for its working set, then the information will be quickly marked for paging out the disk after the application has started. If the value for the Pages/sec counter is over 12 pages/sec over a sustained period of time (typically on the order of minutes), this is a good indication of a memory problem or that there is beginning to be a memory shortage.

Observing the pagefile size in the Page File Size counter is important. If the pagefile on NT is set to too small a range for the purpose of the applications and the demands placed on it, the pagefile will have to be grown by NT as it operates. This is an intensive procedure. You will want to ensure that the pagefile is the correct size. The pagefile will be addressed shortly as you learn more about observing the problems and resolving them.

The Available Bytes counter indicates the amount of memory that NT has to play with. The memory is neither reserved nor committed to some other process. NT likes to maintain this amount of RAM in case it needs to resize the system cache or if an abundant and sudden number of requests for memory are seen. Again, the stress here is for sustained observation. The amount of available RAM can drop drastically at the onset of a large file transfer to disk locations or over the network. So sudden valleys in the amount of available memory are expected (see Figure 7.4).

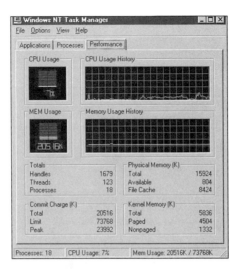

Figure 7.4   Available memory (804KB) diminishes during large file transfers as memory is given to the file system cache (8424KB).

Figure 7.4 illustrates the Task Manager. Most of the initial counters mentioned up to this point are observable very quickly through the Task Manager. An often unassuming and overlooked tool, the Task Manager is quite nice and readily available to use for observation. Being able to start the Task Manager by pressing Ctrl+Alt+Delete and clicking on the Task Manager button is often a great boon for the performance troubleshooter. Hitting Ctrl+Shift+Esc will also start the Task Manager. When the system is going pathetically slow, trying to open the Start menu and running Performance Monitor can be a real strain on the system as well as the troubleshooter's patience. But, pressing the good old three-finger salute will often interrupt even the most intensive processing and allow you to open the Task Manager to get an idea of what is going on. Once in Task Manager, you may also launch another application, Performance Monitor for example. The position of the Task Manager always on top of the windows stack on the desktop enables you to get the attention of the system a little more readily than the Start menu.

In the case presented in Figure 7.4, a 50MB file is moved repeatedly over the network. This quickly causes the file system cache to grow in size. Figure 7.5 illustrates what the system looks like under a "nominal" load.

Notice that the system in general is still quite stressed as the available memory is at less than 4MB. We have adjusted the machine to operate with only 16MB of RAM to assist in exaggerating some of the values displayed in the figures.

This brings to mind another important point, the power of comparison. If you don't have a feel for what the system behaves like under normal conditions, you will have no idea when you are starting to have a problem. This is more important on servers than on the individual workstations. You'll want to observe servers on a regular basis to make sure that you see trends in behavior. In this way, identifying a sudden problem will occur quicker and potentially before the users get an idea that the server is failing them in its promise of good performance. Anticipating need is the mark of a true optimization guru.

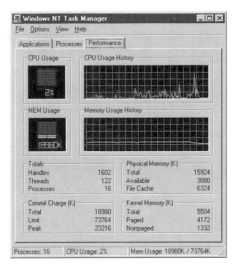

Figure 7.5 Task Manager view of same system under a normal load on a machine with barely enough memory for NT (16MB).

This last counter from Table 7.2 concerns committed bytes. Commited bytes refers to the amount of memory that is marked as in use by a process and cannot be used for any other purpose. Should this value reach the amount of physical RAM in your system, rest-assured you will know it. The system will be plagued by excessively slow performance and incredible disk I/O, also know as *trashing*. Should the value for the Committed Bytes counter exceed RAM and approach the commit limit—the amount of physical RAM plus the maximum size for your pagefile—the system will more than likely come to a complete halt. When it does, you may see the ominous blue screen of death. You may not. A system that has gone this far may simply stop dead in its tracks—the black screen of oblivion. This type of behavior is often indicative of a memory leak as opposed to general memory shortages.

Now that you are familiar with the basic logistics and counters for identifying memory problems, the next logical step is to be able to isolate the memory problem in question.

Isolating the Memory Problem

At this point we have spent some time describing the various ways of identifying that we have a memory issue. This of course helps to leads us in another direction and to our next step. The next step, however, may lead us down several distinct paths. In the case of memory, we have to find out if the disk is contributing to the memory problem or even creating it. We will need to also see if it is a mob of hungry applications raiding the memory store or a single thieving application stealing the precious resource. In either case, there will be specific counters to analyze.

All of this will be geared towards getting us to the next step, figuring out who to blame. After all as administrators that is one of our major goals is finding out who to blame for our system inadequacies. Well, perhaps not. But in this case we will need to know what application is causing the problem. After that we will need to know which vendor to contact to correct the problem, provided it isn't our own internal development staff.

Counters for Detailed Analysis of Memory Performance

The first thing you need to do is examine the paging a little more closely, which will help determine that what you are encountering is not a disk problem. Examining the memory paging will also help you to understand the type of paging that is occurring, consequently allowing you to more accurately pinpoint the causes (See Figure 7.6).

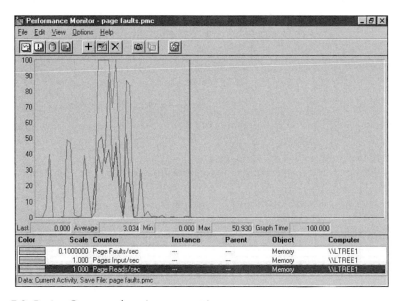

Figure 7.6 Paging Counters observing memory issues.

Figure 7.6 charts the following memory counters:

- Memory: Page Faults/sec
- Memory: Pages Input/sec
- Memory: Page Reads/sec

> Dust off those math skills folks—you're gonna need them. Raw numbers are great, but usually only after you have a strong feel for what is considered normal for various system loads and the types of servers you may be using. Minor calculations, and sometimes not so minor ones, will help make the relationships between various counters more clear. Percentages often will help us figure out more readily what is a bad situation. For example, if I said the disk was doing 24 Page Faults/sec, that might not say much. But if I say 80% of all disk activity is related to paging, that is more likely to make you think that the disk is not as much of a problem as the lack of memory is.

These three counters will enable you to determine the type of paging. First off, you need to examine Page Faults/sec and Pages Input/sec:

Pages Input/sec / Page Faults/sec = % Hard page faults

13.5 / 63.0= 21.4%

Thus, 21% of the paging operations are hard page faults. This is not a bad number. Typically if you encounter more than 50%, you might consider the memory to be more of a problem. For now, it still looks like this problem, if it is even a problem, could be related to disk issues. Next you need to look at the Page Reads/sec counter. This value is around 3 Page Reads/sec on average. This is pretty nominal. Ideally, you want a value of 5 or less for this counter. If you compare the values of Pages Input/sec to Page Reads/sec, you will get the following:

Pages Input/sec / Page Reads/sec = Pages / Read

13.5 / 3 = 4.5 Pages/Read

This result reveals that you are getting about 4.5 pages satisfied per read of the disk. Ideally, you would like to see this value around 3 or so, although you can expect this value to be exceptionally prone to fluctuation. This value can point to a several different causes like paging done by many programs (as opposed to one), fragmentation of the pagefile, hard disk errors, and inefficiently written code that is calling functions broken up among too many DLLs. The one to look for first? Well my bet is usually on the fragmented pagefile. After that, the poorly written program.

> Nowadays I just think that sometimes it is a little too easy to write code. Tools that provide the ability to quickly write code that looks good are tempting many more people to do programming. However, it takes more than a nice look and feel to make quality programs. You must keep a watchful eye on resource consumption and make valiant efforts to try and make code efficient in execution as well as pretty to the eye. Truly elegant code to me is code that accomplishes the most with the fewest commands and simplest methods. Optimization should start at the time you write that first line of code and never end.

If there are multiple programs that are requesting information from memory, it is highly likely that they are stored in varying positions on the hardware and that the requests are coming in sporadically. This points to a general shortage of memory, or an inability for the disk to be able to respond to paging requests quickly. Low seek times, aging hardware, or other disk demands can be the cause. If this were a single application causing the page faults, you would more likely see a much higher sustained value for this particular calculation. In these cases, it is usually a program that is requesting data sets repetitively. Often this will either be a configuration issue with the particular program or a problem with the way that the code was written in general.

Before moving on to more a more in depth discussion on the pagefile, consider Figure 7.6 one more time. So, is there a problem with this system or not? Well, the counters that we see indicate that all seems to be running fine. Certainly the values appear to be well within our parameters for a optimized system. But, we must keep in mind how the system works. Clearly, there is a couple of sudden bursts of activity on this chart. So why not a corresponding paging? Chances are the information being requested already existed in the file system cache. Thus, most of the page faults are soft page faults that don't affect the system's performance.

> Finding a performance problem will often depend on when you look. In this text we are artificially gener-ating various scenarios and producing little snippets and screen shots. In the real world keep in mind that performance analysis involves the examination of data, usually logged, stretching over a period of hours, days, or weeks. Taking a quick peak in Performance Monitor or Task Manager is good for when you know a problem is occurring. But, if the system is being described as slow periodically, the only way to get a real handle on what is going on is to log data over an appropriate time period.

Troubleshooting Pagefile Fragmentation

If you had underestimated the size of the pagefile to begin with and the pagefile was forced to grow to over the initial size of RAM+12, there is a chance of the pagefile becoming fragmented across the disk. If you suspect this, take a look at the size of the pagefile to determine whether it is greater than the original minimum size that you had set. If so, the pagefile may be fragmented. There are a couple of different tactics to correcting this. One tactic would be to do the following:

1. You can create a new pagefile on another drive with enough space for a mini-mal pagefile, around 40MB. Create a bigger pagefile if you can manage it. The pagefile will be deleted shortly so that the space will be returned to the disk.

2. Set the size of the old pagefile to 0, effectively deleting it.

3. Reboot the system.

4. When the system comes up, re-create your old pagefile specifying the minimum size as the size that the pagefile had grown to.

5. Set the size of the temporary pagefile to 0, again deleting it.

6. Reboot the system.

Now you should have a new pagefile in the old location, but on contiguous disk space, and of the appropriate size.

Okay, so let's have a little look at a different problem. Figure 7.7 presents a look at what the system is doing when the pagefile has to be grown. While the system is con-tinuing to page massively (Pages/sec), you can also see that the pagefile is being grown (Usage Peak Bytes). Clearly understanding how to get the size of the pagefile correct will be the key to avoiding many memory issues.

Examining Paging: The Separation of Disk and Memory

While paging is a problem, you still need to make sure and check to see if the root of the problem is not really a disk issue. We are going to jump ahead just a little bit and look at a couple of disk counters to check on the memory versus disk issue. The following are some counters that you will want to chart from the PhysicalDisk object in Performance Monitor:

- % Disk Read Time
- Avg. Disk Read Queue Length
- Disk Reads/sec
- Avg. Disk Bytes/Read

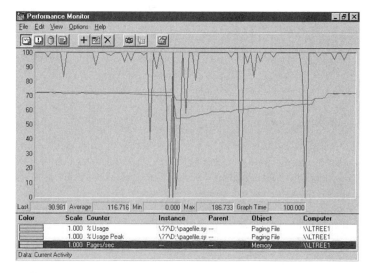

Figure 7.7   Effects on system resource when the pagefile must be increased in size.

When doing this, if you have multiple pagefiles spread over multiple physical disks you may want to look at the **_Total** instance for all the disks. Then you may generalize. You will have to know your disk configuration and location of the pagefiles to make this decision. For example, suppose you had 5 disks, not in a fault-tolerant configuration, and a pagefile on 2 of them. You might want to look at just the values for the 2 disks that have pagefiles on them when performing your calculations. In this case, it would be beneficial to use the Report View of the Performance Monitor as opposed to the Graph View. The Report View offers a view of the counters that is more amiable to calculations (see Figure 7.8).

Figure 7.8 illustrates the display of the memory and the disk counters. The Avg. Disk Read Queue Length value is a general indication of disk congestion. If there is a sustained value over 2, then the disk is not able to service the queue that is being produced. Hold on there. Don't run out and buy that new low seek time drive with the kick butt controller yet. You need to finish your analysis. Okay, so your disk is a little pressed for time to get the information onto or off of the physical media. You'll need to gather some more information. Compare the Disk Reads/sec to the Page Reads/sec counter:

Page Reads/sec / Disk Reads/sec = % Reads due to Paging

35 / 37 = 94.5%   disk reads due to paging

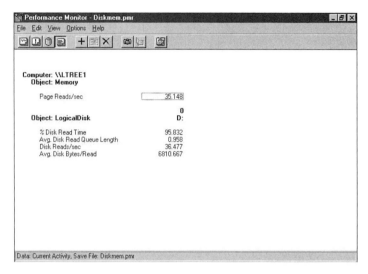

Figure 7.8 Report view of the Disk and Memory Counter.

This is a solid indication that the disk congestion is due to the memory paging. If the value had been lower, say <50%, it might indicate that there may be some other application or activity going on that is causing the problem. Perhaps someone keeps downloading excessively large files or large numbers of files to this system. If this is a file server, you know that this would cause an increase in the file system cache, leaving less room for applications as well as generating high disk activity in the course of copying files.

You might also have a little peak at the Avg. Disk Bytes/Read counter. If you multiply this counter by the Disk Reads/sec counter, you will get the Disk Bytes/sec. This calculation provides a rough indication of how well the disk subsystem is moving information. This will be covered in greater detail later, but if you compare this resulting value to some values under controlled circumstances, you may be able to support the file and pagefile fragmentation hypothesis. Again, this stresses the need to have a baseline for comparison in times of need.

Lastly, reconsider the value of the Disk Reads/sec counter. In general a computer's disk subsystem can handle between 30–60 I/Os per second, a physical limitation of the current hardware technology. If the Disk Reads/sec, or worse, the Page Inputs/sec counter approaches 40, you will be close to the physical maximum of most hardware.

Again, a lot of conditional factors exist here. If you have a high performance RAID controller with 2MB of cache memory and its own RISC processor, your system may be beyond the 60 I/Os mentioned here. Again, you have to know your system to know how to measure performance against it. Chapter 8 will go into determining this value.

So if you look back at the example results from Figure 7.8, you can see that this particular system is mostly having a memory problem. The paging is creating a minimal disk queue that could further affect system performance should other systems require access to the disk. You have indications that the problem may be due to an incorrectly sized or fragmented pagefile. Now you have a little to work with. Of course, determining the exact cause of the memory shortage will take a little more effort. First, you'll need to consider the details of the pagefile sizing/fragmentation issue.

Optimizing Our Pagefile's Size

Determining the proper size of the pagefile is not too difficult of a task. Initially, you want the pagefile to have the size of RAM+12MB. This seems reasonable, until the memory begins to get close to 1GB as on some server systems, which would mean you would need a 1GB + 12MB pagefile! Whoa! So, you'll need to find out about "right sizing" your pagefiles. You need to consider the operating system function (server/workstation), the amount of RAM, and the type of applications.

Sizing the pagefile on an NT Workstation and an NT Server are similar until you exceed 128MBs of RAM. Normally, NT Workstations do not benefit much over that amount of RAM unless they are specifically running applications that are exceptionally memory intensive. Anything below the 128MB mark and you should start with the RAM+12MB idea. This will generally take care of most of the system needs in a good portion of the cases. Once you approach 128MB, you will need to intervene a little more.

With 128MB RAM, you may wish to observe the pagefile over a little time of normal use to make sure that you have the right size. On an NT Workstation, you might consider making the pagefile smaller than the amount of RAM, depending on the average usage of the memory. Over a time period, you should observe the Paging File Objects: % Usage and Usage Peak. This value on most workstations will be considerably less than the total amount of physical RAM. You should consider making the pagefile this size + 12MB. This will be the initial size of the pagefile with the maximum size being RAM+12. If you begin to get a low virtual memory message, you will need to adjust the minimum pagefile size upward until you stop getting the messages. On NT Servers, it is not considered a good practice to set the pagefile size less than RAM+12. Demands on servers tend to be more varying in nature.

Lastly, you must consider the applications that you are going to be running. On NT Workstation, memory-intensive applications like AutoCAD or high-intensity multimedia applications will create much greater and concentrated demands on memory, the pagefile, and system cache. In these cases, RAM x 2 is a typical staring point. For NT Servers, BackOffice applications like SQL Server and Exchange will operate much better when the pagefile is set to RAM x 2 or even x 3, depending on the size of databases or the number of users on the Exchange Server.

Identifying a Memory Leak

So here's the problem. You have a production server that seems well suited for the job of running SQL Server for use with the corporate accounting program. You have a dual Pentium processor (100Mhz each—not exceedingly fast but vary respectable in a dual processor configuration), 128MB of RAM, a 10GB hardware RAID 5 configuration. Approximately 20 users are on the system on average with a peak of around 50 during major accounting time periods—end of month and year end. The server is not a domain controller or a file server. SQL in general seems to perform well. The server, however, has a nasty little habit of rebooting every two weeks. The previous system's administrators had taken the stance of doing a scheduled shutdown and reboot every week. This cures the problem most of the time, but not always. Your new boss has asked that you put your talents to the test and figure out why this is happening. He mentions that the reason the last guy got fired was because he too often couldn't answer your boss' simple questions—which seem to always be one word, "why?"

You're under the gun on this one. First, you discontinue the scheduled reboots of the system. Then you start by monitoring the system under normal conditions. Everything seems fine. The system does not appear to be straining its limits of memory, disk, network, or processor. Recall that in many cases the only way to get an idea of what a system is doing is to watch it for more than a couple of minutes while you are trying to figure out what is going on.

Process for Identifying Memory Leaks

In this case, you would be relying on the Performance Monitor logs over time. Then when you notice that one of those mysterious reboots occurs, you could observe the Performance Monitor logs leading up to the very moment that the system rebooted.

Given the scenario presented, you would probably set the log to collect information every 60 seconds. Considering the duration of the problem, two weeks between reboots, you wouldn't want to overburden the system or the disk space with a log consisting of entries every second or two. Also, you would probably want to collect the four main objects plus a couple more:

- Memory
- Processor
- Physical Disk
- Network
- SQL Server
- Process

These objects should provide you with enough information to figure out what is exactly going on up to the point of failure. The addition of the SQL Server is simply to see if SQL Server is not kicking into some type of operation, whether it is a complex stored procedure or an external program you should be able to see evidence in this counter. The Process object will enable you to observe the system processes outside of SQL Server. This way, you can see if there is another program doing something less than friendly.

Zeroing In on the Culprit

Scanning a performance log can be a tricky business. The best thing to do is start with some basic counters. Look at the Memory, Disk, Processor, and Network objects. Set Performance Monitor Alert for the typical trouble values of the following:

- Memory: Pages/sec   > 16
- Disk: Disk Queue Length > 2
- Processor: % Processor Time > 80%
- Network: % Network Utilization > 60%

See what alerts pop up. Figure 7.9 provides a sample of what you might see.

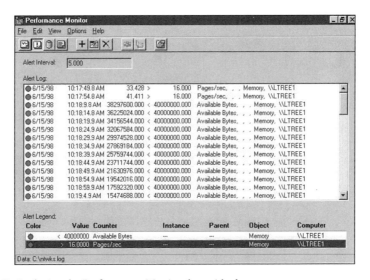

Figure 7.9 Analyzing the Performance Monitor log with alerts.

You'll notice in the log that about half way through our observation period, the Memory and the Disk objects both appear to be having some problems keeping up with demand. This problem appears to get steadily worse until finally a failure occurs.

This behavior is indicative of what is called a memory leak. A memory leak occurs when applications, processes, services, or drivers request memory and then do not return it when they are done. Often this process happens on the order of bytes at a time and can extend over a period of days or weeks. Searching these little buggers out can be a little time-consuming as you will need to collect a log over the entire period to really see who it is.

So, now you have an indication of what the problem is. To zero in on the issue, you need to confirm your hypothesis of continued memory utilization. Return to using Performance Monitor alerts. Set an alert to find the point when available Memory < 4MB. Remember, this is NT's desire, keep available memory around 4MB if possible. Only in time of desperate need will the system surrender its 4MB. Once you have found this point, you will probably want to adjust the Performance Monitor's Time window to look at the period around this time in order to focus your attention on a critical point. Figure 7.10 illustrates what this might look like.

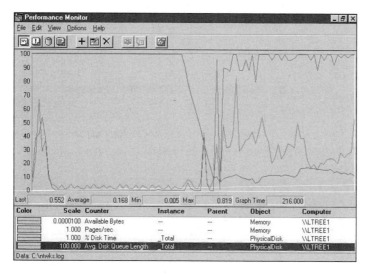

Figure 7.10 Zeroing in on the memory leak.

Notice the steady decline of the available memory. Keep in mind that Figure 7.10 is not really dealing in days or minutes—but for purposes here, deals in seconds. Now that you see the steady decline, you may be curious where to start looking for the culprit. Recall that a memory leak can be a driver as well as a foreground application. So you will look at all of the processes that are currently on the system. So for the time period you have set in the Time windows, you look at the Process: Working set for all of the applications individually. Another helpful tip is to adjust the Performance Monitor Chart view to be a histogram instead of a graph. It is sort of a police line-up of processes, as illustrated in Figure 7.11. With this done, you can zero in on the process with the largest working set.

Notice how one process stands out past the others in the size of its working set. You can further identify this subject as the process leaking memory by comparing the changes in its working set with the decrease in available memory in the Chart view as illustrated in Figure 7.12.

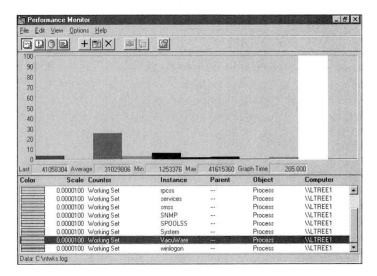

Figure 7.11 Lining up all of the processes' working sets in Histogram view helps identify a single program causing the memory shortage.

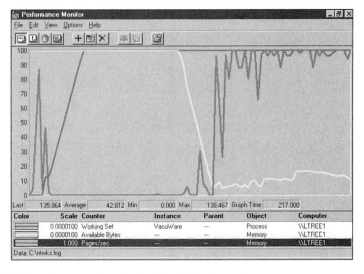

Figure 7.12 Complementary lines in the Graph view finger the suspect.

The lines on the graph pretty much nailed this one down. The process is using up memory and reducing the Available Bytes. With the offending process identified, you must now turn to the program developers for resolution. Occasionally, there are configuration changes that can assist in resolving the issue. Typically, though, the program needs to be repaired in the code. At least you can send them a copy of the Performance Monitor log so that they may analyze the problem.

In addition, determining where the leak is occurring may further assist developers and help you cope with the problem. Recall that there are two types of memory pools: pageable and nonpageable. In the Performance Monitor, for the entire period (as opposed to the adjusted Time window period), chart the Memory object counters, Pool Page Bytes and Pool Nonpage Bytes. Observe how these counters change over the duration of the log's collection period. One of these will steadily grow. Recall that typically Kernel mode services and drivers will be in the nonpage pool whereas other service types and user applications will have most of their memory in the pageable memory area. If you previously identified the system as the process taking all of the memory and the nonpage pool as the one growing, you should search the available Microsoft materials like TechNet or the Microsoft Web site for information on the leak. There may be patches to the leak or you may need to install the most recent service pack. Other unusual configuration options may produce memory leaks in some applications, so checking with the vendor of the application or service is a good start.

Sizing Up Memory

This section discusses some of the available options when it comes to adjusting memory usage and also looks at how you can figure out just how much memory is right for your machine. This section also offers a few insightful little tips about memory when dealing with other applications.

Determining How Much Memory You Need

After all this talk about memory shortages, you should at least understand a little bit about how to figure out how much is a good amount of memory to have. Ideally, the more memory you can get, the better. Of course you don't always have that luxury.

In general, if you have a working machine and are concerned, after your proper analysis of the system using techniques in this chapter, that you need more memory, you'll need to figure out how much. In general, you can use the Page File Object counters, %Usage and Usage Peak, to figure out about how much more memory you need to satisfy the hunger of the services and applications that you are running. The steps to determine this value are as follows:

1. Add up the size of all your pagefiles on the system.
2. Take %Usage x Size of All Pagefiles.

This should be how much memory you would want to add to make sure that all applications have enough physical RAM to run without paging.

Adjusting Memory Consumption

Prior to purchasing memory, you should make sure that you are clear on what the memory needs of your system are. You should have analyzed the system and made sure that you don't have a memory leak. You should also make sure that you reduce the memory requirements. This is possible by removing unnecessary protocols and services from the system. Of course, you must first be clear on what you want your server to do. If you have a BDC that is sharing printers and running the office SQL Server, you may wish to make a decision about moving some of these services to another machine or even purchasing a machine for a specific purpose like SQL Server. Other services like DHCP, WINS, DNS can usually be easily offloaded to a server more suitable for the task. PDC and BDC are generally memory needy machines. Storing user accounts, groups, and trust relationships in memory will keep most authentication duties running nicely. But mixing this with something like the memory hungry SQL Server could be bad news.

Reducing the number of loaded protocols is often a good strategy for memory as well as other resources like network and processor. Also, unneeded drivers and services, even idle ones, can affect memory. Make sure that the production servers are not used for testing applications, beta software, or demo software. Often these programs do not get uninstalled properly, leaving behind services that consume memory but go unnoticed.

Special Software Concerns with Memory

While there is much too much software to be concerned about in this world to mention all of them here, a few of the standard Microsoft BackOffice components deserve some mention. Take these as samples of similar pieces of software. Consider that although different vendors of MS SQL and say Oracle Database exist for Windows NT, they will still function much the same when it comes to memory concerns.

MS SQL Server is a very memory-intensive application. The more that it has, the better the performance of the machine. While it is not financially suitable in all occasions, you should consider putting MS SQL on a separate machine if it requires running enterprise-level applications on it. MS SQL in general likes to take half the available memory for itself. When it starts, it will claim this memory and never relinquish it again to NT. So for a machine with 128MB of RAM, MS SQL Server will claim 64MB. Often this is good for the performance of the application, but not so good for the other services that might need some memory as well.

Exchange is not as memory intensive, but will still need to run in bursts that will require large amounts of memory and usually expand the pagefiles if they were left at default. For any production-level system, the pagefile should be set minimally to twice the amount of RAM.

IIS is another application that will steal away memory, although perhaps not as savagely as SQL Server. IIS has an object cache, which is directly related to the performance of the system. The object cache is part of the working set of the IIS process and will not normally be visible separately in Performance Monitor unless viewing the IIS object. The object cache is typically 10% of the total physical RAM in the system. Again this is good for IIS, but not necessarily good for the other applications running on NT.

Additional Techniques for Sniffing Out Memory Issues

This chapter concentrated on the use of the two major tools on Windows NT to examine memory bottlenecks; however, there are several other tools that are worthy of using to examine information. This section provides a brief look at some of the NT Resource Kit tools that make analysis just a little bit easier. I have chosen to examine the Resource Kit here instead of looking for other third-party tools because of the basic probability that as a person supporting multiple NT machines, you either have the Resource Kits or TechNet at your disposal.

Not to sound too much like a commercial, but TechNet is really a "must have" for anyone supporting Microsoft BackOffice applications. TechNet supplies you with all the most recent service packs, knowledgebase articles, technical white papers, Resource Kit information, and a whole set of tools including all of those in the Resource Kits (BackOffice, NT, Office, and Windows 95). All of this is supplied on a monthly basis for around $300/year subscription. This is not to say that there are not third-party tools worthy of reviewing. Check with the current trade magazines and their Web sites for information on recent tools for assisting in the performance analysis and capacity planning for Windows NT sites. If you install the Resource Kit, there is a directory created on your system called NTRekit\PerfTool. In this directory, there are a number of subdirectories that contain a host of tools for analysis. The following sections examine these tools in groups: quick analysis tools, detailed memory tools, and tools for programmers. Remember that the focus here is on memory detection tools.

Quick Analysis Tools

These tools offer the capability to provide information on the use of memory much as Performance Monitor does, but in a quick, text-mode fashion. These tools come in useful should you desire to have a quick look at the performance on a particular aspect of a system without having to open Performance Monitor and set it up. In addition, I have had occasion to use the quick tools to produce information in a small file for emailing or loading onto floppies. Also, if you're a UNIX convert (or subject of forced service as sometimes we all are) you may simply be more comfortable with the text interface. The quick analysis tools include tlist, pfmon, and perfmtr.

Tlist

Tlist displays information on the Process IDs (PIDs) for applications. Using `tlist -t` will display information in a way that allows you to see the relationships of the processes to parent processes. You may also specify a particular PID and get more detailed information about it. The cousin to the tlist is the pulist. The pulist program will display in a text form the PID and the process user associated with the process. This will allow you to check permission information on your processes. Both tlist and pulist are good for finding out some quick information about a process. One nice little tidbit is the name of the executable that the process is running. Often in the graphical tools this is displayed as a "friendly name" that masks what the executable might be called. You might often use tlist to begin the analysis of individual processes and their memory usage.

pfmon

The pfmon tool displays information about the page faults that a particular application is creating. You attach it to a particular process. You get the PID from using tlist. Then while you are running the program, it collects information about the hard and soft page faults generated by the application. When you are done and close the application, pfmon will display information about the page faults as depicted in Figure 7.13.

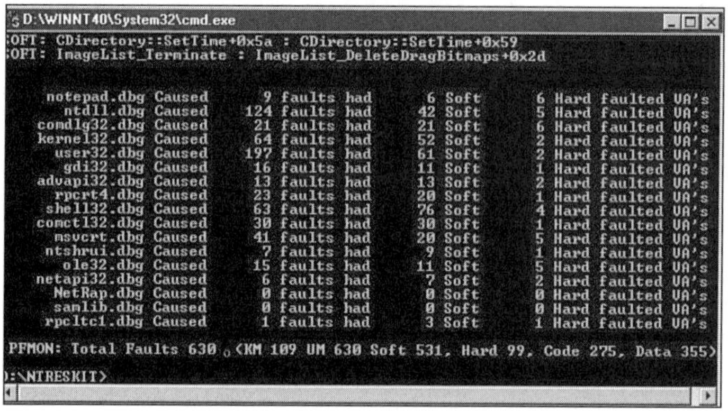

Figure 7.13   PFMON (Page Fault Monitor) display of Notepad's page faults while running.

This type of information helps you to understand the behavior of the particular application. If you are having a problem with unusually high page fault activity and have zeroed in on a particular application as doing most of the page faults, you may want to examine the application or service on another system in a controlled environment. You can get an idea of what is normal for an application as far as page fault activity. Then you can compare it to the other machine and see what the differences there are.

perfmtr

perfmtr is a text-based tool that displays continuous statistics about some of the standard counters for objects that you select, as illustrated in Figure 7.14.

Figure 7.14   perfmtr displays a variety of statistics in a scrolling text fashion.

The display will scroll constantly with the numbers until you hit (q)uit. You can switch between the various objects by hitting the corresponding letters. This is generally an unobtrusive way of getting information about the health of the system without having to open Performance Monitor. If you are having real problems with the graphical tool as graphics tend to affect the system more severely than the text based counterparts, you may wish to perfmtr instead.

Detailed Memory Tools

The Process Explode (pview.exe) and Process Viewer (pviewer.exe) are a couple of graphical tools that enable you to examine more deeply the interaction of the process with memory. These tools often are used more appropriately by programmers that can actually affect the programs use of memory, however, they can sometimes point you in the right direction if you are trying to figure out how to configure the application or service best for the memory configuration that we have. My favorite happens to be pview for the level of detail that it will show you, as illustrated in Figure 7.15.

In many cases, this particular tool will be most valuable to programmers that have a more intimate knowledge of the various modules that are being run in the code. However, notice that there are buttons that will display information about Thread IDs, Process IDs, and also security token information.

When programming in Windows (NT, 95, or Windows for Workgroups for that matter) you generally gain access to various objects through the use of a handle. The handle to the objects is generally tied to some unique ID generated by the system at the time of creation of the object. Knowing these IDs, like Thread ID and Process ID, enable you to single out a particular thread or process on the system. Your ability to analyze these items in the Performance Monitor is thus enhanced. Recall from Chapter 6 when we made good use of these IDs to identify which process was causing problems for us.

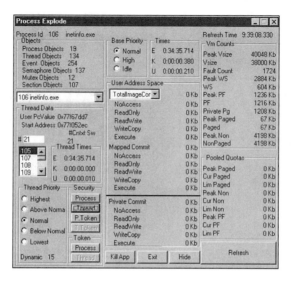

Figure 7.15 Process Explode displays detailed information about the process and threads running in that process.

    The process of optimization actually begins with the programmer. This book is primarily aimed at administrators, so we won't go into the details of how to code for optimization. Performance Monitor remains a powerful tool at this level. The programmer can observer the performance of a system with their program running on the system. Monitoring resource consumption during the pergrams operations would be an excellent first step. Developing your own Performance Monitor counters would be a huge step in the right direction. Counter development is documented in a variety of locations; Resource Kit, Win32 Software Development Kit (SDK), and MSDN Library's to name a few of the main sources.

Summary

This chapter took a good hard look at how memory works in a computer and how NT uses memory. We looked again at the VMM and the methods used to simulate memory. From there we began our serious investigation of the causes for poor memory performance. We tracked down the fugitive programs that had been running amuck and hoarding memory. We learned how memory issues affect the disk, and also how disk performance may contirbute to memory issues. In regard to the disk/memory performance issues, we addresses some of the problems facing using a disk file, pagefile.sys, to provide temporary storage of information. We learned much about paging and how to use the Performance Monitor paging counters to determine where the problem is and how to potentially correct it.

The only way to really get a handle on performance monitoring and optimization is to practice it. Try to simulate one of the issues described in this chapter. One tool for memory reduction simulations is LeakyApp.exe. This tool slowly devours memory, hence simulating a memory leak. You can use the Performance Monitor counters as described above to see how your systems react to the slow consumption of memory. LeakyApp is exceptionally good at allowing one to stop the consumption of memory at a particular point. This gives you time to really analyze what is going on with the system at any point of the memory consumption. Use the Explain button on the Performance Monitor Add Counter display to learn more about the counters that you're looking at. There are hunderds of counters! Keeping them all straight in your head is a daunting task, so why bother. Help is right there in the context of the Explain button, as well as in the pages of this chapter.

8

Optimizing Disk Performance

This chapter covers the following topics:

- **Hardware: Disk Architecture.** This section reviews the current disk subsystems including controller cards and various disk standards like EIDE and SCSI.

- **Disk and the Operating System.** This section analyzes how the operating system works with the device. You will see how the NT operating tries to compensate for the slowest piece of equipment on the machine. Of course, this section reviews some of the memory issues since disk and memory are so closely related.

- **Monitoring Disk Activity.** This section covers disk activity on a system. Disk activity is much more of a comparison value than the other counters, so you will need to see how to simulate activity to set some good baselines.

This chapter focuses on the disk subsystem, the slowest component on the computer (aside from the user at the keyboard). Chapter 6, "Optimizing CPU Performance" examined how caching is used to attempt to compensate for the disk's lack of speed in comparison to the memory and CPU. This chapter begins with some discussion about the hardware architecture of the disk subsystem. You will then learn how to analyze the disk's performance, which often begins with getting an idea of what your disk can do. The chapter ends by disclosing some techniques for enhancing the memory/disk relationship.

Hardware: Disk Architecture

This section covers how the various PC Bus types fit into the overall architecture. We will then focus on the various controller types, IDE/EIDE and SCSI variations.

General PC Architecture

The communication method for the rest of the system to talk to the disk is via the System Bus. The System Bus is different from the Memory Bus, which operates at a higher speed. The System Bus is in charge of communicating with the rest of the hardware aside from the memory and the CPU. Each of the devices on the bus communicates at various speeds managed by the individual components (see Table 9.1). In general, the System Bus will depend on the model (ISA vs. PCI) when you are concerned with the disk. In these cases, the speed of the bus will vary depending on the architecture.

Table 9.1   **Estimated Transfer Speeds for Bus Types**

Bus Type	**Speed Range (MB/s)**
PCMCIA (PC Card)	2–2
ISA non–Bus-mastering	.5–2
ISA Bus-mastering	2.5–3
EISA Bus-mastering	5–12
PCI Local Bus	32–132

Note that the values in Table 9.1 are based on specifications and should be treated as close estimates. Manufacturer techniques and improvements can offer better throughput than mentioned here, although comparatively speaking you get the idea. Clearly the PCI Bus is the fastest as far as operation is concerned. So, at the vary least you would like to see the disk controllers using the PCI Bus. Most computers come with a combination these days of PCI and EISA. This allows users to keep using those ISA cards instead of having to buy all new hardware.

The controllers are the boards that are plugged into the motherboard expansion slots. Nowadays most of the disk controllers, despite what type they are, will be integrated directly into the motherboard. Most motherboards, especially server class systems, will have a SCSI and two EIDE controllers, a primary EIDE and a secondary EIDE. In turn, the hard drives are plugged into the controllers to complete the chain. The sections that follow examine the various controller types.

Controllers

Controllers come in several varieties, IDE/EDIE, PCI, and SCSI. SCSI controllers in themselves have a few different types. In addition, the controllers will be either of the ISA or the PCI nature. Before moving onto the various types of controllers, you'll need to become familiar with what a PIO device is.

PIO Devices

A PIO (Programmable I/O) device is one that relies on the processor to assist in moving the information back and forth from the hardware device (see Chapter 6, "Optimizing CPU Performance"). You would like to remove this burden from the CPU, so you should always try to have a Bus-mastering controller. A PIO device takes the information from the hardware device and places it in a section of memory. The standard PIO device then alerts the processor and expects the processor to move the information from this section of memory to a more appropriate place where it was requested. Unlike the a standard PIO device, the Bus-master device will use DMA (Direct Memory Access) Technology, which allows the device to automatically address the memory and place the information in the requested location without affecting the processor. DMA technology is available with non-Bus mastering controllers, however, they will rely more on the processor than the Bus-mastering device.

The next factor is of course how much memory the device can understand. Consider the ISA card, which is 8-bit or 16-bit. Some of these devices can only see a memory address space up to the first 16MB of RAM. For the standard ISA non-Bus mastering device, NT can provide additional support to be able to allow the device to access higher memory locations. Providing this support, of course, affects the performance of the operating system. Devices like PCI Bus-mastering devices using a 32-bit addressing scheme can access 4GB of memory space.

EIDE Controllers

Enhanced IDE, as the name suggests, is an enhancement over the IDE standard disk device. The enhancements include support for larger drives. In general, the technology is older (more established) and cheaper than current SCSI technology. The seek times and communication speeds are slower than SCSI and present some problems. The EIDE controller is currently limited to two devices. In addition, the EIDE controller will adjust the speed of the controller and the Bus, based on the slowest device on the channel. Thus, if you put a CD-ROM and the hard drive on the same controller card, the controller's communication speed will be adjusted down to the speed of the CD-ROM. Thus, it is generally suggested that the CD-ROM and other slower devices be put on to the secondary EIDE controller. In addition, you should be careful about purchasing second hard drives. The second hard drive should match the speed of the first. If it doesn't, the disk subsystem in general will reduce its performance to that of the slowest drive.

When you are thinking about purchasing a system or new drives and you need to decide between EIDE and SCSI, consider the performance issues, but also consider the cost issues. Currently, and most likely for some time in the future, the EIDE has a pretty good price advantage over SCSI. I have seen 6GB EIDE drives at half of what a SCSI would cost. For home system, EIDE will probably be the way to go. Even for business workstations that do not have extreme performance requirements, the ease and the cost of using EIDE make it an excellent choice. For those servers, though, you want every bit of performance, expandability, and controller throughput that you can muster.

SCSI Controllers

SCSI devices are the predominant controller and device selection for the standard server or advanced workstation. The SCSI speed is based on several documented standards.

Of course, you would want to use the fastest available technology on your systems; however, without unlimited funds you must consider the importance of each component in the communication chain. Consider that in the course of communication with each other, the device that all drives and the operating system must communicate with is the controller card. Thus, it would be wise to make sure that the most attention is paid to this as opposed to the SCSI drives that may be connected to the card. A SCSI controller card with a good amount of cache (anything more than 2MB) is typically a good choice.

Hardware RAID

Many modern PC servers include disk subsystems for automatic hardware RAID configurations for both mirroring and RAID 5. Redundant Array of Inexpensive Disks (RAID) is a technology that utilizes multiple disk drives to enhance the fault tolerance of the disk subsystem. The different RAID levels offer various configurations of these disks. NT can provide a software version of this technology, but this requires resources from the processor. Currently there are RAID specifications beyond RAID 5, but RAID 1 and 5 demonstrate the basics of the technology nicely.

RAID 1 is called mirroring, which is named from a copy of a disk partition automatically maintained on another disk. Usually this is applied to the operating system drive. RAID 5 is disk striping with parity where a collection of three or more disks has data spread across each one. On one of the drives there is a parity bit. Think of the parity bit as a answer to some mathematically equation: $A + B = C$. A and B represent data, and C will represent the parity bit. If you have three disks for example, the data is put on to two of them and the parity is put on the other as illustrated in Figure 8.1.

Which disk ends up with the parity bit rotates in round-robin type fashion. That way one disk isn't responsible for the parity bits. Should a disk fail, the system can use the parity bit to figure out what the information on the disk is. So it would do something like, $A - C = B$. So, despite the failure of a single drive, the system can continue to operate.

The hardware version of RAID configurations offer superior performance over the comparable NT software options. In these cases, as with the general SCSI interface, the controller technology and cache levels are paramount to the performance of the overall system.

RAID 5 technology is far superior to software cases. Thus, it should be used when at all possible. The hardware solution often offers the added benefits of *hot swappable* drives that can be replaced while the system is running. Again, this is an important improvement over the software counterparts. Often, this added performance is slightly abused, since the overall performance of the RAID systems allows us to neglect the analysis of disk configuration and proper configuration of partitions. We will be reviewing the disk configuration schemes later in this chapter.

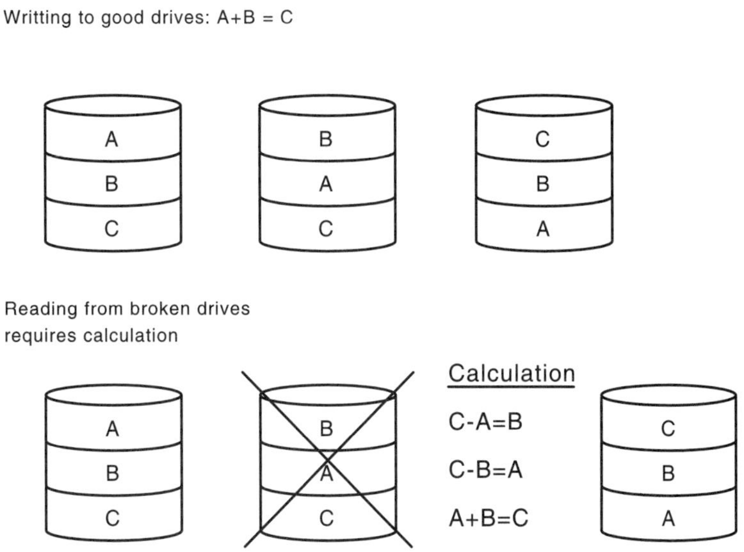

Writting to good drives: A+B = C

Reading from broken drives
requires calculation

Calculation

C-A=B

C-B=A

A+B=C

Figure 8.1 RAID 5 spreads the data across the disks using a parity bit to ensure data recovery.

RAID 1 systems also have some benefits over the comparable software mirroring in Windows NT; however, these benefits of speed are less dramatic given proper configuration of the software/hardware in the NT solution. In addition, the server vendors sometimes will not allow the hardware mirroring to be done on a per partition basis. Instead, the controller configurations only allow the entire physical disk to be mirrored. This sometimes results in a loss of valuable disk space as well as preventing the use of some performance tricks with the pagefile.

Generally, the RAID performance for hardware is superior, however, as you will learn, sometimes some configuration and memory configuration issues result in favoring the software configuration in Windows NT with a more flexible hardware configuration relying on less expensive and less complex hardware configurations.

The Disk and the Operating System

This section takes a look at how the operating system views the disk configurations. First you might need a refresher on the I/O Manager and its interactions with the system. You should also know how the file system cache fits into the whole process. Finally, you'll get more information on how the disk systems can affect the other resources that the operating system is utilizing.

I/O Manager and the File System Cache

The I/O Manager is in charge not just of the disk subsystem but of the I/O for many of the devices on the system. The I/O Manager is involved in the coordination of the drivers necessary to deliver and retrieve information. This includes the network I/O as well as disk I/O. The I/O Manager is also in charge of moving information in and out of the file system cache. However, recall that the VMM is in charge of changing the size of the file system cache based on demand from the system for memory. This balancing act sometimes leads to information disappearing from the file system cache.

When the VMM needs to reduce the size of the cache, it can't simply cut it off. There could be important stuff in there that has not been delivered to its respective devices. The VMM must first flush the cache and then it may reduce the size of the cache. In this way, any data in the cache that had not been written to disk or to the network gets flushed out. The system overall roughly treats the file system cache as part of the I/O Managers working set. In this sense, when an application or service looks to its working set for a piece of information and it is not present, it is counted as a page fault.

So, in your examination you will consider the file system cache. There can be file system cache bottlenecks, but these are fairly rare and often have their origins in other system resource issues. For example, if the file server is very low on memory, the file system cache will be reduced. When the file server's natural usage of moving files across the network is realized, however, the system will not have enough cache available to feed the system. This results in many "cache misses." In other words, data that the system would expect to be present in the cache is missing.

Effects of Disk Usage on Other Systems

The disk activity can be easily seen to affect other components, namely memory and the processor. You'll need to keep your eye on these items as you observe the disk issues.

Memory performance is very much tied to the disk performance. By know, you should be very clear on this. The pagefiles are on the disk and the VMM uses these pagefiles to offer each process 4GB of virtual memory.

If you recall from Chapter 6, "Optimizing CPU Performance," the processor performance is related to the disk in that it can mask disk problems. From the initial discussion of hardware in this chapter, you know that some of the controller cards are PIO devices that actually use the processor to assist in moving the data back and forth. Besides just that, recall that a system's processor is not just in charge of running code, it is responsible for handling hardware interrupts. Excessive disk or network activity can cause the processor to appear excessively busy. Thus, you need to observe all of the counters before moving forward to examining the disk activity.

Monitoring Disk Activity

The hard drive is the container for all of the information on a computer. The hard disk contains your code, your data, and your pagefiles. All in all the hard disk is a library that contains volumes of information that can show the rest of the system how to do things, or provide reference material to be anlyzed and displayed to a user. At a library, there are really only two functions, check out a book and return a book. With the hard drive it is the same, read from the disk and write to the disk. When observing disk performance, reads from the disk account for generally around 70-80% of all disk activity. Thus you will generally focus on reads when monitoring disk activity.

This chapter looks at the steps to analyze the disk performance, which is a little different from the other components covered in Chapters 6, 7, and 10. You will see how to examine what the disk is doing. The disk subsystem is basically serving a queue if you'll remember the queuing theory discussions from Chapter 6, "Optmizing CPU Performance." However, the disk is much more sensitive to queues than the quick little processor. Once again you will learn how to zero in on the troublemaker. Lastly, this section looks at some tips for configuring disk subsystems to assist in optimizing disk and memory performance in a couple if different scenarios. In addition, you will learn to consider those situations that are affected by different software components in the BackOffice suite.

Steps to Analyzing Disk Performance

The steps to disk analysis are much the same as for memory and processors:

1. Establish baselines.
2. Observe overall activity.
3. Eliminate other sources of performance degradation.
4. Zero in on the disk.
5. Zero in on the cause.

When monitoring disk activity, probably more so than the other resources, step 1 will be paramount to being able to understand what the disk counters mean. Take a look at a typical scenario.

Case Study

I was working with a client, that despite ample monetary resources, was reluctant to generate funds for non-production machines. Thus, the system administrators were often left to build development and test servers out of desktop machines that would have additional hard drives and memory put in them to act as servers. This practice, although effective if demands are not placed on the machines, is not recommended when the system will be servicing larger groups as it was in this case. The issue arose when the department began development on an SQL server application. They had installed SQL server on a converted workstation with 8GB of drives and a good 128MB of RAM. The users complained that the system was slow. Despite the fact that this was a workstation that was converted, given the amount of resources the system should operate well enough for this small group of developers to do their work.

When the systems performance was observed, the processor was most notably in excess closing in on 95% at times during routine SQL server operations. Initially, you start to think that the processor needs to be upgraded. However, closer examination revealed that the value for the Disk Queue Length counter was hovering around 2 and often climbed above that for sustained periods of time. If you recall from Chapter 6, "Optimizing CPU Performance," you know that that hardware interrupts were greater than the system calls. Well, at this point I started to wonder just what was inside the box. I opened the case a found a couple of things. This was an older workstation which despite the presence of Pentium processor, was an ISA bus. The hard drives were operating off of an ISA/EIDE controller card. This card was producing a good portion of the processor problems. In addition, we found a problem that you are familiar with by now. We found that the system had a memory upgrade but not a L2-Cache upgrade. The system now running on 128MB of RAM was still working with a 256 L2-Cache. The issues mentioned considered with the cost of the upgrades to correct them allowed us to finally get the okay to purchase a departmental server that could handle this and other tasks.

Observing Disk Activity

Before launching into the process of monitoring disk activity, you must enable the monitoring of disk activity in the operating system. The other objects such as memory and processor did not require this activation step. Microsoft has left this a manual procedure since the monitoring of the disk activity on 386 machines could affect the performance of the system as much as 1.5%. Microsoft has determined that on a 486 machine, the counters could affect the system's performance no more than about 1%. Thus, on Pentium class servers that you are typically dealing with, there is no real reason to turn these counters off once you have enabled them. When you turn the counters on it is like flipping a switch within the disk drivers. To make the drivers read the switch, you will have to restart them. This of course means a reboot of the computer. In order to enable the disk counters you simple do the following steps:

1. Open a command prompt.
2. Type `diskperf -y`.
3. Reboot the machine.

Note that if you are running any kind of software RAID (mirroring, strip sets, strip sets with parity) you will need to run `diskperf -ye`. This will enable the counters to be used with these types of configurations. If you don't use the `ye` argument, the activity of the disk will generally be grossly exaggerated. Note that this conditional is only to be used with software RAID. If you are using a hardware RAID solution, you should use the standard command `diskperf -y` instead, which will present accurate results. Keep in mind that the system does not know anything about your disk subsystem past the hardware controller card. This means that when NT writes the data to the controller card on a hardware RAID configuration, it considers that data written to the disk.

General Counters in Performance Monitor

Disk activity is usually a process of elimination. You will want to first recall how to recognize the difference between the processor and the disk. First, you need to understand how to eliminate the memory as a problem. You will also have to watch for those rare system cache issues. To begin, you need to establish the counters that will be earmarks for disk performance. The counters below are all associated with either the PhysicalDisk object or the LogicalDisk object.

- **Current Disk Queue Length.** This counter provides a primary measure of disk congestion. Just as the processor queue was an indication of waiting threads, the disk queue is an indication of the number of transactions that are waiting to be processed. Recall that the queue is an important measure for services that operate on a transaction basis. Just like the line at the super market, the queue will be representative of not only the number of transactions, but also the length and frequency of each transaction.

- **% Disk Time.** Much like % Processor time, this counter is a general mark of how busy the disk is. You will see many similarities between the disk and processor since they are both transaction-based services. This counter indicatesa disk problem, but must be observed in conjunction with the Current Disk Queue Length counter to be truly informative. Recall also that the disk could be a bottleneck prior to the % Disk Time reaching 100%.

- **Avg. Disk Queue Length.** This counter is actually strongly related to the %Disk Time counter. This counter converts the %Disk Time to a decimal value and displays it. This counter will be needed in times when the disk configuration employs multiple controllers for multiple physical disks. In these cases, the overall performance of the disk I/O system, which consists of two controllers, could exceed that of an individual disk. Thus, if you were looking at the %Disk Time counter, you would only see a value of 100%, which wouldn't represent the total potential of the entire system, but only that it had reached the potential of a single disk on a single controller. The real value may be 120% which the Avg. Disk Queue Length counter would display as 1.2.

- **Disk Reads/sec.** This counter is used to compare to the Memory: Page Inputs/sec counter. You need to compare the two counters to determine how much of the Disk Reads are actually attributed to satisfying page faults.

Other counters (which will be reviewed shortly) are used for setting the performance standards for the particular disk configuration. Keep in mind that with all of these counters there are two objects, PhysicalDisk and LogicalDisk. The PhysicalDisk object refers to the piece of hardware that is installed in the computer, no matter how you have divided the disk into various partitions. In the Performance Monitor, you will see instances for the PhysicalDisk object referring to the number of hard drives installed in the system, starting with drive 0. A logical disk is one of the partitions that the physical disk has been divided into. These are usually referred to as drive C:, D:, E:, or as many as you have. A single physical disk can contain several partitions.

In general, when observing overall disk system performance of the entire hardware configuration, you will be looking at the PhysicalDisk object. When looking into issues of pagefile activity, you generally examine the PhysicalDisk object. When you are trying to isolate particular issues of usage with an application or perform more specific analysis on selected partitions you would use the LogicalDisk object. For example, say you have isolated intensive non-memory disk activity to a database application. You would want to isolate the disk activity to the partition where the database was so that other factors such as pagefiles and other disk oriented applications do not interfere with your analysis.

Establishing Disk Capabilities

You should create a baseline by gathering initial data for the resource under controlled conditions. This is especially critical for disk subsystems. The disk subsystem is comprised of the disk, the controller card, and the computer I/O Bus structure. When you are measuring the performance of a disk you must consider all of these. Since each of these components has its own performance ranges, and since it is the combinations that we are actually measuring with the Performance Monitor, stating simple rules of good and bad performance is difficult. Thus, you must establish baselines for each of the servers that you are concerned about, before you put them into production. Knowing how the system performs under controlled conditions will allow you to determine what is good and bad in the production environment. In establishing a baseline for disk performance, you first want to identify the counters to use:

- **Disk Reads Bytes/sec.** Primarily, you'll use this counter to describe the performance of disk throughput for the disk subsystem. Remember that you are generally measuring the capability of the entire disk hardware subsystem to respond to requests for information.

- **Avg. Disk Bytes/Read.** This counter is used primarily to let you know the average number of bytes transferred per read of the disk system. This helps distinguish between random reads of the disk and the more efficient sequential file reads. A smaller value generally indicates random reads. The value for this counter can also be an indicator of file fragmentation.

- **Avg. Disk sec/Read.** The value for this counter is generally the number of seconds it takes to do each read. On less complex disk subsystems involving controllers that do not have intelligent management of the I/O, this value is a multiple of the disk's rotation per minute. This does not negate the rule that the entire system is being observed. The rotational speed of the hard drive will be the predominant factor in the value with the delays imposed by the controller card and Support Bus system.

- **Disk Reads/sec.** The value for this counter is the number of reads that the disk was able to accomplish per second. Changes in this value indicate the amount of random access to the disk. The disk is a mechanical device that is capable of only so much activity. When files are closer together, the disk is permitted to get to the files quicker than if the files are spread throughout the disk. In addition, disk fragmentation can contribute to an increased value here.

In order to exercise these values, you can use a program called Response Probe that is contained in the NT Resource Kit. If you have a little programming skills, you could easily write a utility to do a similar activity reading information from a file sequentially or randomly. Given the number of sample files that the Resource Kit provides for the Response Probe, it is just as easy to use this utility. To set up Response Probe to exercise disk activity, you'll need to do the following:

1. Create a directory for the test files.

2. Copy the following files into this directory:

   - \NTReskit\PerfTool\Probe\Creatfil.exe

   - \NTReskit\PerfTool\Probe\Probeprc.exe

   - \NTReskit\PerfTool\Probe\Probe.exe

   - \NTReskit\PerfTool\Probe\timerw32.dll

   - \NTReskit\PerfTool\Probe\statw32.dll

   - \NTReskit\PerfTool\Probe\Examples\DiskMax.scp

   - \NTReskit\PerfTool\Probe\Examples\Diskmax.scr

   - \NTReskit\PerfTool\Probe\Examples\Diskmax.sct

3. Open a command prompt and move to the directory that you created.

4. Create a large file, typically 60MB is a good starting point. The Resource Kit contains a program CREATFIL.EXE that will allow the creation of a file filled with zeros. At a command prompt type: CREATFIL WORKFIL.DAT 60000.

5. Open the Performance Monitor and go to the Log view. You will be recording the counters previously listed. Start the logging file.

   For best results you should try to avoid logging the data to the same disk that you are exercising for this test. Even better, avoid using the same controller that the test is working on.

6. Returning to the command prompt, start the Response Probe test. The syntax is probe ProcessFileName.SCR TrialTime [OutputFileName]. PROBE DISKMAX.SCR 900 DISKMAX.OUT. The value of 900 is the trial time in seconds. This translates to 15 minutes of test time. This is pretty much the lowest value for producing a reasonable test. Doing longer trial times will increase the accuracy of the testing.

7. When the test completes, stop the Performance Monitor log and examine the results (see Figure 9.2).

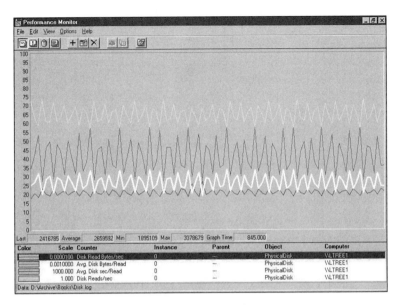

Figure 8.2 Sample Results from a disk configuration trial.

This test was run using a SCSI-2 internal hard drive.

Although this information is interesting, it does not indicate what the actual disk throughput for either drive is. You must vary the trials to get an idea at the very least of when the disk is used to read sequentially, randomly, small record sizes, and large record sizes. Although time consuming, this test involves little user interaction and results in an excellent description of the overall performance of the disk. Varying these items is done by adjusting the Response Probe scripts.

The next section examines the various values for the performance issues indicated from the preceding test.

Isolating the Disk

A lot of the examination of disk issues is the elimination of other issues that have affected the disk performance—primarily memory. The chart in Figure 8.3 displays information regarding the Memory: Input Pages/sec and the Physical Disk: Disk Reads/sec counters.

From Figure 8.3, you can see that the memory is representing a small portion of the overall disk activity, indicating that the memory is not causing the problem. However, you should also notice that the disk is still having a problem due to the size of the Disk Queue Length. Thus, you determine that the load on this disk is more than the disk can handle—the general definition of a bottleneck.

At this point, the analysis gets a little more subjective. You must determine if the job is inappropriate for the disk or if the disk is inappropriate for the job. Let us consider a scenario.

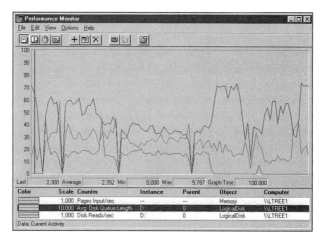

Figure 8.3 Separating disk from memory.

Suppose you're in a work environment where you are forced to convert PC work-stations to servers. In this case, you would want to create a file server out of a PC that used to be on a co-workers desk. The PC has a PCI-based I/O bus with an EIDE controller integrated into the motherboard. The system is supplied with an ample 64MB of RAM and a respectable Pentium 100MHz processor. The system is actually okay as a file server, with the understanding that the files are not excessively large or used by a large number of users simultaneously. Suppose in this case that it is a small departmental file server supporting some 40 users. This is actually an acceptable sce-nario. However, if you take the same system and install IIS as an Intranet Server for the department and it gets numerous hits from inside as well as outside the depart-ment, you may expect to see the disk subsystem strained to its limitations.

When looking at performance issues, you must always consider the intended use of the hardware. Sometimes the performance potential of the machine can be wasted due to inappropriate use. Suppose you have a dual Pentium processor (200MHz) that you are using as a file server. The file server has 128MB of RAM and a very nice 8GB RAID controller. Certainly this is a suitable file server for almost any department. However, the dual processor configuration makes it even more appropriate as an appli-cation server. Perhaps there is a swap that could occur within the department to get a different machine for a file server and this one as an application server.

Sometimes it is necessary to try and determine what the application is that is causing the problem. There are times when a particular application may be causing the disk activity as opposed to a general system overload. You can get this information using the Process: %Disk Time counter which will give an indication of which applications are generating the most calls to the hard drive if those calls are primarily related to paging operations.

After you eliminate the possibility of a memory issue, it is down to examining each process and understanding what the process' functions are. Occasionally, you may find it necessary to enable security auditing to determine which process is modifying a particular series of files—a trick I have used to find users copying large amounts of data that perhaps they shouldn't.

Once you identify the application, you then want to determine why that application is working the way that it is. Sometimes this is a task left to the developers who will need to improve their programming to better utilize the operating and the disk subsystem. However, there are many times that high performance applications such as enterprise database systems, email systems, and web servers that require attention be paid to the disk configurations. This could mean adjusting the adapter card, creating partitions in a particular way, placing pagefiles in particular locations, or configuration of the applications components to use different disks. The next few sections cover these situations and configurations.

Disk Configurations

The performance of the disk subsystem can affect the entire performance of the system. This section looks at some various disk configurations given the goals for the configuration in optimizing the disk configuration.

General Fault Tolerant Configurations

There are several RAID configurations that are possible with Windows NT Server: RAID 0, RAID 1, and RAID 5. These configurations each have their merits although, if incorrectly utilized, they can be less than appropriate.

RAID 0 is disk striping without parity. This configuration actually offers no fault tolerance at all, consequently increasing the likeliness of loss of data given the failure of a single drive. Figure 8.4 illustrates how information is spread across several physical disks.

Physical Hard Disks

Figure 8.4 Disk striping.

The data is written across several volumes in order to allow the operating disk to have the opportunity to access the drives more readily. As stated, the RAID 0 disk configuration does not have any value in fault tolerance. However, this configuration does tend to speed up the disk access for writes and reads, which can be useful under certain circumstances.

RAID 1 is mirroring. This is the process of using the space on another drive to maintain a duplicate copy of the some files. This can be done in hardware or software.

The hardware configurations are more expensive, but provide additional speed. However, the software version in Windows NT can be useful as well and sometimes allow for configurations that the hardware version does not allow. With disk mirroring, the system is constantly writing to both drives which causes duplicate efforts on the part of the operating system.

Hardware solutions have a slight advantage here. However, if the drives are configured on individual controllers, the disk system will not have the drain on the system that is typically associated with dual writes since the operating system is free to access either drive doing the work close to simultaneously. This often competes nicely with the speed of a hardware configuration.

The next item is that the software solution can be configured to mirror disk partitions. Often the hardware solutions are implemented on the entire disk. This can be a drawback to the system depending on the placement of the pagefile on the system. If you wanted to segregate the pagefile on the same physical disk but in a different partition so that the pagefile is not being mirrored, it might not be possible on the hardware solution.

Mirroring is normally employed to mirror the operating system for fault tolerance as well as performance reasons. When mirroring is used, write performance slightly decreases where read performance actually increases. This discrepancy occurs because the system will be able to read from either drive depending on which one is least busy at the time. Using separate controllers can further enhance this performance. The OS files hardly ever change with the exception of the `pagefile.sys`. Most of the activity is thus reads. This consideration also points out how important the need is to keep the pagefile off of a mirrored partition.

RAID 5 is disk striping with parity (see Figure 8.5).

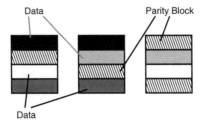

Figure 8.5 Disk striping with parity.

The software version in the case of RAID 5 has a hard time competing with the hardware version. The software version offers little in the way of additional configuration features like the mirrored configuration. The software version does offer a little price relief, but with the increased performance that hardware solutions offer, this is not much of a motivator.

Maximizing the Pagefile

You should know by now that the disk performance and in particular the performance for accessing the pagefile can greatly affect the memory performance of the system. So, you need to know about the configurations that are best suited for the pagefile. Here are a few little tips:

- Do not mirror the pagefile or put on RAID 5 configurations.
- Separate the pagefile among different physical drives.
- Separate the pagefile among different controllers if possible.
- Keep the pagefile on a different drive from the operating system.
- Put the pagefile on a FAT partition of 300 MB or less.

So let's talk about these a moment. First, as you can probably determine, mirroring the pagefile is silly. First off, the pagefile is nothing you would ever want to save. Secondly, the pagefile is constantly being written to. Mirroring is best for drives that are primarily read from and not written to. Typically the operating system partition is mirrored. Even in a RAID 5 configuration, the pagefile will create an almost constant flurry of activity. Undoubtedly, a hardware RAID 5 configuration will be able to handle it, but there is also a cost for this activity. Even though you might have a powerful RAID 5 system, that is no need to waste the power on such an activity.

Separating the pagefile among different physical drives and controllers can offer great increases in overall system performance. The capability to access the pagefile more readily is always well accepted by the system and always capitalized on.

Keeping the pagefile on a different partition from the operating system will give the already busy operating system drive a break. The drive will be able to focus on reading from a specific area of the drive as opposed to reading and writing to all sorts of locations within the pagefile. Often this keeps the pagefile from being mirrored as well, since it is the operating system drive that is usually the focus for fault tolerance in a mirror configuration. One concern in this case though is that if the operating system partition does not have a pagefile on it that matches the size of physical RAM, then the system will not be able to write a memory dump file in the event of a Blue Screen. This is often something you might simply accept. Should you need such a dump file, you should temporarily create a pagefile on the operating system drive and wait for the error to occur again, which usually isn't too long. If the system has produced a Blue Screen once, it is typically going to happen again readily.

Despite the distinct advances of the NT File System (NTFS), FAT remains faster to access the disk on partitions less than 300MB. So if you are going to put the pagefile on a separate partition, it might as well be a FAT partition. The pagefile is not interested in the file permissions or compression functionality that NTFS offers, so why force it.

Figure 8.6 illustrates a conceptual disk configuration based on the information covered so far in this section.

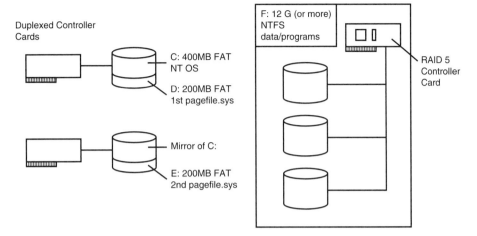

Figure 8.6 Conceptual Disk Configuration.

Now, there is nothing that says you cannot implement some of the suggestions and squeeze out a little more performance from your system. So consider your choices, your resources, and the time that you have to put into building the solution.

Special Software Concerns

This section offer a few little pieces of wisdom regarding various other BackOffice components. The BackOffice components are covered becasues of their inherent integration with NT and for the availability of data on the configuration and performance of these systems. Other systems with like functionality will often benefit from similar disk configurations.

SQL

In general, the Microsoft SQL server likes to have the system's database devices on one disk and the log devices on another. A SQL device is a preallocated section of disk that is used for storing the tables, user information, store procedures, and other objects that make up an entire database. Each database must have a log where transactions for the database are stored. It is both a wise fault tolerant move as well as a good performance move to put the two on different physical drives. Again, the use of addition controllers is beneficial. Advance RAID 5 controllers can keep up with the demand, but if possible, putting the logs on a separate disk and controller will still offer some benefits.

Exchange

Much as SQL server has databases and logs, so does Exchange. The same rules apply. Keeping the Exchange stores, which contain the email messages for all of the users on the system, on a separate drive from the transaction logs will assist in the performance of the system overall. In addition, this will offer a higher degree of fault tolerance. For both SQL Server and Exchange, it is suggested that the write caching on the controller card is actually turned off. This will result in a slight decrease in performance, so before trying it in production you may want to try some simulations. However, both SQL and Exchange rely on many disk writes to be "real" writes that are insured to have gone to the physical media as opposed to a volatile cache.

IIS

The system primarily reads from the file system. This is one of the few times when using a stripe set without parity may be a good choice. The information on the web site should actually be stored somewhere else. This is often the case with web servers, as in any configuration (secure Firewall or not) the web server is the most exposed machine in the company to Internet "bad guys". Thus, the total web site's pages and configurations should be stored on tape at the very least, or on a file server for faster recovery. With this in mind, the content of the web server is not considered critical data. Thus, you can use a stripe set to get the advantages of the increased disk read performance without concern for the fault tolerance issues created.

Summary

This chapter analyzed the disk activity on a system. We built our knowledge of the disk subsystem from the ground up, beginning with the disk hardware components. The operating system was seen to react to the disk subsystem in a couple of different ways. First, NT attempts to compensate for the relative slow speed of the disk component by using the File System Cache. Second, virtual memory strategies use the pagefile (or files) on the hard drives to attempt to provide ample room in the virtual memory space for all applications. When viewing disk activity, it is always critical to have a baseline, more so with disk than any of the other components. This chapter demonstrated how to establish the baseline for disks and concluded with a discussion of the various disk counters and issues.

On Your Own

As with the previous two chapters, it is always best to try these techniques out to really get a good feel for how they work. Take a test machine and run the Response Probe against it to check the throughput of the system. Change the some of the conditions of the tests to see if you can find the maximum throughput of the disk subsystem for the machine. If you have other system in your enterprise like SQL or mail systems, load these up on a test server. Make some adjustments to the server based on the recommendation for these components in this chapter. Measure how these changes affect the performance of the disk and the other software. Lastly, adjust the configuration of NT and see how moving the pagefile around affects both the disk performance and well as the memory performance for the computer.

## 9

Optimizing Network Interface Performance

This chapter covers the following topics:

- **Hardware Architecture.** This section addresses the interaction of the Network Interface Card (NIC) with the rest of the hardware. In addition, some of the basic network architecture is examined.

- **Networking and the Operating System.** The NT operating system has several components, clients, and services that rely and interact with the network. Together, these components take care of all the communication on the network. The interaction of these components, the user, and the NIC will be important as our discussion unfolds into an analysis of Network Performance.

- **Monitoring the Network Interface.** With an established understanding of the hardware and operating system components, you are ready to analyze network performance. Topics in this section will not be limited to situations of heavy network traffic, but will include how the operating system and components are affected by traffic on the network.

First, notice that this chapter is not named "Optimizing Network Performance." Network performance consists of more than simply what goes in and out of a single machine. The topic of entire network performance is more a matter of examining all the varieties of services, components, and infrastructure designs that contribute to an overall network. This, of course, is far too involved a topic to cover here. This chapter refers to networking that is under the direct control of the Windows NT base operating system, which includes components within the operating system that interact with the network outside of the computer.

Most of the discussion within this chapter will focus on TCP/IP and, in general, Ethernet. This is one of the most common network architectures that you will run across. When appropriate, you will see mention of a major departure in technology: for example, in the case of Token Ring networks as opposed to Ethernet.

All that being said, the first thing you need to be familiar with are the hardware basics. The network interface card is essentially a simple device. As you will see, however, the hardware is changing and offers its own complexities in integrating with other components in the operating system. After you understand hardware, you will need to turn your attention to the operating system, which must cope with the unseen burdens the network places on it. With all these concepts established, it is time again to turn to the Performance Monitor in order to decipher the various clues of performance issues.

Hardware Architecture

The network interface card (NIC) is one of the simpler devices when looking at the computer. It has no moving parts, it is generally small, and it is dedicated to a single task. The sections that follow describe this unassuming device and its role as a component in the computer.

System Layout

As far as the rest of the computer goes, the NIC is simply another card that drops into one of the expansion slots on your computer. Most NICs are either PCI or ISA. Rarely, you may see the occasional EISA network card. Table 8.1 in Chapter 8, "Optimizing Disk Performance," discloses that ISA is a 16-bit (2.5–3.0 MB/s), relatively slow moving interface, whereas the PCI is a 32-bit fast moving (32–132 MB/s) interface. The NIC sits in the expansion slot that is provided for access to the system bus, which connects to the rest of the hardware components in the computer. This should be very familiar to anyone who has ever opened a computer before. Thinking of performance, you would want to consider the fastest bus architecture; however, pointing at your ISA card and shouting "bottleneck!" isn't really going to be the solution here. PCI is great, but consider that most current network speeds are 10 MB/s, ISA doesn't sound all that much worse. The 16-bit vs. 32-bit, however, does change the discussion a little.

Consider that the operating system is speaking in 32-bit "words." It would be beneficial for it to be able to talk to the other components using the same 32-bit words as opposed to saying it with twice as many 16-bit words. Although this does not cut the performance in half, it does slow things down a touch. Also, you must remember that we are in part slaves to the vendor's standards. NIC vendors tend to throw more of their development efforts and thus the little extras into the newer technology. Thus, the PCI cards seem to have a few more features that allow for better operation. Considering all this, it generally is not worth the time and effort to replace all those NICs in your workstations with 32-bit PCI ones, unless you are moving to a faster network architecture like 100MB/s.

Recall that previous chapters warned of accepting all of the bits of wisdom as hard and fast rules. This remains the case in this chapter. For example, suggesting that you might not want to put your money into a bunch of new NICs is good advice if you have other more pressing issues and a limited budget as IT administrators usually have. If your users utilize the network for heavy file transfers or major database applications, however, those faster NICs are going to be a very appropriate expenditure. Remember, always consider the entire situation before applying the rules found in these chapters.

The next thing to consider is how the NIC fits in to the rest of the network system, how it might transfer data, communicate with the processor, or react to transmissions on the network wire. Life begins to get a little more complicated for the little NIC.

How the Network Card Fits In

The network card serves as a bridge to worlds outside your own. It connects you to the rest of the business and sometimes to the rest of the world. Often the NIC is underrated, lacking the pizzazz of a 400MHz processor or the ego boost of 256MB of RAM. To most, this lackluster component in the computer is little more and a passive device that somehow achieves the mundane task of converting information to electrical impulses on a wire. Consider, however, the complexities of simple network traffic: picking up packets, making sure they are not for this computer, sometimes reacting to them without the computers knowledge; passing information to the processor; other times curbing interruptions to the system; all this while trying to move information as fast as possible. Perhaps this unassuming little character is more important than it first seems.

Recall that this chapter analyzes the network interface. While the NIC is a major part of this subsystem, the entire subsystem is being considered. As much as you need to include coverage of controller card, bus architecture, and disk drives, you must consider all the software and hardware components involved in moving information out over the network. The network card vendors, in an effort to continue to offer better performance and more features, have changed the way some of the NICs work.

The new NICs have a focus of speeding up throughput. Caching agents and algorithms programmed into the chips on the card assist in reading and writing to and from the network in a simultaneous fashion. In addition, features built into the card can be used by drivers to provide additional throughput defenses, such as prioritizing packets, avoiding multicast traffic and caching of networking traffic on the card.

Other features beginning to emerge have to do with assisting in the management of networks and computers on the network. NIC vendors have partnered with software vendors to provide client and network management features. Utilizing Simple Network Manager Protocols (SNMP), software can be used to monitor the health of the network or the computer using the network card.

Lastly, how could we forget the very much-hyped Plug and Play? This is where the network card communicates seamlessly with the operating system to install itself without user interaction. This is all well and good if your operating system supports it. Windows NT's support for such features has been lagging to say the least. This topic is addressed again in the sections that follow.

Some big PC vendors have integrated some vendors' NICs onto the motherboard. This has been a bit of a mixed blessing. You may encounter when a business has standardized on a NIC and refuses to use even the integrated one. Businesses see no benefit in having the NIC integrated, which is only a perceived cost that can't be avoided. You may also run into companies using Token Ring. The integrated cards tend to be Ethernet. This might cost a great deal of time each time a user adjusts their network settings and disables the wrong interface. Often, the integrated card will be found first, or will be the only one found automatically. The unknowing user disables the wrong interface and thus their network connectivity.

Many of these features are partially built into the network card and partially in the driver. The network card driver is a component that is tightly integrated within the operating system, which is the topic of the next section.

> Prior to buying any NIC, the first step is to make sure that it appears on the NT hardware compatibility list (HCL). You can find the list posted on the Microsoft Web site (www.microsoft.com). (Note that you'll have to do a search for HCL as it seems to move around a little.) Also, if you get TechNet, the most recent HCL can usually be found on it.

The Operating System

The Windows NT operating system is responsible for responding to the user's request for information. If that information is out on the network, it is the responsibility of the operating system and its supporting services to be able to retrieve the information in a timely manner. NT is built with networks in mind.

There are several components and services that are involved in servicing connections and communications. Much of the system is a duplicate of the Disk I/O. Unlike the disk, there are many ways of communicating. There are different protocols, there are variations within the protocols, there are different hardware configurations, different clients, and different applications trying to communicate. All this results in a rather complex layering of the network communication components. In the following sections, do the following:

- Review the NT network architecture.

- See in detail how some of the new components are related.

- Learn how NT must react to network communications through interrupt mechanisms.

- Come to understand how a variety of client services utilize the supporting network communication services.

General I/O

The network I/O for Windows NT generally is the same as that for the Disk I/O. Information is passed through the system cache and then sent out over the network. Recall that this is done within the I/O Manager, a Windows NT Executive Service (refer Chapter 8 "Optimizing Disk Performance" or Chapter 1, "Understanding NT Architecture" for a refresher). Inside the I/O manager, however, is a complex seven-layered cake of services and drivers that work to pass information back and forth to the network, as illustrated in Figure 9.1.

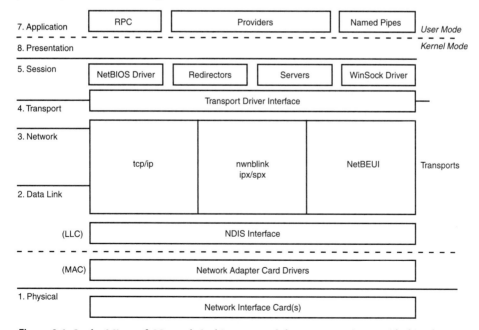

Figure 9.1 In the Microsoft Network Architecture, each layer communicates with the other to pass information to and from the network.

As you recall, this architecture is loosely based on the OSI 7-layer model. While the layers have changed and some boundaries have crossed, the concept remains the same. The layers only know how to communicate with the layer above and below them. Each layer generally speaks to the rest of the system as if it were actually talking to a corresponding component on another machine. It is like speaking through a translator. If you are giving a speech in another country, you face the crowd and speak to them. The translator standing next to you transforms your words into the language of the crowd. The listening crowd looks at you while you speak but listens to the translator speaking in their tongue.

When talking about performance, remember that generally you want to concern yourself with components, services, and software that you have the power to change. While it is nice to be able to take an analysis of some service and call the vendor (usually Microsoft) complaining that it isn't coded right, it usually doesn't get you very far in improving the performance of your system.

Drivers

Drivers are one of those items that you can't usually do much about, except perhaps get an updated one. However, the importance of the driver and the interaction of the protocol are important concepts to understand. The driver sits in between what Microsoft calls a NDIS wrapper. NDIS.sys (which is referred to simply as NDIS from here on) is an important component in the collection of components that are interacting to provide network services. The driver and NDIS are working to move information back from the physical layer. Proper communication between these layers is very important. As you will learn later, NDIS is also responsible for interrupting the processor. For now, back to the driver.

Poorly configured NICs are probably one of the biggest causes of network errors and performance. There are many forms of poorly configured NICs, as in the following:

- Wrong/outdated drivers
- Plug and Play issues
- Poor installation routines

Having the wrong or outdated driver often can get the computer started but produces poor performance or even errors. The best place to get updated drivers is from the vendors. This can be somewhat difficult if you purchase computers from a more generic vendor. Generally, for business customers you might consider buying from one of the big name brands in order to ensure availability and support for the card in the future.

Plug and Play (PnP) is a method for providing a service through files and programming to allow for hardware components to work with the operating system to automatically configure themselves. Windows NT does not currently support this type of configuration on its own. On older cards, it was usually necessary to turn the PnP features off on the card. If this wasn't done, then the operating system would usually report some type of hardware conflict and disable the hardware, if you were lucky. If you weren't so lucky, you would get a blue screen. Microsoft has yet to include PnP features into Windows NT, but has supported the efforts of other software vendors to do so. Several of the big names, such as DELL, IBM, and Compaq, have included PnP features into NT to work with their hardware. Most often you see this with laptops as opposed to desktop machines.

When a hardware vendor writes a driver for Windows NT, they are required to supply installation files in the form of `*.INF` files. These files supply information that supports the installation of the drivers. It will usually contain files listings, configuration options, and registry settings. However, these files can sometimes have errors. In these cases, it is not really the driver, but the installation that produces the problem. One such case involves a NIC that was reporting its name one way, but in the `.INF` file, the name of the component was listed differently. For example, when the hardware was queried by Windows NT it reported its name as "Widget Network Card." If you looked in the INF file supplied on a disk that came with the hardware you would see, "Widget Inc Network Card." Since the two didn't match, NT would never acknowledge the existence of the card.

Now that you perhaps have our driver installed, take a look and see how it might be communicating with the rest of the system.

Interrupts (Getting Noticed)

The network card needs to let the rest of the system know when communications are coming in or when it has completed the transmission of data. To do this, the NIC produces interrupts that it sends to the processor. The processor must then respond to the interrupts. With a network card potentially producing thousands of interrupts, this can become time-consuming as far as the processor is concerned. Software and hardware components ease the burden. To understand this, you have to delve a little deeper into the architecture.

Interrupts, as you recall from Chapter 6, "Optimizing CPU Performance," allow the processor to stop what it is doing and respond to the hardware. Interrupts are assigned levels called IRQLs (Interrupt Request Levels). Various pieces of hardware put in reservations for the various IRQLs. This way the operating system can tell which piece of hardware is making a request based on the IRQL. The Hardware Abstract Layer (HAL) is generally responsible for keeping track of the IRQLs.

After the processor receives the request, some basic processing might be done, and then the rest of the processing may be deferred. Thus, we have Deferred Procedure Calls (DPCs). The management of the DPCs involves many components. The processors themselves often have programmed into them methods for dealing with DPCs. In addition, the NICs now have some sense of DPCs and management of excessive interrupts. Essentially, the NIC driver watches the number of interrupts, and if the processor becomes overloaded, the NIC driver will disable interrupts and begin caching them while the processor is able to finish what it was doing.

The data has now come across the wire and is ready for processing on the system. Some application or component must have requested the information to begin with. The request applications and services exist in the application and sessions layers of the NT architecture. These are the layers where the users begin to have more control over their destiny and their system's performance.

Understanding Network Services

After the processor has been notified that there is information, it is up to the remaining services and drivers to move the information into a position so that the applications and thus the users can see it. Consider these layers from a perspective of performance.

The Transport and Network layer primarily consist of the transport protocol. This usually is TCP/IP, NWLink (IPX), or NetBEUI. Each of the protocols has a strength. NetBEUI still has a purpose in the life of some organizations and actually is quite a nice fit for single office locations without Internet connections. NetBEUI is small and efficient for transporting numerous small packets of data that would be the norm for most network traffic. In addition, it is very low maintenance. There is little to configure—just install and go. NetBEUI, however, is not a routable protocol. Thus, it is not a good choice for many medium to large companies.

NWLink or NBNWLink are the Microsoft versions of IPX/SPX. NBNWLink is the NetWare Link protocol with NetBIOS support. This protocol is a little larger, but again does not require too much in the way of maintenance. You install it, choose a frame type, and you're done. The NBNWLink is a routable protocol so it is suitable for medium to large networks.

TCP/IP is the de facto standard for any company using internets. The protocol is flexible and very capable for transporting large packets of data over a network. It is, of course, a routable protocol; however, there is a price for its flexibility. TCP/IP comes with a high amount of maintenance. You have to maintain lists of IP addresses being assigned. You also need a way to resolve the host names to IP addresses. This is done either through DNS or WINS for NetBIOS-based names. There also is the ever-popular broadcast.

WINS, DNS, and DHCP are key to the health and performance of the entire TCP/IP network. The proper configuration and deployment of these servers is more a topic for a book on network infrastructure. Name resolution in general is an important part of the network performance. If a system cannot find the host or service on the network, the user will experience many delays waiting for timeouts to occur. Take the time to read up on these server components that are included in Windows NT Server. Make sure that you consider the way the users utilize resources on the network.

The transport protocols work with NDIS to move the information from the applications out to the network. The applications must communicate with a variety of connectivity services in order to make connections and establish conversations with other machines on the network. This is where a number of the services come into play. Much of network communications is based on a client-server paradigm, thus on one end we have the client requesting information, and on the other the server supplying it. During any performance review of network connectivity, you must keep in mind that it is not necessarily the client machine that is slow, it might be the server portion of the communication on the other machine. In the discussions here, *server* is any system that is sharing a folder, printer, or any services that are used by other machine on the network. The client is the machine making the request.

The client, protocols, and network cards all are connected loosely through the layering of the Microsoft network architecture. This layering allows for the various components to utilize any other service or component on the system. For example, you can configure a single network card to communicate via TCP/IP and NetBEUI. You can have two network cards each using the same protocol. You can have a client service utilizing various protocols associated with various network cards. All of this makes NT networking flexible, but complex. There are a some basic rules for maintaining good system performance, which is discussed in the following sections.

Reduce Protocol Overhead

Don't install protocols unless you really need them. There have been countless times when I have walked into a company, looked at their production servers, and have found TCP/IP, NetBEUI, and NWLink all installed. They don't have NetWare and they require a routable protocol. The only one they need is either NWLink (IPX/SPX is routable) or TCP/IP. They certainly don't need all three. Loading extra protocols will cost you more than the memory it takes to load them. When an application or service request information on the network, NT will look for the server or service requested on all loaded protocols. It will, by default, wait for the protocols to respond before selecting one to make the connection. Suppose that you are looking for a server across a router. You have TCP/IP and NetBEUI installed. NT will send lookup information via both protocols. If this lookup is a broadcast, all your machines will be responding to the broadcasts on each protocol. Even if the TCP/IP were to respond with a message indicating that it found the server, if it is not the default protocol, the system waits for NetBEUI to time out on finding the network host before allowing transmission on TCP/IP.

Binding Order Is Important

As mentioned previously, clients, protocols, and adapters are all somehow associated. These associations are called *bindings*. When a protocol is bound to an adapter, it is allowed to use the adapter for those types of transmissions. If multiple protocols are bound to an adapter, the first one is generally considered the default protocol, as illustrated in Figure 9.2.

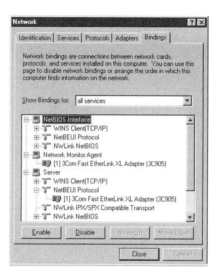

Figure 9.2 The binding order determines which protocol is favored in communications to other machines on the network.

If you use TCP/IP connections to the Internet more than NetBEUI connections to local machines, you would want the TCP/IP protocol to be higher in the binding order.

> Bindings are also important for the client services as well. If you have both the NetWare client and the Microsoft Client installed, you will want the one you use most to appear higher on the binding order.

Protocol Configurations

Protocols typically do not have that much to configure. For TCP/IP one configuration item, however, you must keep in mind is the *name resolution* issue. Resolving names to IP addresses is time consuming and often uses up precious bandwidth and resources on other machines besides the one requesting information. Having a good overall strategy for name resolution on your network is a must for any network with more than one router. The main concerns of name resolution are speed and accuracy. You want names to be resolved quickly and at the same time accurately. Hopefully, all this is achieved without too much effort on your part. WINS, DHCP, and DNS are commonly used in this respect to keep the effort to a minimum at the same time reduce the amount of traffic and especially broadcast traffic.

The NetWare client and related protocol also need to be considered closely when designing the network. There have been many NetWare installations where the administrators have not selected a particular frame type. Thus in NT, they have left the default frame type to be automatic. NT treats each frame type as a different protocol. All the information regarding transmitting broadcasts and name request over every protocol applies to each frame type. Again, this is a waste of resources. Decide on a frame type and apply it consistently across the network.

Reduce Broadcasts When Possible

In order to find machines on the network, the Microsoft operating system will default to a method called *browsing*. This is not the browse-the-Web browsing, but a method used all the way back to Windows for Workgroups in order to locate other machines on the network. For each segment on your network and for each loaded protocol, there will be a machine that is acting as a master browser. This machine maintains a list of all the other machines on the segment that might have something to share. It communicates to other machines called *backup browsers*. The backup browsers have a copy of the list. Every time that you look for a server on the network, your machine will find the backup browser and ask it for the information. Master browsers get their title through a process called an *election*. The term makes it sound very civil, but it isn't. It generally is a shouting match between several computers that each think they have a chance at being king of the hill. This shouting match of course is open to the public, in other words it is based on a series of broadcast messages. Every Microsoft operating system, with the exception of DOS will attempt to become the master browser. So when your 200 users start their machines in the morning, you should basically hear the words "Let's get ready to ruuuummmmmbbbbblllleeee!" All those machines begin the battle for king of the hill. TCP/IP WINS virtually eliminates the need for such broadcast methods, but it is good to have a backup; however, you don't need this broadcast melee going on throughout the day. The following sections provide some general recommendations for reducing such noise.

Disabling Client Machine Capability to Become Master Browsers or Backup Browsers

Disabling the client machine capability to become Master Browsers or Backup Browsers will be a little different, based on the various client configurations.

With Windows for Workgroups clients, edit the `SYSTEM.INI` , `[NETWORK]` section. Set the parameter `MaintainServerList=no`.

With Windows 95 clients, edit the Registry as follows:

```
KEY_LOCAL_MACHINE\System\CurrentControlSet\Services\VxD\
Vnetsetup\MaintainServerList=No
```

In Windows 95, if file and printer sharing is installed, you may also turn this parameter off from the Network applet in the Control Panel, as in the following:

1. Highlight File and Printer sharing for Microsoft Networks and click Properties.

2. Select BrowseMaster from the Properties list box.

3. Clear the check box.

For Windows NT, edit the Registry as follows:

```
HKEY_LOCAL_MACHINE\SYSTEM\CurrentControlSet\Services\Browser\Parameters\
MaintainServerList = False
```

Disabling Server Sharing Capability

A server is any machine that has the capability to share files. The browse list that is being broadcast around the network is a list of servers. Usually, client machines are not sharing folders or printers. Turn off the sharing functionality and these machines will no longer announce themselves to the master browser. This will reduce the size of the list and the amount of broadcasts on the network. In Windows for Workgroups and Windows 95, you go into the Control Panel | Networking and remove the functionality to share files and printers. In Windows NT, you can disable the Server Service through the Control Panel | Services. Highlight the Server Service and click on Startup. and then set the Startup option to disabled.

Ensuring the Quality of Your Name Resolution Scheme

There is no substitute for planning. If you set up WINS and DNS servers in the right way, broadcasts for NetBIOS name resolutions virtually can be eliminated.

This section has surpassed simply explaining how the operating system works with networking—it has given you some strong recommendations for the improving your network performance rather easily and quickly. Next you look at how you might observe the performance of your servers networking components.

Monitoring Activity

Much as the disk activity was related to the entire disk subsystem, the network performance is related to the entire system of components, through which the network data must pass. There are several key ones that the previous sections have pointed out. You will want to be able to observe the performance of the various components in order to determine where improvements might be needed.

Your network has a maximum bandwidth. This value could be 10MBs, 16MBs, or 100MBs. Perhaps you have invested in some advance technology and are looking at a different speed. Nonetheless, knowing the limitation of the network is not the same as knowing the limitation of your servers capability to put traffic onto the network.

Steps to Analysis

You will be using the Performance Monitor to observe network performance; however, there are a few other tools and options that you may want to consider. Oddly enough, several of the counters you might want to look at won't be present unless you install extra services. One of the services is *SNMP* (Simple Network Management Protocol). This is installed from the Control Panel's Network applet. Click on the Services tab and click Add. You don't have to configure anything in the SNMP dialog when it appears. When SNMP is installed, it will add an Extended Object called Network Interface. This is useful for observing the activity in the Data Link layer of networking. Another service to consider installing is the Network Monitor Agent. Installing this service adds the Network Object and enables you to observe network bandwidth usage. It is installed the same way that SNMP was installed.

The Network Monitor Agent allows anyone using the Network Monitor software to observe traffic on the network. This can be a security issue. Although the Network Monitor Agent can have passwords assigned to it, it can still be compromised and allow unwanted persons to observe network traffic. My tactic has been to install the service and set it to Manual Startup in the Control Panel's Services applet. You then can start the service when you need it and turn it off when you don't. A second recommendation would be to install the service only on selected servers that will be key to observing particular segments of your network.

With these two network objects now in the Performance Monitor's list, you can begin to analyze the network traffic.

You already know that the network actually is a layered set of components. When you want to observe the activity, you will need to decide with which layer you are most concerned. In these next few sections, you will see how to observe the network and diagnose problems at each level.

Physical/Data Link Layer Observations

Observation of the network begins with analysis of the Physical layer. In order to observe the Physical layer, you need to install the SNMP services. These services allow the inclusion of the Network Interface Object. Following are several counters you should use:

- **Bytes Sent/sec.** This is how many bytes of data are sent to the NIC. You really are measuring the information sent to the interface, which is the lowest point you can measure. If you have multiple NIC, you will see multiple instances of this particular counter.

- **Bytes Received/sec.** This, of course, is how many bytes you get from the NIC. In measuring the bytes, NT isn't too particular at this level, so no matter what the byte is, it is counted. This includes the framing bytes as opposed to just the data.

- **Bytes Total/sec.** This is simply a combination of the other two counters.

If you have a 10MBs network, you would want this to be able to approach 10MBs if traffic were really heavy. In reality, this typically won't happen. Figure 9.3 shows the performance monitor report view of a fairly typical file transfer where the information is copied to the server. You also will see another counter that displays the current bandwidth.

From Figure 9.3, you can see that the current bandwidth of my network is 10MBs. You also can see that the information is being transferred quite quickly. Notice that the interface 1 is pretty empty. This interface is connected to a different network that is running only IPX. The NetWare server was not running and thus there was no traffic.

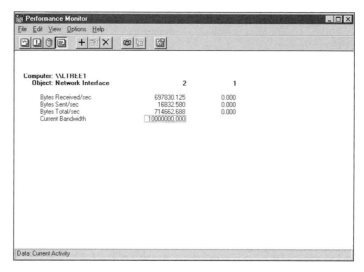

Figure 9.3 Network traffic.

When you are looking at network traffic, you will want to see not only how the traffic is being moving through the interface cards, but you will also want to have a look at how the traffic is affecting the performance of the processor that must handle the interrupts. In these cases, you will want to observe a few of the Processor object counters:

- **% Interrupt Time**. This counter indicates how much time the processor is busy handling interrupts as opposed to servicing system services and applications. An interrupt will occur each time the NIC receives data or when a client has requested data be sent out. The interrupt for outbound traffic occurs at the end of the transmission.

- **% DPC Time**. Remember that interrupts can be handled later. These are called *Deferred Procedure Calls*. You will want to keep track of these as well. The combination of this time with the % Interrupt Time will give you a strong idea of how much of the precious processor time is going to servicing the network.

- **DPCs queued/sec**. This counter provides you the rate at which DPC are being sent to the process queue. Unlike the Processor Queue Length and the Disk Queue Length, this value only shows you the rate at which the DPCs are being added to the queue, not how many are in the queue. Still, observing this value can give you an indication of a growing problem.

You generally will want to look at the processor whenever the network seems to be moving a little slower. Figure 9.4 presents a picture of high network utilization.

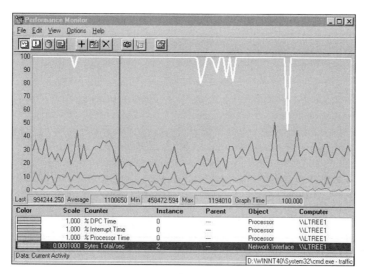

Figure 9.4 Processor and network usage.

In general, the bandwidth of the network is all but gone; however, notice that the processor, which is around 50 percent utilized, is handling the network portion of the load nicely. The %Interrupts is only around 7 percent. Notice how the % DPC Time is higher. More time must be spent on the DPCs than is spent processing the initial hardware interrupt.

What this really tells you is that the interrupts are more a function of the frequency of the connections as opposed to the amount of data. You probably suspected this already, so you can see that many more small packets can affect the processor more while leaving the network looking like everything is fine.

There are several applications that run on NT that can affect the processor in just the way that has been described here. One of the more prominent is *IIS*. SQL databases and email programs can also produce traffic patterns that will produce the small repetitive packets that were just described; however, they tend to occur in bursts. IIS is subject to large volumes of network traffic and relatively small packets of data. More so than the other applications, you will want to observe these counters on IIS and other Web servers.

DPCs are a little more involved. There actually are various strategies for handling DPCs. Some systems will distribute that DPCs evenly among the processors. Other systems will distribute the them in accordance to ties established between the processors and the NICs when the system is booted. This DPC distribution is typically handled at the NDIS level; however, some processors actually provide the functionality. The whole concept of DPC distribution really doesn't affect you until you have more than one processor. If you have two processors, a common strategy would be for the system to send all interrupts to the first processor and ship DPCs to the second processor. Using the counters introduced in this section, you could observe this behavior by watching the counters for each instance of processor. If you notice one processor being overloaded, getting another NIC may be a solution. The second NIC would associate itself with the other processor and thus distribute the load.

> In a multiple processor system, another method would be to modify the registry. You should be very clear on the problem being the DPC and Interrupt handling being the root of your processor issues. You will need to modify the following key in the Registry:
>
> HKEY_LOCAL_MACHINE\System\CurrentControlSet\Services\NDIS\Parameters\ProcessorA
> ffinityMask = 0
>
> This turns off the association of NICs with particular processors. Thus, not matter how many NICs or processors, the processor that accepted the interrupt handles the DPC. You will want to monitor the system closely after making this change to ensure that you have indeed improved the system performance.

The examples in this section show a network whose bandwidth was used up. The next section reviews bandwidth situations.

Observing Bandwidth Issues

Bandwidth is the amount of traffic that is conceptually permissible along a particular segment of a network. To date, Ethernet is usually 10Mbps or 100Mbps with 1Gbps Ethernet looming on the horizon. Token Ring is 4Mbps or 16Mbps. Conditions where this bandwidth is completely utilized produces problems for everyone connected to the wire. You will want to observe and look for particular causes of network traffic. Following are a few simple counters from the Network Segment Object to get started:

- ▪ **%Network Utilization**. Shows you how much of the available bandwidth is being utilized. Generally speaking, any network that is around 60 percent utilized will have a bandwidth issue. This statement assume that the 60 percent is original traffic. The Performance Monitor counter makes no such assumptions about the traffic. It sees all bytes and frames and compares them to the theoretical limit of the network to produce a value.

- **%Broadcasts**. Tells you how much of the network bandwidth is dedicated to broadcast traffic.

- **%Multicasts**. Tells you how much of the network bandwidth is dedicated to multicast traffic.

These counters can give you a good idea of the type of traffic and what the origins might be. Broadcasts are packets of information that are transmitted with no particular destination in mind. Think of broadcasts as a lost person standing in a crowd, yelling out a friend's name in hopes of locating them. When a broadcast is sent on the network, every system assumes that the data is meant for them, thus each machine spends processor cycles retrieving and analyzing the information.

Broadcasts generally are associated with name resolutions, which are finding out what name goes with what IP address. There are other broadcasts on the system and from various types of operating systems. Some broadcasts announce the availability of services to other systems that might be interested. Sometimes you may hear the term *broadcast storm*. A broadcast storm is a surge of broadcast traffic that devours network bandwidth and slows the systems to a crawl. These types of issues again usually are related to name resolutions or poorly selected IP addresses. Giving a Windows NT workstation the IP address of the default router for the segment, for example, could result in a variety of problems, including a broadcast storm.

Multicasts are traffic that is sent to groups of machines that have indicated an interest in the information being sent out. This type of information dissemination is usually used in video conferencing situations. Multicasts tend to be a little more predictable and controllable than the broadcasts; however, the nature of the multicast type traffic means it is worth watching out for.

You can expect that the broadcasts will have many peaks and valleys. If, however, you see a value over 20 percent for sustained broadcasts, you may start to worry.

In addition to using the Performance Monitor to view broadcast traffic, you can use the Network Monitor to view information about the origins of the broadcasts. In Figure 9.5, the Network Monitor is being used to capture some traffic on a small network. Looking at the bottom pane, you can see that there is a column for Broadcasts. If you click on the column, you can sort the listing of machines based on amount of broadcasts sent.

If you can eliminate the broadcasts and multicasts as causes of the traffic problems, you then will need to locate the machine transmitting the most traffic. This too can be achieved by looking at the Network Monitor.

After general bandwidth issues, you may want to consider the amount of traffic that the system itself can sustain. This might not be as much as the network can supply. The discussion moves upward along the layers to the transports section.

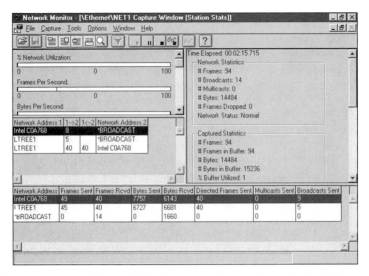

Figure 9.5 You can use the Network Monitor to view the machine with the highest amount of broadcast traffic.

Transport Issues

Transports are the network protocols such as TCP/IP or NetBEUI. The focus in this section is on TCP/IP, but you will get the general idea and be able to apply it to other protocols. So far, discussions have involved the lower level network traffic and primarily the hardware components. At this new level of the evolutionary chain of network traffic, more of the operating system and services are involved in dictating how fast the information will be moving. Much like the disk optimization that was discussed earlier, it is a very good idea to get a baseline for network traffic. You want to use a network application that your are concerned about, such as IIS or possibly Exchange, and simulate a number of users on the network. Monitor the traffic and see what is normal for the type of activity you are generating. After you get your system into production, you will want to continue to monitor the system to see how the performance changes over time. Following are some of the basic counters that you should use for TCP:

- **Segments Sent/sec**. Rate at which TCP segments are sent.
- **Segments Received/sec**. Rate at which segments are received for the protocol.
- **Segments/sec**. Total of the previous two counters.
- **Segments Retransmitted/sec**. Rate at which retransmissions occur. Retransmissions are measured based on bytes in the data that are recognized as being transmitted before. On a Ethernet/TCP/IP network, retransmissions are a fact of life; however, excessive retransmissions indicate a distinct reduction in bandwidth.

While testing, you will want to generate traffic. Generating traffic can be as simple as copying large files from multiple computers. Depending on the software, it can be more complicated. Both MS SQL Server and Exchange Server have LoadSim programs that simulate usage on the network. These programs can become quite detailed, but can also provide a variety of traffic as well as exercise the applications to provide you with a good baseline for what your configuration can do.

When testing, make sure to keep an eye on the interrupts and DPCs. You also will want to watch the retransmissions. Take a look at the ratio of Segments Retransmitted/sec / Segments Transmitted/sec. This gives you a percentage of the traffic that is on the network due to retransmissions. Recall that retransmissions usually occur because of collisions, or when a system is trying to write information onto the network, but is cut off by the packets from another system coming in. If the percentage is over 30 percent, you may want to throttle back your test so that you don't generate a situation in which your server is simply waiting for data to arrive and not really testing its processor prowess. If you balance it well, the retransmits will stabilize and the Segments/Sec will plateau out. This will be the capacity of your system given the type and frequency of the traffic.

Remember your queuing theory. Network traffic is about as complex as it gets. The traffic arrives from multiple sources, at different frequencies, and the segments have a range of byte sizes. All of this means that baselines of one situation must be compared carefully with different situations. A system may run great when moving small packets of data quickly, but may suffer when the segments are larger but are coming slower.

Following is another set of counters involved in connections to observe:

- **Connection Failures**. The raw number of TCP connections that have failed since the server was started. A failure usually indicates a loss of data somewhere in the process. Data lose can occur at many locations. This could be an indication of another device being down, or problems with the client side configuration of the software.

- **Connections Reset**. Typically a result of a timeout as opposed to an erroneous set of information. The reset results from the a lack of any information over a period of time.

- **Connections Established**. Represents the number of connections. Unlike the other two counters, this is an instantaneous counter of how many TCP connections are currently on the system as opposed to a count of the number of successful connections.

The primary point of these counters is to watch the failures and resets. They are the majority of problems on the network or bandwidth issues, more than transport issues.

Consider, for example, a IIS server that is running with dual Pentium II processors. You have a single network card. Observing the system, notice that the response is rather slow. At this point, there are several things to check. It is usually good to start from the bottom up. Check out the %Utilization and also the Network Segment counters. This will give you an idea whether you have a bandwidth issue. If there is a lot of traffic, you will want check the %Interrupt time on the processor. This tells you whether the processors are having a problem keeping up. If this all seems fine, you will want to look at the TCP counters and connections. This helps you determine whether the operating system is keeping up its end of the bargain by transmitting and receiving packets. You also will be able to determine if there are connection errors.

Now that you have all the background stuff, you are ready to have a look at the application issues.

Application Layer Issues

Application issues are concerned with the various applications that you might be running. You might, for example, have IIS running on your system, or perhaps SQL. Each of these applications will bring with them performance objects that can be used to measure their performance in conjunction with the network.

Consider a few rules about tuning network applications. Recall that the network traffic is perhaps the most unpredictable type of transaction that you can consider. Yet, you somehow must get a picture of what the average traffic to a particular server or service looks like. This can only come through continued observation, which means creating Performance Monitor logs to collect the information over time and then look at it. Most administrators get the "collection part" down, but somehow forget the "look at the data" part. Remember that with the network, many pieces that are involved in the transmission and receipt of data. You will want to observe the various layers by using the techniques laid out in this chapter. Sometimes it is good just to capture some of the packets using the Network Monitor and then sift through them. This will help you become more familiar with the type of traffic and will give you a better understanding of the type of problems that can occur while system are trying to communicate.

When observing other applications, including simple Windows NT file transfers, always get a picture of what the system must do to communicate. Then analyze each part, establishing baselines for various conditions. You then will be ready to observe production cases.

On Your Own

To get the additional network objects you need to really observe the network, install the Network Monitor and the SNMP services. Take a look at one of your production machines using each of the counters in the chapter. See if it looks like it is really performing well, or simply getting by. Get a server or workstation on an isolated network and see how the system reacts to various traffic requests. Following are a few traffic requests that are good to try:

- Transfers of large files
- Repeated transfers of small files
- Transfers in FTP
- Transfers using TCP/IP and then NetBEUI

Use the Network Monitor and examine some traffic-like file transfers, or what happens when you are logging on to the network.

Summary

This chapter dealt with the network architecture and the internals of how the network operates. You learned how the network card affects other hardware components, such as the processor. You also saw how the operating system attempts to balance the load of the interrupts and the DPCs. You read about the NT networking architecture and how it affects the capability and quest to understand the performance of the network. Network communications, cabling, technologies, architecture, protocols, and various hardware components all work together yet differently to move information around the network. Understanding all of it may take some time, but you have a strong beginning to view and analyze how the traffic is affecting you.

10

NT Performance Tuning Techniques: Practical Applications

This chapter covers the following topics:

- **Guide to Performance Analysis.** This section summarizes many of the rules and tips discussed throughout the book.

- **Performance Tuning: Staying Ahead of the Game.** This section takes performance monitoring to a different level, using it to anticipate need instead of resolving immediate problems.

- **Performance for the Small Business Office.** This section discusses some of the issues that small business offices face.

- **Additional Resources on NT Optimization.** Many places offer additional help, sometimes for free. This section reviews some of my favorites and discusses their merits.

In this chapter, you will find a review of sorts, bringing together the tips and techniques explored throughout this book. You will combine the techniques to provide a rare service to yourself and your company, proactive performance maintenance. You will also have an opportunity to see how techniques might differ in a small business or single office scenario. Lastly, because no one can know everything, I'll mention some of the Web sites and information resources used in troubleshooting and writing this book.

Guide to Performance Analysis

Throughout this book, you have been subjected to all sorts of information regarding the analysis of NT and the techniques for bottleneck detection. This chapter attempts to describe the basic framework that you have already put to use throughout this book. tPerhaps you will learn a few new things, and perhaps you will just be reminded of a few old ones you forgot. Reviewing these topics certainly can't hurt. Let us begin with what I, along with my seventh-grade science teacher, like to call the scientific method.

The Scientific Method

Whenever you are attempting to figure out a problem or expose a model of behavior for some process or mechanism, you use a process. Some people are consciously aware of this process; others call it intuition or guesswork. In any case, each of us has a process for figuring out how the world around us works. When troubleshooting computer problems, you use a process as well. However, as problems and variables become more complex, the process of figuring out the behavior of the problem must rise to the occasion. It is no longer sufficient to "guess," rely on old methods, or try a couple things and then give in or reinstall. If you really want to be good at troubleshooting, you must first instill within yourself a desire to never surrender. I like to think of it as a "savage pursuit of the truth." When you have such a desire, you do not expect or accept the response "it just works that way." Such an answer must be first backed by hours of relentless testing to ensure that no answer can be deduced or exposed through experimentation. I can promise you that the problem to which you simply say, "It just works that way," will be the one that pops up repeatedly and at the most awkward moments.

The scientific method is a simple set of rules roughly applied to problem solving. If you follow the rules, you can solve almost any problem or at least be sure that you have exhausted all the avenues to a solution, which then warrants calling in other resources if the problem is worth solving. The model for the scientific method follows:

1. Get the overall picture.
2. Formulate a hypothesis.
3. Test the hypothesis.
4. Refine the hypothesis.
5. Design a solution.
6. Test a solution.
7. Reevaluate the system (return to step 1).

Getting the Overall Picture

Think about what the problem is and why you want to solve it. For example, developers are having a problem connecting the SQL database system. Their connections periodically drop while they are using TCP/IP sockets. The named pipes appear to be working correctly, however. They could use named pipes connections without worrying further. Is there a problem?

Your first reaction should be to start asking questions. Why are they trying to use TCP/IP sockets at all if they know named pipes work? What is it costing the developers in time and effort while this solution is not working? These questions are important. They help to describe the motivation and effort level you might need to put into a solution. Perhaps the developers are using TCP/IP sockets because clients use that type, or perhaps TCP/IP sockets offer other features that the other connection type doesn't. Cost can never be ignored. Every problem and every downtime has a cost. If a development team sits idle for 30 minutes, you can bet that is going to cost the company in real dollars and cost the developers in frustration and motivation. However, suppose only one developer is experiencing the connection problem. He is trying to use the TCP/IP sockets to satisfy his own curiosity and not for any job requirement. This puts the issue in a different light.

Getting the big picture is more than just assessing cost and how much effort you must put into a solution. After you decide to actually tackle the problem, you must assess the entire situation, not just the details. All too often, we lunge at the problem without first looking at what is going on with the entire system or network. It is like chasing your child's pet rabbit in a field because she left the cage door open again. You get so focused on trying to grab the rabbit you don't realize you are rolling around in poison ivy.

In a more topical analogy, consider a client I was working with. The client had a server failure. The application that the client was trying to make work simply was not working. The application was a client/server database application. The person troubleshooting the problem focused on the server and the network card. He replaced the card, reconfigured the server, and reconfigured the software until he had exhausted all options. This server had given us network problems in the past that were hardware related. The issues had concerned the chipset on the motherboard for the PCI interface. The server was old and was under consideration for replacement in the next budget cycle. However, with this sudden failure and the support person failing to find a solution, the company decided to buy a new server. While the buyers were out shopping, a more senior engineer came in, looked at the system, and plugged the ethernet cable back into the hub where it had become loose. Wham! Everything started working. The lesson is that you always evaluate the entire situation.

In the world of optimization and bottleneck detection, what this means is that you want to get a complete picture of the computer, the purpose the computer was built for, and the environment where the system is running. If the server is an application server, you expect certain resources, such as the processor, to be more heavily utilized than the disk. A file server, as you have seen, is more active on the network and the disk than the memory or processor. (Chapter 6, "Optimizing CPU Performance," presented this information originally.) You will want to know about the network and the client software that the system is exposed to. These components affect the server directly. Chapter 9, "Optimizing Network Interface Performance," demonstrated how the network and NIC interrupts can affect the processor. After collecting all that information, which actually takes only a few moments, you will want to start the Performance Monitor. Take a look at the four basic computer groups:

- **CPU.** Processor object : % Processor Time counter
- **Memory.** Memory object : Pages/sec counter
- **Disk.** PhysicalDisk/Logical Disk object : Disk Queue Length counter
- **Network.** Network Segment object : % Network Utilization counter

Taking a look at these counters will give you an overall picture of what resources are being utilized.

Formulating a Hypothesis

Formulating a hypothesis is basically a fancy way of saying that from what you have learned, you take a guess at where the problem lies. From reading Chapters 6–9, you should have a good idea where the numbers are leading you. For example, if the Memory Pages/sec is 23 and is sustained over the duration of your observation, memory issues are the likely target. At this point, don't make your guess, or hypothesis, too refined. You do not want to box yourself into a cause without further investigation.

Testing the Hypothesis

Testing the hypothesis is little more than taking the next step. You adjust the counters on the Performance Monitor to turn a critical eye on the component that is probably the problem. In the preceding example, memory seemed to be the issue. What do we know about memory problems? Chapter 7, "Optimizing Memory Performance," indicates there are basically three possibilities:

- You just don't have enough memory.
- You have a memory leak in some application or service.
- You have a misconfigured application (or poorly written one).

At this point, you should investigate all the possibilities using the techniques of this book. Based on what you learn, can you guess what you will do next?

Refining the Hypothesis

Adjust your hypothesis to better suit what you have observed. Let us continue the memory issues scenario. You see that the available memory is low and decreasing ever so slightly as you observe the system. It might be a memory leak. Next step: Find out which application is creating the problem. At this point, you will end up spending a few cycles in step 3, "Testing the Hypothesis," and step 4, "Refining the Hypothesis." You will continue to refine your guess until it is no longer a guess. You end up with the solution to which application is causing the problem. You may even end up with a pretty good guess of what type of code the programmer wrote to produce the problem. Furthermore, because you went through this process step- by -step, you have proof or validation of your claim. All right, now what? You design a solution, of course!

Designing a Solution

Based on all the information you have collected, you will usually have a pretty good idea how to fix the problem. You may be able to adjust some configuration of NT; adjust the program, service, or driver; or simply stop using the application causing the problem. Keep in mind everything that you do will affect the system somehow, usually in more than one way. You might reconfigure the application based on information from a vendor white paper. You might make a Registry change based on a Microsoft white paper. You might upgrade software components or drivers. You might do a BIOS upgrade on an adapter card or system BIOS. You might do nothing more than put a service call into the vendor regarding the problem. Whatever solution you apply, you want to make sure you do it gradually. Avoid trying multiple things at once. For example, the vendor says updating the driver might fix the problem, but you also find a Microsoft article that says changing a Registry setting may alleviate the problem. Do you do both? No, of course not. You test one possible solution at a time.

Testing a Solution

You may stay in a bit of a loop between step 5, "Designing a Solution," and step 6, "Testing a Solution," for a while. However, I am sure you want more than to simply fix the problem. You must know exactly what the problem is so that in the future you can recognize it and resolve it more quickly. Computers, software, and users come in all sorts of configurations. The same problem may pop up in slightly different forms within your enterprise. If you understand the true nature of the problem, you will be able to detect it even though it may be camouflaged in the dense brush of varied software configurations and user preferences. At some point, you will get to a solution. Then, you are done, right? Wrong!

Reevaluating the System: Back to Step 1

It's time to return to the big picture. More than any other step, the reevaluation step is often missed in a rush to fix a problem and move on to the next item on the agenda. Remember that everything you change on a computer is bound to affect some other component or resource. You must reevaluate the entire system before dusting off your hands and calling it a done deal. You may have fixed the memory issue but caused processor performance to suffer because of it. Say you decide to add more memory because the system was simply being overworked by the growing use of the applications by the users. If you don't reevaluate the system, you might not realize that the processor is running less efficiently. You forgot that you should check your L2-Cache levels, and you have a new problem with L2-Cache/memory ratios that is creating overhead for the processor (see Chapter 6).

Using a scientific process of setting a hypothesis and experimenting will help you treat problems consistently and achieve accuracy in finding solutions the first time. You will also begin to see your hypothesis/testing and solution/testing loops get shorter as you improve in your ability to guess or hypothesize. No matter how good you think you are, never skip a step. The one time you skip the step, you'll end up having to go back and fix a problem you caused because you did not properly reevaluate or test.

Now that you have a method of problem evaluation and resolution, let's review some general tips and tricks for performance monitoring.

Performance Monitoring Considerations

The last section discussed the rules for working through a problem. The topics in this section deal with a more specific issue of performance monitoring. You must keep in mind some general bits of wisdom while you are performance monitoring. You will perhaps guess some of the tips from reading the rest of this book; others may not have been so obvious.

One Bottleneck Masking Another

Masking is generally the principle behind "getting the big picture." Remember to think about how the various hardware and software components relate to one another. Memory problems might really be memory problems, but they might also be manifestations of a disk problem. If the VMM cannot get information to the disk quickly enough because of contention or bad pagefile configuration, don't blame the memory. Also, if you notice that the disk has an excessive disk queue, your first thought might be that you need a better disk subsystem (controller and disk). Of course, after reading this book, your first thought should be to make sure that the disk queue isn't being caused by excessive page faults.

How about this one: A user complains that since she installed IE 4.0, her system has been exceptionally slow. She knows a little about the NT Performance Monitor, so she shows you how the system uses almost 75% of the CPU time since adding IE 4.0. She has a Pentium 100MHz machine—not the fastest, but such awful performance can't be related to speed. Are you thinking of the big picture yet? You start Performance Monitor and look at all the counters. You notice that not only is the processor at 79%, but also the Processor: % Interrupt time is 55%. Did IE 4.0 do that? No.

However, you find out that the user installed the full version. You start IE 4.0 and point it to the user's machine because she installed Peer Web services. She built her own Web page to offer a cute little game for downloading. Needless to say, eight other folks downloaded the little game, which wasn't so little. This older machine had an ISA NIC and an ISA EIDE controller. The NIC and disk controller interrupted the processor so much that it had a noticeable effect on the performance of the system.

Seeing a Bottleneck Because of When You Are Looking

This book provides many case studies. Don't be fooled by these seemingly straightforward examples. It takes time to track down a bottleneck on a system. NT is as complex an operating system as any other, so the bottleneck causes can be elusive. Become familiar with not only interactively observing performance, but also logging data. The Performance Monitor will log information to a file so that you can view it later. This feature is extremely helpful when you have more than one user.

Understanding Performance Calculations

Your mother told you that you need rudimentary math skills. Although most of the performance-monitoring calculations you need to understand are rudimentary, you should get used to looking at fractions, percentages, and ratios. You may also want to get a small book on statistics. If you are really going to get down and dirty in the dark regions of NT performance, you may find yourself in need of a correlation coefficient or two. You might even find yourself running an all-out linear regression test on some data. Hey, it could happen! Luckily, some software packages are readily available to do this kind of analysis for you. Spreadsheet programs such as Lotus 123 and Excel can do the job. Other programs offer more sophistication, but spreadsheets usually are sufficient for the task.

Ratios and Minor Calculations and the Details of a Bottleneck

Speaking of calculations, some of the most minor calculations often have revealing results. Often, it is difficult to conceptualize some of the absolute numbers that you will get from the Performance Monitor. For example, if you are getting 24 Page Faults/sec, is that good or bad? Comparing the Input Pages/sec with the Page Faults/sec gives you the percentage of hard page faults. This percentage usually has more meaning than the raw number, but it also leads to the next tip.

Averages and Generalities

You no doubt recall that among the available counters in Performance Monitor are average values. You must also be aware that some counters are averages that don't explicitly say that they are averages. This is especially true of some of the raw counters, such as Disk Queue Length. Averages will reveal trends and general activity but will hide details about what is going on.

Using the Time Window in Performance Monitor

As much as generalities lack details, using too many data points while viewing a chart also hides the details. Remember that the chart will display only 100 data points across. If you have 10,000 data points in a performance log file, you will see only every 100th data point. You could be missing valuable details. To avoid this, you use the Performance Monitor Time window. The steps for using the Time windows effectively follow:

1. Set the alert for appropriate values (such as % Processor Time > 80%).
2. Adjust the Time window to focus on the value in question.

3. Adjust the width of the Time window so that it includes 100 data points or fewer to see more details. When you have fewer than 100 data points, the data ends before the right side of the screen.

Understanding the Heisenberg Principle

Roughly speaking, the Heisenberg principle states that the act of measuring something inherently changes the results. Whenever you use Performance Monitor, you are adding to the drain on resources. The trick is to not affect the same component that you are trying to analyze. For example, suppose you want to check the throughput on the disk drive you just installed. While doing this, you do not want Performance Monitor to be logging data to the same physical drive on which you are testing throughput. This would skew the data. No matter what you do, you will affect the performance. Even if you monitor the system from a remote location, you are still affecting memory, network, and processor resources.

Bottlenecks at Less than 100 Percent Utilization

As documented in Chapter 6, "Optimizing CPU Performance," and Chapter 8, "Optimizing Disk Performance," many components are based on servicing a queue. Remember the clerk at the grocery store? The effects of queuing theory basically dictate two important truths:

- Random use of a resource for irregular intervals can form long queues at less than 100% utilization.

- The more regular the intervals and the more consistent the duration of use, the more you can accomplish at a lower utilization.

Testing Incremental Changes and Controls

I know you got an earful of this in the last section, but I just think that it is exceptionally important in troubleshooting, performance monitoring, and life in general. When you are trying to correct a problem, make sure you follow a set of rules, as outlined in the previous section. Incremental changes will allow you to exactly determine what fixed the problem and also help you confirm the cause of the problem in most cases.

Systems and Their Differences

Machines all operate differently. Considering all the hardware options, software revisions, BIOS revisions, configuration options, and just plain human fallacy, there seems actually to be little chance that any two systems will behave in an identical fashion. Although you can expect some system to operate within certain parameters, you must avoid hastily making generalized statements about what is good and bad performance. A machine's performance depends on what it is being used for. You may recall that Chapters 8 and 9 place a lot of emphasis on getting performance baselines. Baselines serve as a reference point for comparing other values. The concept of baselines and their uses is covered in more detail in the next section.

Performance Tuning: Staying Ahead of the Game

You have read about baselines and profiling your systems several times throughout this book. In this section, the concepts are brought into full bloom. Almost every situation with computer performance tuning requires you to have a reference point, a place where you completely understand the conditions that the machine was working under. When you have this information, you have a baseline of what the performance of the machine is supposed to be. When you compare a more recent collection of performance data with the baseline, you can tell how the usage of your system has changed over time. You can also tell where you are getting into trouble with potential bottlenecks. The process is collectively called *capacity planning*.

Capacity Planning

The goals of capacity planning depend on the goals and needs of your company and department. In general, however, the idea is to provide a structured approach to collecting data, performing regular analysis, and maintaining records. The goals ensure that you can predict and provide for future system and resource demands prior to the demands affecting the performance of the systems and the business in general.

The first action to perform in capacity planning is to make sure that the personnel with a stake in the operations of the computers are aware of the goals. System administrators have long fallen into the pitfall of being reactive. System administrators react to problems. Your printer does not work; call the system administrator. You can't connect to a network share; call the system administrator. You just installed a new game and it messed up your entire system; call the system administrator and go to lunch before he gets there. System administrators are the fixit folks. It breaks; they fix it. For most cases, this might be a decent concept for the end user. For a company's administration to have the same concept is detrimental to the department and the health of the company's critical computer systems. For this reason, capacity planning goals and procedures should be documented and regularly put in front of the company administration.

Capacity planning is proactive. It is a process whereby the company's business side and computing side attempt to work together to achieve a common goal of a stable computing environment that leads to a successful business. Yes, I know you probably cringed at *documentation* and becoming involved with the *business side* of the company. All that I can say is, too bad. It is no longer sufficient, if it ever was, for a company simply to add computers as the business grows. A concept of the system's current capacities and abilities is required as a first step in knowing what needs to change in the coming years to accommodate a growing and changing business. Adaptation to adversity seems to be a key phrase separating the successful business from the failing business. Computer systems in many cases play a key role in a company's ability to adapt. After you have the first documentation, you will want to continue a trend of documenting and record keeping, which make up the next step to capacity planning.

Record Keeping

Write it down. Whenever you make a change to a server, router, or other network component, you should write it down. Basically, you should have a binder containing a collection of information about each system. Whether this binder is a physical folder, a three-ring binder, or a set of electronic documents is irrelevant—as long as there is one for each component on your network. You need this binder system no matter how many administrators there are. For a group of many administrators, you want to make sure that each person is aware of changes made to servers or other components. This alleviates the problem of trying to find out who changed whatever is making the system perform so much differently than it did before rebooting. For a site with only one administrator, record keeping is especially critical because people move on, sometimes abruptly. Without information about each of the systems, the new administrator has no starting point. What should the binders contain?

- **Log pages.** Log pages are useful so that people can record changes to anything on the system.
- **Printout of IPCONFIG.EXE/All.** This printout will show all the computers' TCP/IP configuration settings.
- **WINMSDP.EXE.** This is a utility from the NT Resource Kit. It pipes the contents of the Windows NT Diagnostic Tool into a text file. The information will contain hardware settings, services loaded, drivers loaded, the OS version information, and more.
- **Screen capture of Disk Administrator.** This record gives you an idea about the disk's configuration in case the system crashes hard. You can find this information in other places, but the graphical display seems easiest to understand.

Now that you have a binder, you will need to create at least four disks for emergencies:

- Emergency repair disk
- NT boot disk
- Disk configuration disk
- Boot sector disk

You need an emergency repair disk for each machine because they tend to be pretty particular. You use a utility called RDISK.EXE to create them. RDISK.EXE is installed when you install NT, but no icon is created for it. You will find it in the %SystemRoot%\System32 folder. When you run the utility, make sure that you click update the repair information prior to making a new disk (see Figure 10.1).

This updates the information from the Registry in the emergency repair file before updating the disk.

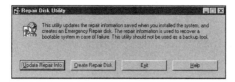

Figure 10.1   The Repair Disk utility interface.

The NT boot disk is a necessity if you are using any kind of mirror set. This disk must be formatted on an NT Workstation or Server and contain the following files:

- NTLDR
- NTDETECT.COM
- BOOTSECT.DOS
- BOOT.INI
- NTBOOTDD.SYS (optional)

The idea is that you can have an NT boot disk on a FAT file system that you can carry around and edit if necessary. Suppose a mirror set fails. You need to boot from the alternate disk. If you had not configured the BOOT.INI on the hard drive to do so, you would not be able to reboot the machine. If your boot partition is NTFS, you would not be able to edit the file easily. You can, however, boot the system from a floppy that contains the right files. You have to modify the BOOT.INI on the floppy to make sure that the path names correctly point to the system partition where you installed the Windows NT. Details on the path names are supplied in Chapter 3, "Simulating System Bottlenecks," and Chapter 7, "Optimizing Memory Performance."

You will generate the disk configuration disk from the Disk Administrator to contain information regarding the current systems and disk configuration information from the Registry.

For the boot sector disks, if you want to get a little fancy, you can use the Disk Save (DISKSAVE.EXE) or Disk Probe (DISKPROBE.EXE) programs to save the boot sector from the hard drive. You can avoid going through the NT install and using the repair option, which is often time consuming. The two utilities are both from the NT Resource Kit. The Disk Save program is DOS-based and thus is useful when the system cannot boot at all and you don't have an NT boot disk. Disk Probe is a graphical tool that allows you to perform low-level editing on the disks, which is useful in a couple of ways. You can make repairs to the Master File Table (MFT) on the NTFS partitions. It is also handy for creating images of floppies. You can create the image of a DOS boot floppy and save it as a file. Then, if you need to make a DOS disk, you can do it from NT.

So far, I've mentioned a lot of information for record keeping, but it is still not enough. As silly as it may sound, keeping a regular journal is a good idea. It isn't a personal diary; it is a log of the events that affect the computer systems currently or in the future. Note business activities that you have been informed of. Note when you have installed new machines on the network. Write notes about moving hardware around. This journal doesn't have to be an extravagant service call system, although it can contain service call information as well. Typical journal entries might resemble the following:

Date: Today

Company announced a merger with another small company 40 miles north of us. No further announcements indicated; however, we anticipate having to integrate the two networks.

This entry is simple, yet says a lot. Behind these lines is a host of preparation to do. Another example might be:

Date: Another Day

Connected WAN through router-5. No further user or server configuration changes were needed. Server seemed to be able to communicate now.

Clearly, this entry records a critical change to the network that would not get recorded in a server log or anywhere else. You capture such events in the journal. It is handy to refer to your journal if you require information about other events or what has occurred in the past. You can always count on some user announcing two months after you made a change, "Oh yeah, my computer hasn't worked ever since I saw an email from you about some WAN thing." Your log should say what, when, and where things changed that may have upset the user's connection or workstation.

Keeping records is hard work. It is simple but hard. Sticking to your guns and recording information in binders, updating disks, and keeping journal entries can seem more like interruptions. However, when you need them, you will be pleased with yourself for making the effort.

Logging Data

After finishing all of the other information collection, you are finally ready to consider collecting performance data. In this case, NT's Performance Monitor will do most of the busy work, but setting it up to collect the information will take some thought.

The starting point of collecting the data is the *baseline*. The baseline is the performance of the system under controlled circumstances. This is your reference point. When you first install a server, you will get a baseline of the server before you ever put it into production. You will install all the services and software that you are going to run on the machine and then establish a baseline for the performance of the system. At that point, you will get an idea of how the system will perform under stress. Remember Chapter 3? We talked about simulating activity on a machine. The time to do it is before the system ever gets into the greedy paws of the users. You can then compare the results of the system under no load, under a regular load, and under extreme duress. This exercise will help you see signs of overuse or unusual usage before they become a problem. How to collect this data is the topic of this section.

Data collection is a theme throughout the book. In your efforts to maintain the performance of your systems, you need to constantly monitor them. You could spend your entire day staring at the Performance Monitor and waiting for something bad to happen, but somehow I don't think you'll have the time to do that. Performance Monitor offers a couple methods for collecting the data.

The first method simply uses a remote machine to monitor the system or systems that concern you. You might have a low-powered machine such as a 486. You probably also have a spare disk or two. That is all that you need to collect information from your machines. Install NT on the machine. Start Performance Monitor in Log view. From here, you will collect the data to a log by following these steps:

1. Add objects to the Performance Monitor for logging.
2. Set the log file storage options.
3. Calculate the log file size.
4. Start the logging procedure.
5. Store log file information and relog if necessary.

Adding Objects to the Performance Monitor for Logging

First, you press the plus sign (+) and add some objects to the Performance Monitor (see Figure 10.2). Make the computer selection in the dialog box first. Other counters will show up only if you have the proper computer selected. The most basic baseline or performance statistics include the following objects:

- Processor
- PhysicalDisk or LogicalDisk
- Memory
- Network

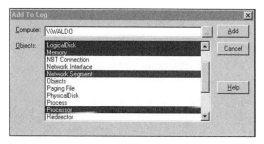

Figure 10.2 Adding the four basic objects for establishing a baseline to the log file list of objects to collect.

You will set more objects based on the type of system that you are monitoring. For example, you might want to include SQL Server objects or Exchange objects according to the primary function of that particular machine.

Setting Log File Storage Options

The next step involves setting the Performance Monitor options to store a log file in a location of your choice (see Figure 10.3). You will also set the interval for collecting data. For now, set the collection time to manual. At this point, you do not want to start the collection.

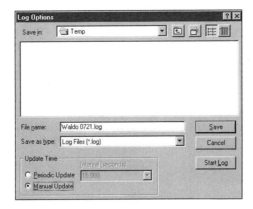

Figure 10.3 Setting the Performance Monitor options for data collection.

Calculating the Log File Size

You will want to calculate the size of the log file prior to actually doing the collection. The calculation is simply:

# of Samples × Size of the Samples = Disk Space Required

The number of samples is a combination of how often you are going to take samples and how long you plan to take the samples. For example, you are going to take samples every 15 seconds for the next hour:

1 sample/15 seconds × 60 secs/1 minute × 60 minutes/hour × 1 hour = # of Samples = 240 samples

You then need to know how big a sample will be. First, check the size of the log file now in the Performance Monitor Log interface. Record the value. Recall that you set the interval to manual. In the Performance Monitor Log interface, click the snapshot icon (the camera). Click the camera four times and record the result. Then, subtract the first value from the last and divide by four. (Every fourth collection contains a little more administrative data that adds to the size of the log.) Multiply the new value by the number of samples to get the amount of disk space that you need.

Starting the Logging Procedure

The next procedure involves simply logging the data. Access the Log options and adjust the interval. Fifteen seconds is a good interval for general logging. For more specific processor or memory problems, you will adjust the collection interval to every second. Keep in mind that such a setting will result in an increased number of samples and thus a larger log file. Then, start your logging.

From a single computer, you may log multiple machines at the same time. All you have to do is start multiple instances of the Performance Monitor. Performance monitoring is not that taxing on a machine, with the exception of the disk activity. You can usually monitor five or six servers from a single 486MHz machine with a PCI Disk controller without fear of crippling the performance to the point of jeopardizing the statistics you are collecting. Remember that the Performance Monitor is just another program. If the machine where you are running it starts to have problems, the collection process may experience problems as well. While you are doing this kind of monitoring, you need a user to stay logged into the NT Workstation that the collection is running from. You can log in and lock the workstation.

The other way to perform the collection is to run a service to take care of the process. You can use the Monitor service from the NT Resource Kit, which consists of two pieces. The first piece is DATALOG.EXE, which is the service that does the collection. The second piece is MONITOR.EXE, which is a command-line interface to the service. Because MONITOR.EXE is command line, you will run it from a batch file. You should be aware of a few procedural items when using the performance monitoring service:

- The service runs on the server whose data is being collected.
- The service will only be able to log data to a local file on the server. You want to make sure that you are logging to a disk where you are not watching the performance and that you have the appropriate amount of disk space.
- The MONITOR.EXE interface can be run from any remote workstation.

To set this up, you will first install the service as follows:

1. From the NT Resource Kit, copy the files DATALOG.EXE and MONITOR.EXE to a floppy disk or a network share.

2. Copy DATALOG.EXE to the %SystemRoot%\System32 directory on each server where you want to monitor the service.

3. On the server where you want to install the service, open a command prompt and run `C:\> MONITOR SETUP` to install the service. The service is set to a manual startup, which is appropriate in most cases.

The service is now ready. You must now prepare the Performance Monitor for collecting data. These steps are similar to the steps in the first method used to log data, with a couple of exceptions:

1. You want to visit the actual server where you are going to collect the data. On the server, start the Performance Monitor and configure all your settings. Save the settings to a ⋆.PML or a ⋆.PMW file. Save the files to the %Systemroot%\System32 folder. Don't forget to consider the disk space that will be used for the collection process.

2. At a command prompt from any machine, enter `C:\> MONITOR [\\COMPUTERNAME] [MYFILE.PML]`. COMPUTERNAME is the name of the computer where you want the service to run. The MYFILE.PML or MYFILE.PMW is the configuration file that you created in Performance Monitor.

3. Start the service.

To start the service, you use the `MONITOR \\COMPUTERNAME START` and `STOP` commands. You can control the DATALOG.EXE service of several machines from a single server or workstation that basically acts as a scheduling machine. Using the Command Scheduler from the NT Resource Kit, you can set the services to start and stop at certain times throughout the day.

For the sake of preserving disk space, you probably do not want to run the service for an entire 24-hour period because the systems are usually not busy during non-business hours. You should pick particular times when the system is expected to be busy or when you are noticing regular performance problems. Keep in mind a couple of things about the scheduler:

- If the server running the scheduler is down for any amount of time and passes the time when one of the services was supposed to stop or start, the scheduler will not perform the scheduled task. The service only performs tasks as it encounters them. If for some reason, it never encounters the time when the action was to be performed, it will not perform the action during that cycle.

- Scheduling too many jobs too close together can cause the scheduler to miss a job. This is a manifestation of the first point. The scheduler waits for a job to start, and if a time passes before it returns to see what task is next, it will miss a job.

Storing Log File Information and Relogging

As you collect information on a regular basis, you will want to review that information. In addition, you need a method for storing the information. For example, you might be collecting the statistics of a particular server on a daily basis. However, you do not want to stockpile logs of data. This situation is when relogging becomes important. When you log information to a file, you can read it back into Alert view, Chart view, and Report view. However, you can also relog the data by reading it into the Log view. This arrangement offers the following benefits:

- You can reduce the size of the logged data by adjusting the objects you want to save. Select the objects from the available objects that appear in the original log. Only the objects selected are collected to the new log.

- You can reduce the size of the logged data by adjusting the time interval for collecting. If originally you were collecting the data at 1-second intervals, you could set the new log to collect the data at 15-second intervals. You get every fifteenth point from the original log, which is usually sufficient for standard record keeping practices. Of course, if you have some event of interest in the log, you want to preserve the interval.

- You can adjust the time window. That is how you limit the data screening from one log to the next to the data collected within the smaller time window that you specified. Adjusting the time window is an excellent way of collecting only the data of specific interest. Perhaps you examined the logs and noticed a 5-minute interval in which the processor was at 95%. You might want to save this time slice and compare it to future similar events. Also, if you were doing a simulation, you might want to save particular segments of the simulation as notes about how the system would react under particular circumstances. Then, if you would run across similar activity in the production world, you could compare your notes and diagnose the situation.

Of course, implementing relogging implies that you are examining the data on a regular basis, which is the topic of the next section.

Data Analysis

You may be collecting data for your capacity planning on a regular basis; however, you cannot forget to analyze the data. This is clearly an important step but one that takes some discipline to achieve on a regular basis. Before getting into the technical methods for collecting data, you should understand the general methodology for analyzing the data:

1. Filter log file data with alerts.
2. Adjust the Performance Monitor time window.
3. Perform a preliminary data analysis.
4. Export the data for critical analysis.

Filtering Log File Data with Alerts

After you have the data you want in a log, start your analysis with the Performance Monitor Alert view. Often, only some of the data points within a log are interesting enough to warrant your attention. Ferret out the interesting points with alerts. The alerts that you will start with will probably resemble the following:

- Process Object : % Processor Time > 80%
- Memory Object : Pages/sec > 16
- Physical Disk Object : Disk Queue Length > 2
- Network Segment Object : % Network Utilization > 50%

The preceding items should look familiar to you. They are the basic objects and counters for most of our initial analyses throughout the book. Some other counters may interest you, depending on the type of software you have installed. After you have a nice set of alerts, save them in the Performance Monitor to a *.PMA or *.PMW file. The *.PMA is a Performance Monitor Alert file. The *.PMW is a Performance Monitor Workspace file. The difference is *.PMA files will only save information regarding the settings for the alerts, whereas *.PMW files will save the settings for all views within the Performance Monitor.

Adjusting the Performance Monitor Time Window

Write down a few of the alerts that are revealed. Adjust the time window around the alerts to get 100 data points. You can figure this out because you will know the collection interval, and the time window displays the time stamps for each data point. Let's say that you were collecting a data point every 15 seconds. You would adjust the time window start and stop times so that they were 150 seconds apart.

> Remember that the Chart view can display only 100 data points across, which is why it is important to adjust the time window to view only 100 data points. Also, understand that the time window displays time stamps to the hundredth's of a second. Don't confuse the seconds with minutes or hundredth of a second.

Performing a Preliminary Data Analysis

After you have a nice section of data, you will look at it with a critical eye. Using all the techniques in this book, determine whether the data you see is a critical problem or simply a manifestation of some user performing an unusual activity. In addition, you'll look at the intervals to see which resource is being used to a critical limit and why. Even if a sign is just a fluke, it is good practice to perform a quick process of figuring out the bottleneck and the possible cause. This exercise will keep your skills sharp.

Exporting the Data for Critical Analysis

For more serious analysis, you might want to export the information to another file type so that it can be loaded into a database, spreadsheet, or statistical package. This step will allow you to analyze the data in a more critical manner. Often, one of the easiest options to use is a spreadsheet program. To get the information to another program, export the data from the log to a tab-delimited file that can be retrieved into almost any package. The steps are simple:

1. Reduce the data set to a section that interests you by adjusting the Performance Monitor alerts and the time window. Of course, if you are looking for more general descriptive statistics on the usage patterns of your system, you will use the entire data set.

2. Click File and Export from the Performance Monitor drop-down menu. Give the file and name, and click OK (see Figure 10.4).

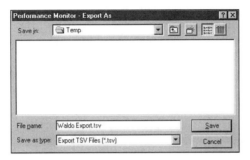

Figure 10.4   Exporting the Performance Monitor data to a tab-delimited file.

3. Now, choose an appropriate tool for editing the file, such as a spreadsheet or a word processor. You especially want to edit the information if you are going to import it into a statistics package or database. The Performance Monitor exports a lot of header information with the data (see Figure 10.5), which could interfere with the import functions of other packages.

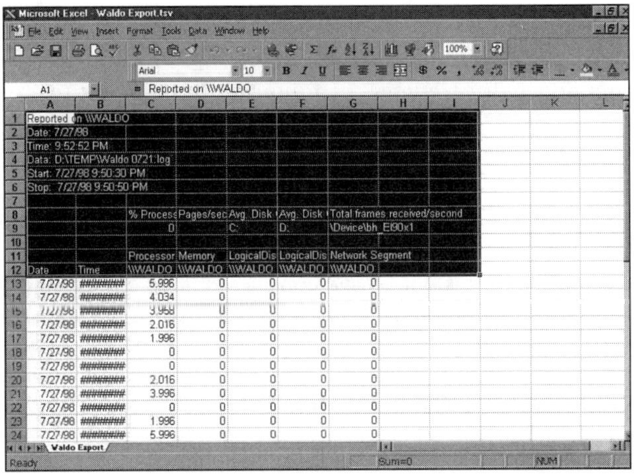

Figure 10.5   Removing extraneous header information from Performance Monitor exported data in a spreadsheet or word processor.

After you have successfully cropped the header information, you will also check the data points themselves. Performance Monitor is only a software application. It can have errors in retrieving data from the local or remote machine's Registry. You will do a quick search of all the data points for blanks. Also, consider the existence of 0 values. Sometimes, the values are significant, and other times, they simply mean that the system could not retrieve a value. You will have to consider this on a case-by-case basis. In general, for raw counts that are 0, you have to consider what you are counting and whether it is reasonable to have a 0. For example, it is certainly plausible to have a Disk Queue Length of 0 at a particular point in time. You may also notice that the number of users connected to SQL or to an Exchange post office is 0. However, it is very unlikely to see Available Memory at 0, which would be a situation of severe consequences.

After you have sorted the data, you can load it into your favorite statistics package. Then, perform your analysis. For a taste of what types of statistics you might perform, here is a list I have used in the past:

- **Descriptive statistics on users connected to Exchange, SQL, and IIS servers.** These are the basics of figuring out system usage patterns.

- **Regression analysis (correlations) on various memory and processor counters.** This is a discovery session for learning how certain counters and NT components are related.

- **Trend analysis.** This is a common step for determining how memory and disk resources usage trends are changing.

Data analysis is more intensive than the other aspects of capacity planning and performance monitoring in general, mostly due to the amount of time you must contribute to the task. The other tasks involve investments in time primarily to get set up and operational. After that, tasks such as record keeping and data logging are relatively modest in terms of the amount of time you have to spend on them. The analysis will require your attention and sometimes deep thought. I find it best to work on such tasks either away from the office or outside normal hours when interruptions are fewer.

Performance for the Small Business Office

Many of the discussions in this book have considered large enterprises with multiple sites and a number of servers. This will not always be the case. You may be running a startup business, a single office of a larger company, or simply a small business franchise not in need of large-scale computing. In any case, the techniques of this book will still work for you. You still need to make sure that the server you have can run at the best performance. This performance may even be more important when you have only one server. There is no option to offload some of the workload to another machine. The machine you have must do it all. For a small office situation, I have a few extra tips:

■ Do not ignore capacity planning and regular monitoring simply because you figure your office will never grow.

■ Analyzing a small system doesn't mean you can forget the scientific method.

■ Be creative when testing.

■ There is typically a limit to the amount of performance you get by upgrading a server.

■ Keep the users informed.

Ignoring capacity planning and regular monitoring simply because you figure your office will never grow is not a good idea. As systems change and the applications that you use change, the resource usage will change. Perhaps the business will alter critical processes that affect the usage of new software or old software in a different way. Without monitoring and capacity planning, you could be caught off guard by the changes. Even in a small business, it is sometimes difficult to predict how changes can affect a system. I suggest reducing the monitoring of the system. I recommend picking one day out of the week to collect data on the system. Rotate this day if possible. If you always monitor Monday, you'll have a very good idea about what occurs on Monday, but not Tuesday. Rotating the days when you collect data will help.

A small business environment does not permit you to omit the proper steps of troubleshooting. The scientific method was not built with a size difference in mind. The same techniques work for small and large businesses.

A small business environment enables you to be creative when testing. You might want to install NT twice on your server. In one situation, you will have a test server, and in another, you will have a production server. They can share the same common boot partition (typically the C: drive), but you will put the operating system partitions on separate logical drives if possible. This might cost you some money for a little more disk space, but it is cheaper than buying a second server. In this situation, you can install software to the test version of NT and mess with it without hurting the production version. Of course, this means that you need to do some off-hours work. However, you still should fight the temptation to test on the production server. Eventually, you will cause a problem.

There is typically a limit to the improvement in performance you will see by upgrading a server. At some point, after you have added several major applications and your server is starting to feel the sting of resource contention, you might want to consider buying another machine instead of pumping more resources into the existing server. Even a cheaper or low-powered machine can be a greater benefit than adding more memory or another CPU to a system. This is especially true if you are looking at adding more server applications. Even in a small office scenario, SQL Server will run better on its own than when sharing resources on a high-powered server that also doubles also as a file and print server.

Most importantly, in a small business environment, you need to keep the users informed. You probably don't have a lot of users, but you need to make sure you keep them informed of your efforts, anyway. Large or small, periodic changes to the system can annoy users. However, I have found that if you keep them well informed of the benefits of optimizing the system, periodic intensive systems data logging, and configuration changes, the users will find it easier to accept. In a small company, you usually don't have any bureaucracy to hide behind.

You'll find that, as an administrator, the small business is usually a good place to learn. Often, you will have the chance to sit down with a book such as this and try a lot of the suggestions and examples. Make a couple goals for yourself and improve your own performance as well as your system's.

Microsoft Operating System Options

When selecting Windows NT, you have several options. You must figure out how you are going to use the server prior to actually purchasing the hardware and software. You must consider how you are going to use the server now and later down the road. Considering this will help you configure a machine that will be useful past its original purpose. When considering a Microsoft operating system such as NT, you should consider the variety of ways to purchase it. Each way has its benefits and limitations. The sections that follow discuss the variety of ways NT is packaged and include some comments on why you might make each selection. When purchasing any of these packages, you should always consider how the company is going to grow and not just the immediate needs.

Windows NT Workstation

No one said your system has to be big to be effective. For a small office of fewer than 15 users, Windows NT Workstation may be a viable solution for a server. NT Workstation will provide many of the security features and other features of Windows NT Server without the big price. Also, the resource requirements of the system aren't quite as intense. Windows NT Workstation has a limitation of 10 concurrent user connections. If you are purchasing a system so that users can connect to it and stay connected, and if you have more than 10 users, consider NT Server instead. In addition, if you are looking for more than file and print services, be cautious about purchasing Windows NT Workstation. Many server-based components detect that they are running on NT Workstation and refuse to install.

Windows NT Server

By itself, NT Server is an excellent choice for almost any type of service. NT really shines as an application server for other products such as Web, database, and email services. How many users NT will support is primarily dependent on the nature of the services and the number of users; this determination of course is the whole nature of optimization and is the topic of this book.

Small Business Server

Microsoft put together a nice bundle of services built on top of Windows NT Server in a single product called the Microsoft Small Business Server (SBS). This product is suitable for businesses with 25 users or fewer. A software limitation on the server keeps it from supporting more than 25 users. However, if the numbers are right, SBS can be a real value for a business. SBS offers NT Server as well as Exchange for email, IIS for Web services, and SQL for database products. Keep in mind the 25-user limit when considering these other powerful components. In addition to these components, SBS includes components geared toward Internet connectivity and communication. One product sadly not found in BackOffice or NT by itself is the Shared Fax Services. This service allows users to send faxes via Exchange through the NT Server and a single fax card. This product is also provided by third parties at quite a cost, in most cases.

BackOffice

Microsoft BackOffice is a suite of products like Microsoft Office. Whereas Office contains Word, Excel, and PowerPoint, BackOffice contains Exchange, SQL Server, Systems Manager Server, IIS, and SNA Server. This extremely powerful combination of software can fulfill many needs of a medium-sized business. Larger, more complex companies often buy the individual products and put them on NT, due to the often highly intensive nature of a larger company's resource usage. Any company with 100 to 1,000 users should consider the BackOffice suite as an excellent beginning.

Additional Resources on NT Optimization

Is this book the end-all-be-all of optimization? I daresay my credibility would suffer greatly to even suggest it. I have provided you with all the information you need to take a hard look at Windows NT and its internals. However, you have much more than simply NT to worry about. You must consider Web services, database services, email servers, and other application and networking services that can run on Windows NT. Many services carry their own set of objects, counters, and methods of optimizing. With the methods outlined in this book, you can easily work with many other products, but to get deep into those other products, you need some other resources.

Online Resources

Many other books offer valuable NT optimization information, however, you should also consider several Web sites for some excellent information. Some tried and true sites include:

- **www.winntmag.com.** *Windows NT Magazine*'s Web site as well as the periodical itself, have proven worthy of mention. Despite the name of the magazine, it also provides fair presentations of non-Microsoft products that run on NT. More than once, I have relied on and been satisfied with the analysis and comparisons of the various software products examined by the folks at *Windows NT Magazine*. The well-developed Web site contains a host of information regarding past articles and software comparisons.

- **www.infoworld.com.** Another magazine also worth mentioning, *InfoWorld* has presented a large variety of ideas consistently throughout its publication. It has a fine staff of professionals who analyze software and the industry in general. Although the magazine and Web site are more industry-news related, they still can be mined for some good analysis of emerging technologies.

- **www.sysinternals.com.** If you are looking for a tool to do a nifty little job on NT and it's not in the NT Resource Kit, visit this site. These folks have put together an excellent collection of NT tools and tips that are beyond the norm of freeware and shareware.

- **www.jerold.com.** This guy has put together an impressive collection of how-tos and tips. Although he is a little overzealous in the promotion of his own site, it certainly deserves a look. Solutions to many commonly reported problems (and a few rare ones) are posted on this site.

- **www.compaq.com.** These guys know their hardware! At their site, you will find all sorts of white papers on the newest chip technologies, integration of the technology into servers and workstations, and how operating systems (NT included) work with the new technology. In addition, they have performed a lot of analysis on their own hardware that can be very informative about how NT works in general.

I am sure that even more sites offer excellent information if you can stomach a little Web searching. Most of the products I have noted are Microsoft BackOffice products. With this in mind, I want to offer a few Microsoft-specific resources.

Microsoft Resources

First off, buy TechNet. It is one of the best resources you can get for a decent price. For a few hundred bucks, you get a stack of CDs with the following items:

- Microsoft Knowledgebase
- Current NT/Win95/Win98 Resource Kits
- Office/IE and other Resource Kits
- All the service packs on CD
- A software library of all sorts of tools

The Resource Kits mentioned have electronic versions of the books on TechNet, as well as copies of all the latest tools. For the price (currently $299.00 U.S.), it is hard to beat. Consider also that when you call Microsoft's front-line support, they generally check TechNet for your problem. If they find it, they'll ship you the article and charge you a service fee.

Another subscription of excellent value, but a little narrower in its scope, is the Microsoft Development Network (MSDN). This CD set in its most basic form contains several CDs with all sorts of sample, solutions, and documentation for writing code for the Microsoft platform. There is some overlap between TechNet and MSDN, but MSDN will contain much more programmer-oriented information, so it isn't for everyone. However, if you are doing some serious development work internally or externally, you'll want to consider at least the basic subscription to MSDN. The various levels of MSDN subscription range from the basic to the universal. I won't bore you with all the details, but the universal subscription contains all the MS platforms, BackOffice products, and development platforms.

This is all well and good, but where are the freebies? Those more monetarily challenged may try the Microsoft Web site (www.microsoft.com). Microsoft has posted a significant portion of the MSDN library on the Web site, although searching there is more tiresome than using the CDs.

One newsgroup to consider is msnews.microsoft.com, hosted, obviously, by Microsoft. You can typically post to the newsgroup and get an answer to your question. Microsoft engineers do not answer the questions, but a host of other people, such as consultants and other professionals in the industry, review the newsgroups on a regular basis. It's free and if you have Internet access, you can usually gain access to a newsgroup. Other Internet service providers, such as AOL and CompuServe, also host forums where you can discuss technology issues. In any case, it's free, and if you have access, you can often get an answer to an important question.

Summary

In this farewell chapter, you have reviewed the various performance tips that were previously mentioned throughout the book. In addition, you have had the opportunity to learn more about methodology and the application of all that you had learned in previous chapters. You were able to take your knowledge one step further and apply it to the process of capacity planning. Capacity planning was the process of staying ahead of the game. The process involves obtaining baselines for performance under controlled conditions. I also presented techniques for data collection.

I have also given you a series of resources where you can find other information. Newsgroups are a favorite resource of mine because I can get answers as well as share my own experience. Finally, I offered more information on the choices available to you when you are purchasing Windows NT. You can purchase a Windows package fit for an enterprise of any size.

Performance Monitor Counters

This appendix covers the following topics:

- **Processor Performance Counters.** This section describes the most significant counters associated with the Processor object.

- **Memory Performance Counters.** This section describes the most significant counters associated with the Memory object.

- **Disk Performance Counters.** This section describes the most significant counters associated with the PhysicalDisk and LogicalDisk objects.

- **Network Performance Counters.** This section describes the most significant counters associated with the network interface, network segment, and TCP/IP components.

This section lists all of the objects and counters that were referenced throughout the text, and some extras that will be of particular interest. There are hundreds of Performance Monitor counters that can be used for a multitude of situations. You might consider this the starter list of ones that you should be using on a regular basis. Explanations and usage of the counters is offered where appropriate. Each listing will have the following format:

[Object] : [Counter Name]. [Explanation/Usage]

Recall that an object refers to a Performance Monitor object. For each object there will be multiple counters—[Counter Name]—and potentially multiple instances. This is the case with multiple processor systems or systems with more than one hard drive. Some of the objects and counters are not present unless an NT component or other software is installed on the system. This is specifically stated in the [Explanation/Usage] section of each object/counter pairing.

Processor Performance Counters

The Processor object is focused primarily on the CPU of the system. Note that some system have multiple processors, which will display as independent instances for each of these counters.

The counters listed in this section are all used to determine processor performance or influence other components are enforcing over the processor.

- **Processor : % Processor Time.** This counter provides a measure of how much time the processor actually spends working on productive threads and how often it was busy servicing requests. This counter actually provides a measurement of how often the system is doing nothing subtracted from 100%. This is a simpler calculation for the processor to make. The processor can never be sitting idle waiting to the next task, unlike our cashier. The CPU must always have something to do. It's like when you turn on the computer, the CPU is a piece of wire that electric current is always running through, thus it must always be doing something. NT give the CPU something to do when there is nothing else waiting in the queue. This is called the idle thread. The system can easily measure how often the idle thread is running as opposed to having to tally the run time of each of the other process threads. Then , the counter simply subtracts the percentage from 100%.

- **Processor : Interrupts /sec.** The numbers of interrupts the processor was asked to respond to. Interrupts are generated from hardware components like hard disk controller adapters and network interface cards. A sustained value over 1000 is usually an indication of a problem. Problems would include a poorly configured drivers, errors in drivers, excessive utilization of a device (like a NIC on an IIS server), or hardware failure. Compare this value with the System : Systems Calls/sec. If the Interrupts/sec is much larger over a sustained period, you probably have a hardware issue.

- **Processor : % Interrupt Time.** This is the percentage of time that the processor is spending on handling Interrupts. Generally, if this value exceeds 50% of the processor time you may have a hardware issue. Some components on the computer can force this issue and not really be a problem. For example a programmable I/O card like an old disk controller card, can take up to 40% of the CPU time. A NIC on a busy IIS server can likewise generate a large percentage of processor activity.

- **Processor: % User Time.** The value of this counter helps to determine the kind of processing that is affecting the system. Of course the resulting value is the total amount of non–idle time that was spent on User mode operations. This generally means application code.

- **Processor : %Privilege Time.** This is the amount of time the processor was busy with Kernel mode operations. If the processor is very busy and this mode is high, it is usually an indication of some type of NT service having difficulty, although user mode programs can make calls to the Kernel mode NT components to occasionally cause this type of performance issue.

- **Processor: %DPC Time.** Much like the other values, this counter shows the amount of time that the processor spends servicing DPC requests. DPC requests are more often than not associated with the network interface.

- **Process : % Processor Time.** This counter is a natural choice that will give use the amount of time that this particular process spends using the processor resource. There are also % Privilege Time and % User Time counters for this object that will help to identify what the program is spending most of its time doing.

- **System : Processor Queue Length.** Oddly enough, this processor counter shows up under the System object, but not without good reason. There is only 1 queue for tasks that need to go to the processor, even if there is more than one CPU. Thus, counter provides a measure of the instantaneous size of the queue for all processors at the moment that the measurement was taken. The resulting value is a measure of how many threads are in the Ready state waiting to be processed. When dealing with queues, if the value exceeds 2 for a sustained period, you are definitely having a problem with the resource in question.

- **System : System Calls/sec.** This counter is a measure of the number of calls made to the system components, Kernel mode services. This is a measure of how busy the system is taking care of applications and services—software stuff. When compared to the Interrupts/Sec it will give you an indication of whether processor issues are hardware or software related. See Processor : Interrupts/Sec for more information.

- **System : % Total Processor Time.** This counter groups the activity of all the processors together to report the total performance of the entire system. On a single processor machine, this value will equal the %Processor Time value of the processor object.

- **System : % Total User Time.** This is the total user time of all the processors on the system. See Processor : % User Time for more details.

- **System : % Total Privledge Time.** This is the total privledge time for all processors on the system collectively. See Processor : % Privledge Time for more details.

- **System : % Total Interrupt Time.** This is the collective amount of time that all of the processors are spending on handling interrupts. See Processor : % Interrupt Time for more details.

- **Thread Object : % Processor Time.** This counter takes the analysis to the next level. Typically, this counter would be for programmers, but occasionally there is a more global use for it. For example, if you are trying to examine the actions of a 16-bit process. The 16-bit application will actually be running as a thread in the NTVDM process. If you wish to see the processor usage by the 16-bit without obscuring it with the processing of the NTVDM and WOWEXEC.exe, you will want to examine the individual thread. BackOffice applications tend to have very distinct multiple threads that sometimes are worth examining individually as opposed to in a group. Often the threads of more sophisticated applications can be configured independently from the entire process.

■ **Thread Object : ID Thread.** When a process creates a thread, the system assigns a Thread ID so that it may distinguish the thread among the other threads on the system. Thread IDs are reassigned upon creation and deletion of the threads. You can not expect a thread to have the same ID each time it is created. It is important to use the Thread ID whenever you are looking at any other counters that are specific to the thread. If the thread is deleted, the performance monitor will *spike* indicating the thread has in fact expired.

■ **Thread Object** : **Priority Base.** The thread gets a base priority from the Process that created it. The priority of the thread can be adjusted by the system or through a program. This priority is used to judge when the thread is going to have access to the process and how many other threads it may *jump ahead of* in the processor queue of ready threads.

■ **Process : Process ID.** Each process on Windows NT gets a Process ID that identifies it as a unique process on the system. You can reference the Process ID counter to gain information about the process through API calls. The Process ID is guaranteed to remain unique to the particular process during the entire time that it is running. But, the process is *not* guaranteed to have the same process ID each time that it is run.

■ **Process : % Processor Time.** Each process will show up as an instance when selecting this counter. This counter will break down how much processor time each process is taking on the CPU. Don't forget to exclude the Idle and the Total counts when looking at all of the instances.

■ **Process** : **% User Time.** This will break down the amount of user time that each process is taking out of the total amount of processor time that the processes is using.

Memory Performance Counters

The following counters all have to do with the management of memory issues. In addition, there will counters that assist in the determination of whether the problem you are having is really a memory issue.

■ **Memory : Page Faults/sec.** This counter gives a general idea of how many times information being requested is not where the application (and VMM) expects it to be. The information must either be retrieved from another location in memory or from the pagefile. Recall that while a sustained value may indicate trouble here, you should be more concerned with hard page faults that represent actual reads or writes to the disk. Remember that the disk access is much slower than RAM.

■ **Memory : Pages Input/sec.** Use this counter in comparison with the Page Faults/sec counter to determine the percentage of the page faults that are hard page faults.

Thus, Pages Input/sec / Page Faults/sec = % Hard Page Faults. Sustained values surpassing 40% are generally indicative of memory shortages of some kind. While you might know at this point that there is memory shortage of some kind on the system, this is not necessarily an indication that the system is in need of an immediate memory upgrade.

■ **Memory : Pages Output/sec.** As memory becomes more in demand, you can expect to see that the amount of information being removed from memory is increasing. This may even begin to occur prior to the hard page faults becoming a problem. As memory begins to run short, the system will attempt to first start reducing the applications to their minimum working set. This means moving more information out to the pagefiles and disk. Thus, if your system is on the verge of being truly strained for memory you may begin to see this value climb. Often the first pages to be removed from memory are data pages. The code pages experience more repetitive reuse.

■ **Memory : Pages/sec.** This value is often confused with Page Faults/sec. The Pages/sec counter is a combination of Pages Input/sec and Pages Output/sec counters. Recall that Page Faults/sec is a combination of hard page faults and soft page faults. This counter, however, is a general indicator of how often the system is using the hard drive to store or retrieve memory associated data.

■ **Memory : Page Reads/sec.** This counter is probably the best indicator of a memory shortage because it indicates how often the system is reading from disk because of hard page faults. The system is always using the pagefile even if there is enough RAM to support all of the applications. Thus, some number of page reads will always be encountered. However, a sustained value over 5 Page Reads/sec is often a strong indicator of a memory shortage. You must be careful about viewing these counters to understand what they are telling you. This counter again indicates the number of reads from the disk that were done to satisfy page faults. The amount of pages read each time the system went to the disk may indeed vary. This will be a function of the application and the proximity of the data on the hard drive. Irrelevant of these facts, a sustained value of over 5 is still a strong indicator of a memory problem. Remember the importance of "sustained." System operations often fluctuate, sometimes widely. So, just because the system has a Page Reads/sec of 24 for a couple of seconds does not mean you have a memory shortage.

- **Memory : Page Writes/sec.** Much like the Page Reads/sec, this counter indicates how many times the disk was written to in an effort to clear unused items out of memory. Again, the numbers of pages per read may change. Increasing values in this counter often indicate a building tension in the battle for memory resources.

- **Memory : Available Memory.** This counter indicates the amount of memory that is left after nonpaged pool allocations, paged pool allocations, process' working sets, and the file system cache have all taken their piece. In general, NT attempts to keep this value around 4 MB. Should it drop below this for a sustained period, on the order of minutes at a time, there may be a memory shortage. Of course, you must always keep an eye out for those times when you are simply attempting to perform memory intensive tasks or large file transfers.

- **Memory : Nonpageable memory pool bytes.** This counter provides an indication of how NT has divided up the physical memory resource. An uncontrolled increase in this value would be indicative of a memory leak in a Kernel level service or driver.

- **Memory : Pageable memory pool bytes.** An uncontrolled increase in this counter, with the corresponding decrease in the available memory, would be indicative of a process taking more memory than it should and not giving it back.

- **Memory : Committed Bytes.** This counter indicates the total amount of memory that has been committed for the exclusive use of any of the services or processes on Windows NT. Should this value approach the committed limit, you will be facing a memory shortage of unknown cause, but of certain severe consequence.

- **Process : Page Faults/sec.** This is a indication of the number of page faults that occurred due to requests from this particular process. Excessive page faults from a particular process is an indication usually of bad coding practices. Either the functions and DLLs are not organized correctly, or the data set that the application is using is being called in a less than efficient manner.

- **Process : Pool Paged Bytes.** This is the amount of memory that the process is using in the pageable memory region. This information can be paged out from physical RAM to the pagefile on the hard drive.

- **Process : Pool NonPaged Bytes.** This is the amount of memory that the process is using that cannot be moved out to the pagefile and thus will remain in physical RAM. Most processes do not use this, however, some real-time applications may find it necessary to keep some DLLs and functions readily available in order to function at the real-time mode.

- **Process : Working Set.** This is the current size of the memory area that the process is utilizing for code, threads, and data. The size of the working set will grow and shrink as the VMM can permit. When memory is becoming scarce the working sets of the applications will be trimmed. When memory is plentiful the working sets are allowed to grow. Larger working sets means more code and data in memory making the overall performance of the applications increase. However, a large working set that does not shrink appropriately is usually an indication of a memory leak.

Disk Performance Counters

The Disk Performance counters help you to evaluate the performance of the disk subsystem. The disk subsystem is more than the disk itself. It will include to disk controller card, the I/O bus of the system, and the disk. When measuring disk performance it is usually better to have a good baseline for performance than simply to try and evaluate the disk performance on a case by case basis.

There are two objects for the disk—PhysicalDisk and LogicalDisk. The counters for the two are identical. However, in some cases they may lead to slightly different conclusions. The PhysicalDisk object is used for the analysis of the overall disk, despite the partitions that may be on the disk. When evaluating overall disk performance this would be the one to select. The LogicalDisk object analyzes information for a single partition. Thus the values will be isolated to activity that is particularly occurring on a single partition and not necessarily representative of the entire load that the disk is burdened with. The LogicalDisk object is useful primarily when looking at the affects or a particular application, like SQL Server, on the disk performance. Again the PhysicalDisk is primarily for looking at the performance of the entire disk subsystem. In the list that follows, the favored object is indicated with the counter. When the LogicalDisk and PhysicalDisk objects are especially different, the counter will be listed twice and the difference specifically mentioned.

- **PhysicalDisk : Current Disk Queue Length.** This counter provides a primary measure of disk congestion. Just as the processor queue was an indication of waiting threads, the disk queue is an indication of the number of transactions that are waiting to be processed. Recall that the queue is an important measure for services that operate on a transaction basis. Just like the line at the supermarket, the queue will be representative of not only the number of transactions, but also the length and frequency of each transaction.

- **PhysicalDisk : % Disk Time.** Much like % Processor time, this counter is a general mark of how busy the disk is. You will see many similarities between the disk and processor since they are both transaction-based services. This counter indicates a disk problem, but must be observed in conjunction with the Current Disk Queue Length counter to be truly informative. Recall also that the disk could be a bottleneck prior to the % Disk Time reaching 100%.

- **PhysicalDisk : Avg. Disk Queue Length.** This counter is actually strongly related to the %Disk Time counter. This counter converts the %Disk Time to a decimal value and displays it. This counter will be needed in times when the disk configuration employs multiple controllers for multiple physical disks. In these cases, the overall performance of the disk I/O system, which consists of two controllers, could exceed that of an individual disk. Thus, if you were looking at the %Disk Time counter, you would only see a value of 100%, which wouldn't represent the total potential of the entire system, but only that it had reached the potential of a single disk on a single controller. The real value may be 120% which the Avg. Disk Queue Length counter would display as 1.2.

- **PhysicalDisk : Disk Reads/sec.** This counter is used to compare to the Memory: Page Inputs/sec counter. You need to compare the two counters to determine how much of the Disk Reads are actually attributed to satisfying page faults.

- **LogicalDisk : Disk Reads/sec.** When observing an individual application (rather a partition) this counter will be an indication of how often the applications on the partition are reading from the disk. This will provide you with a more exact measure of the contribution of the various processes on the partition that are affecting the disk.

- **PhysicalDisk : Disk Reads Bytes/sec.** Primarily, you'll use this counter to describe the performance of disk throughput for the disk subsystem. Remember that you are generally measuring the capability of the entire disk hardware subsystem to respond to requests for information.

- **LogicalDisk : Disk Reads Bytes/sec.** For the partition, this will be an indication of the rate that data is being transferred. This will be an indication of what type of activity the partition is experiencing. A smaller value will indicate more random reads of smaller sections.

- **PhysicalDisk : Avg. Disk Bytes/Read.** This counter is used primarily to let you know the average number of bytes transferred per read of the disk system. This helps distinguish between random reads of the disk and the more efficient sequential file reads. A smaller value generally indicates random reads. The value for this counter can also be an indicator of file fragmentation.

- **PhysicalDisk : Avg. Disk sec/Read.** The value for this counter is generally the number of seconds it takes to do each read. On less-complex disk subsystems involving controllers that do not have intelligent management of the I/O, this value is a multiple of the disk's rotation per minute. This does not negate the rule that the entire system is being observed. The rotational speed of the hard drive will be the predominant factor in the value with the delays imposed by the controller card and support bus system.

- **PhysicalDisk: Disk Reads/sec.** The value for this counter is the number of reads that the disk was able to accomplish per second. Changes in this value indicate the amount of random access to the disk. The disk is a mechanical device that is capable of only so much activity. When files are closer together, the disk is permitted to get to the files quicker than if the files are spread throughout the disk. In addition, disk fragmentation can contribute to an increased value here.

Network Performance Counters

The network performance counters are not typically installed. The Network Segment object that is referred to here is installed when the Network Monitor Agent is installed. The network interface is installed when the SNMP service is installed. Many of the counters have to do with TCP/IP components, such as the SNMP service which relies on TCP/IP.

- **Network Interface : Bytes Sent/sec.** This is how many bytes of data are sent to the NIC. This is a raw measure of throughput for the network interface. We are really measuring the information sent to the interface which is the lowest point we can measure. If you have multiple NIC, you will see multiple instances of this particular counter.

- **Network Interface: Bytes Received/sec.** This, of course, is how many bytes you get from the NIC. This is a measure of the inbound traffic In measuring the bytes, NT isn't too particular at this level. So, no matter what the byte is, it is counted. This will include the framing bytes as opposed to just the data.

- **Network Interface : Bytes Total/sec.** This is simply a combination of the other two counters. This will tell you overall how much information is going in and out of the interface. Typically, you can use this to get a general feel, but will want to look at the Bytes Sent/sec and the Bytes Received/sec for a more exact detail of the type of traffic.

- **Processor : % DPC Time.** Interrupts can be handled later. These are called Deferred Procedure Calls. You will want to keep track of these as well. The combination of this time with the % Interrupt Time will give you a strong idea of how much of the precious processor time is going to servicing the network.

- **Processor : DPCs queued/sec.** This will give you the rate at which DPC are being sent to the process queue. Unlike the Processor Queue Length and the Disk Queue Length, this value only shows you the rate at which the DPCs are being added to the queue, no how many are in the queue. Still, observing this value can give you an indication of a growing problem.

- **Network Segment : %Broadcasts.** This value will let you know how much of the network bandwidth is dedicated to broadcast traffic. Broadcasts are network packets that have been designated as intended for all machines on the segment. Often, it is this type of traffic that has a detrimental affect on the network.

- **Network Segment : %Multicasts.** This is a measure of the % of the network bandwidth that multicast traffic is taking. Multicast traffic is similar to the broadcast, however, there is a limited number of intended recipients. The idea was that if you can identify multiple recipients you can reduce the repetitive transmission of data. This type of transfer is used most commonly with video conferencing.

- **TCP** : **Segments Sent/sec.** This is the rate at which TCP segments are sent. This is how much information that is being sent out for TCP/IP transmissions.

- **TCP** : **Segments Received/sec.** Of course, the rate at which segments are received for the protocol.

- **TCP** : **Segments/sec.** This is just the total of the previous two counters. This is the information being sent and received. This is a general indication of how busy the TCP/IP traffic is. The segment size is variable and thus, this does not translate easily to bytes.

- **TCP** : **Segments Retransmitted/sec.** This is the rate at which retransmissions occur. Retransmissions are measured based on bytes in the data that are recognized as being transmitted before. On a Ethernet/TCP/IP network retransmissions are a fact of life. However, excessive retransmissions indicate a distinct reduction in bandwidth.

- **TCP** : **Connection Failures.** This is the raw number of TCP connections that have failed since the server was started. A failure usually indicates a loss of data somewhere in the process. Data lose can occur at many locations. This could be an indication of another device being down, or problems with the client-side configuration of the software.

- **TCP** : **Connections Reset.** This is typically a result of a timeout as opposed to an erroneous set of information. The reset results from the a lack of any information over a period of time.

- **TCP** : **Connections Established.** This counter represents them number of connections. Unlike the other two this is more and instantaneous counter of how many TCP connections are currently on the system as opposed to a count of the number of successful connections.

Index

Books for Networking Professionals

New Riders

Windows NT Titles

Windows NT TCP/IP
By Karanjit Siyan
1st Edition Summer 1998
500 pages, $29.99
ISBN: 1-56205-887-8

If you're still looking for good documentation on Microsoft TCP/IP, then look no further—this is your book. *Windows NT TCP/IP* cuts through the complexities and provides the most informative and complete reference book on Windows-based TCP/IP. Concepts essential to TCP/IP administration are explained thoroughly, then related to the practical use of Microsoft TCP/IP in a real-world networking environment. The book begins by covering TCP/IP architecture, advanced installation and configuration issues, then moves on to routing with TCP/IP, DHCP Management, and WINS/DNS Name Resolution.

Windows NT DNS
By Michael Masterson, Herman L. Knief, Scott Vinick, and Eric Roul
1st Edition Summer 1998
325 pages, $29.99
ISBN: 1-56205-943-2

Have you ever opened a Windows NT book looking for detailed information about DNS only to discover that it doesn't even begin to scratch the surface? DNS is probably one of the most complicated subjects for NT administrators, and there are few books on the market that really address it in detail. This book answers your most complex DNS questions, focusing on the implementation of the Domain Name Service within Windows NT, treating it thoroughly from the viewpoint of an experienced Windows NT professional. Many detailed, real-world examples illustrate further the understanding of the material throughout. The book covers the details of how DNS functions within NT, then explores specific interactions with critical network components. Finally, proven procedures to design and set up DNS are demonstrated. You'll also find coverage of related topics, such as maintenance, security, and troubleshooting.

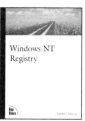

Windows NT Registry
By Sandra Osborne
1st Edition Summer 1998
500 pages, $29.99
ISBN: 1-56205-941-6

The NT Registry can be a very powerful tool for those capable of using it wisely. Unfortunately, there is very little information regarding the NT Registry, due to Microsoft's insistence that their source code be kept secret. If you're looking to optimize your use of the registry, you're usually forced to search the Web for bits of information. This book is your resource. It covers critical issues and settings used for configuring network protocols, including NWLink, PTP, TCP/IP, and DHCP. This book approaches the material from a unique point of view, discussing the problems related to a particular component, and then discussing settings, which are the actual changes necessary for implementing robust solutions. There is also a comprehensive reference of registry settings and commands, making this the perfect addition to your technical bookshelf.

Windows NT Performance Monitoring, Benchmarking, and Tuning

By Mark Edmead and Paul Hinsberg

1st Edition Fall 1998

400 pages, $29.99

ISBN: 1-56205-942-4

Performance monitoring is a little like preventative medicine for the administrator: no one enjoys a checkup, but it's a good thing to do on a regular basis. This book helps you focus on the critical aspects of improving the performance of your NT system, showing you how to monitor the system, implement benchmarking, and tune your network. The book is organized by resource components, which makes it easy to use as a reference tool.

Windows NT Terminal Server

By Ted Harwood

1st Edition Winter 1998

500 pages, $29.99

ISBN: 1-56205-944-0

It's no surprise that most administration headaches revolve around integration with other networks and clients. This book addresses these types of real-world issues on a case-by-case basis, giving tools and advice on solving each problem. The author also offers the real nuts and bolts of thin client administration on multiple systems, covering such relevant issues as installation, configuration, network connection, management, and application distribution.

Windows NT Security

By Richard Puckett

1st Edition Winter 1998

600 pages, $29.99

ISBN: 1-56205-945-9

Swiss cheese. That's what some people say Windows NT security is like. And they may be right, because they only know what the NT documentation says about implementing security. Who has the time to research alternatives; play around with the features, service packs, hot fixes and add-on tools, and figure out what makes NT rock solid? Well, Richard Puckett does. He's been researching Windows NT Security for the University of Virginia for a while now, and he's got pretty good news. He's going to show you how to make NT secure in your environment, and we mean really secure.

Windows NT Administration Handbook

By Eric Svetcov

1st Edition Winter 1998

400 pages, $29.99

ISBN: 1-56205-946-7

Administering a Windows NT network is kind of like trying to herd cats—an impossible task characterized by constant motion, exhausting labor and lots of hairballs. Author Eric Svetcov knows all about it—he's administered NT networks for some of the fastest growing companies around Silicon Valley. So we asked Eric to put together a concise manual of best practices, a book of tools and ideas that other administrators can turn to again and again in administering their own NT networks. Eric's experience shines through as he shares his secrets for administering users, for getting domain and groups set up quickly and for troubleshooting the thorniest NT problems. Daily, weekly, and monthly task lists help organize routine tasks and preventative maintenance.

Planning for Windows NT 5

By David Lafferty and Eric K. Cone
1st Edition Spring 1999
400 pages, $29.99
ISBN: 0-73570-048-6

Windows NT 5 is poised to be one of the largest and most important software releases of the next decade, and you are charged with planning, testing, and deploying it in your enterprise. Are you ready? With this book, you will be. *Planning for Windows NT 5* lets you know what the upgrade hurdles will be, informs you how to clear them, guides you through effective Active Directory design, and presents you with detailed rollout procedures. MCSEs David Lafferty and Eric K. Cone give you the benefit of their extensive experiences as Windows NT 5 Rapid Deployment Program members, sharing problems and solutions they've encountered on the job.

MCSE Core Essential Reference

By Matthew Shepker
1st Edition Fall 1998
500 pages, $19.99
ISBN: 0-7357-0006-0

You're sitting in the first session of your Networking Essentials class and the instructor starts talking about RAS and you have no idea what that means. You think about raising your hand to ask about RAS, but you reconsider—you'd feel pretty foolish asking a question in front of all these people. You turn to your handy *MCSE Core Essential Reference* and find a quick summary on Remote Access Services. Question answered. It's a couple months later and you're taking your Networking Essentials exam the next day. You're reviewing practice tests and you keep forgetting the maximum lengths for the various commonly used cable types. Once again, you turn to the *MCSE Core Essential Reference* and find a table on cables, including all of the characteristics you need to memorize in order to pass the test.

BackOffice Titles

Implementing Exchange Server

By Doug Hauger, Marywynne Leon, and William C. Wade III
1st Edition Fall 1998
450 pages, $29.99
ISBN: 1-56205-931-9

If you're interested in connectivity and maintenance issues for Exchange Server, then this book is for you. Exchange's power lies in its ability to be connected to multiple email subsystems to create a "universal email backbone." It's not unusual to have several different and complex systems all connected via email gateways, including Lotus Notes or cc:Mail, Microsoft Mail, legacy mainframe systems, and Internet mail. This book covers all of the problems and issues associated with getting an integrated system running smoothly and addresses troubleshooting and diagnosis of email problems with an eye towards prevention and best practices.

SQL Server System Administration

By Sean Baird, Chris Miller, et al.
1st Edition Fall 1998
400 pages, $29.99
ISBN: 1-56205-955-6

How often does your SQL Server go down during the day when everyone wants to access the data? Do you spend most of your time being a "report monkey" for your co-workers and bosses? *SQL Server System Administration* helps you keep data consistently available to your users. This book omits the introductory information. The authors don't spend time explaining queries and how they work. Instead they focus on the information that you can't get anywhere else, like how to choose the correct replication topology and achieve high availability of information.

Internet Information Server Administration

By Kelli Adam, et. al.
1st Edition Winter 1998
300 pages, $29.99
ISBN: 0-73570-022-2

Are the new Internet technologies in Internet Information Server 4.0 giving you headaches? Does protecting security on the Web take up all of your time? Then this is the book for you. With hands-on configuration training, advanced study of the new protocols in IIS 4, and detailed instructions on authenticating users with the new Certificate Server and implementing and managing the new e-commerce features, *Internet Information Server Administration* gives you the real-life solutions you need. This definitive resource also prepares you for the release of Windows NT 5 by giving you detailed advice on working with Microsoft Management Console, which was first used by IIS 4.

Unix/Linux Titles

Solaris Essential Reference

By John Mulligan
1st Edition Winter 1998
350 pages, $19.99
ISBN: 0-7357-0230-7

Looking for the fastest, easiest way to find the Solaris command you need? Need a few pointers on shell scripting? How about advanced administration tips and sound, practical expertise on security issues? Are you looking for trustworthy information about available third-party software packages that will enhance your operating system? Author John Mulligan—creator of the popular Unofficial Guide to Solaris Web site (sun.icsnet.com)—delivers all that and more in one attractive, easy-to-use reference book. With clear and concise instructions on how to perform important administration and management tasks and key information on powerful commands and advanced topics, *Solaris Essential Reference* is the reference you need when you know what you want to do and you just need to know how.

Linux System Administration

By James T. Dennis
1st Edition Winter 1998
450 pages, $29.99
ISBN: 1-56205-934-3

As an administrator, you probably feel that most of your time and energy is spent in endless firefighting. If your network has become a fragile quilt of temporary patches and workarounds, then this book is for you. For example, have you had trouble sending or receiving your email lately? Are you looking for a way to keep your network running smoothly with enhanced performance? Are your users always hankering for more storage, more services, and more speed? *Linux System Administration* advises you on the many intricacies of maintaining a secure, stable system. In this definitive work, the author addresses all the issues related to system administration, from adding users and managing files permission to internet services and Web hosting to recovery planning and security. This book fulfills the need for expert advice that will ensure a trouble-free Linux environment.

Linux Security

By John S. Flowers
1st Edition Spring 1999
400 pages, $29.99
ISBN: 0-7357-0035-4

New Riders is proud to offer the first book aimed specifically at Linux security issues. While there are a host of general UNIX security books, we thought it was time to address the practical needs of the Linux network. In this definitive work, author John Flowers takes a balanced approach to system security, from discussing topics like planning a secure environment to firewalls to utilizing security scripts. With comprehensive information on specific system compromises, and advice on how to prevent and repair them, this is one book that every Linux administrator should have on the shelf.

Linux GUI Application Development

By Eric Harlow
1st Edition Spring 1999
400 pages, $34.99
ISBN: 0-7357-0214-7

We all know that Linux is one of the most powerful and solid operating systems in existence. And as the success of Linux grows, there is an increasing interest in developing applications with graphical user interfaces that really take advantage of the power of Linux. In this book, software developer Eric Harlow gives you an indispensable development handbook focusing on the GTK+ toolkit. More than an overview on the elements of application or GUI design, this is a hands-on book that delves deeply into the technology. With in-depth material on the various GUI programming tools, a strong emphasis on CORBA and CGI programming, and loads of examples, this book's unique focus will give you the information you need to design and launch professional-quality applications.

Lotus Notes and Domino Titles

Domino System Administration

By Rob Kirkland
1st Edition Winter 1998
500 pages, $29.99
ISBN: 1-56205-948-3

Your boss has just announced that you will be upgrading to the newest version of Notes and Domino when it ships. As a Premium Lotus Business Partner, Lotus has offered a substantial price break to keep your company away from Microsoft's Exchange Server. How are you supposed to get this new system installed, configured, and rolled out to all of your end users? You understand how Lotus Notes works—you've been administering it for years. What you need is a concise, practical explanation about the new features, and how to make some of the advanced stuff really work. You need answers and solutions from someone like you, who has worked with the product for years, and understands what it is you need to know. *Domino System Administration* is the answer—the first book on Domino that attacks the technology at the professional level, with practical, hands-on assistance to get Domino running in your organization.

Lotus Notes and Domino Essential Reference

By Dave Hatter & Tim Bankes
1st Edition Winter 1998
500 pages, $19.99
ISBN: 0-7357-0007-9

You're in a bind because you've been asked to design and program a new database in Notes for an important client that will keep track of and itemize a myriad of inventory and shipping data. The client wants a user-friendly interface, without sacrificing speed or functionality. You are experienced (and could develop this app in your sleep), but feel that you need to take your talents to the next level. You need something to facilitate your creative and technical abilities, something to perfect your programming skills. Your answer is waiting for you: *Lotus Notes and Domino Essential Reference*. It's compact and simply designed. It's loaded with information. All of the objects, classes, functions, and methods are listed. It shows you the object hierarchy and the overlaying relationship between each one. It's perfect for you. Problem solved.

Networking Titles

Cisco Router Configuration and Troubleshooting

By Pablo Espinosa and Mark Tripod
1st Edition Winter 1998
300 pages, $34.99
ISBN: 0-7357-0024-9

Want the real story on making your Cisco routers run like a dream? Why not pick up a copy of *Cisco Router Configuration and Troubleshooting* and see what Pablo Espinosa and Mark Tripod have to say? They're the folks responsible for making some of the largest sites on the Net scream, like Amazon.com, Hotmail, USAToday, Geocities, and Sony. In this book, they provide advanced configuration issues, sprinkled with advice and preferred practices. You won't see a general overview on TCP/IP—we talk about more meaty issues like security, monitoring, traffic management, and more. In the troubleshooting section, the authors provide a unique methodology and lots of sample problems to illustrate. By providing real-world insight and examples instead of rehashing Cisco's documentation, Pablo and Mark give network administrators information they can start using today.

Implementing and Troubleshooting LDAP

By Robert Lamothe
1st Edition Spring 1999
400 pages, $29.99
ISBN: 1-56205-947-5

While there is some limited information available about LDAP, most of it is RFCs, white papers and books about programming LDAP into your networking applications. That leaves the people who most need information—administrators—out in the cold. What do you do if you need to know how to make LDAP work in your system? You ask Bob Lamothe. Bob is a UNIX administrator with hands-on experience in setting up a corporate-wide directory service using LDAP. Bob's book is NOT a guide to the protocol; rather, it is designed to be an aid to administrators to help them understand the most efficient way to structure, encrypt, authenticate, administer and troubleshoot LDAP in a mixed network environment. The book shows you how to work with the major implementations of LDAP and get them to coexist.

Implementing Virtual Private Networks:

A Practitioner's Guide
By Tina Bird and Ted Stockwell
1st Edition Spring 1999
300 pages, $29.99
ISBN: 0-73570-047-8

Tired of looking for decent, practical, up-to-date information on virtual private networks? *Implementing Virtual Private Networks*, by noted authorities Dr. Tina Bird and Ted Stockwell, finally gives you what you need—an authoritative guide on the design, implementation, and maintenance of Internet-based access to private networks. This book focuses on real-world solutions, demonstrating how the choice of VPN architecture should align with an organization's business and technological requirements. Tina and Ted give you the information you need to determine whether a VPN is right for your organization, select the VPN that suits your needs, and design and implement the VPN you have chosen.

New Riders | How to Contact Us

Visit Our Web Site

www.newriders.com

On our Web site you'll find information about our other books, authors, tables of contents, indexes, and book errata. You can also place orders for books through our Web site.

Email Us

Contact us at this address:

newriders@mcp.com

- If you have comments or questions about this book
- To report errors that you have found in this book
- If you have a book proposal to submit or are interested in writing for New Riders
- If you would like to have an author kit sent to you
- If you are an expert in a computer topic or technology and are interested in being a technical editor who reviews manuscripts for technical accuracy

international@mcp.com

- To find a distributor in your area, please contact our international department at the address above.

pr@mcp.com

- For instructors from educational institutions who wish to preview Macmillan Computer Publishing books for classroom use. Email should include your name, title, school, department, address, phone number, office days/hours, text in use, and enrollment in the body of your text along with your request for desk/examination copies and/or additional information.

Write to Us

New Riders Publishing
201 W. 103rd St.
Indianapolis, IN 46290-1097

Call Us

Toll-free (800) 571-5840 + 9 + 4557
If outside U.S. (317) 581-3500. Ask for New Riders.

Fax Us

(317) 581-4663

New Riders
We Want to Know What You Think

To better serve you, we would like your opinion on the content and quality of this book. Please complete this card and mail it to us or fax it to 317-581-4663.

Name _____

Address _____

City _____ State _____ Zip _____

Phone _____

Email Address _____

Occupation _____

Operating System(s) that you use _____

What influenced your purchase of this book?
❑ Recommendation　　❑ Cover Design
❑ Table of Contents　❑ Index
❑ Magazine Review　　❑ Advertisement
❑ Reputation of New Riders　❑ Author Name

How would you rate the contents of this book?
❑ Excellent　　❑ Very Good
❑ Good　　　　❑ Fair
❑ Below Average　❑ Poor

How do you plan to use this book?
❑ Quick reference　❑ Self-training
❑ Classroom　　　❑ Other

What do you like most about this book?
Check all that apply.
❑ Content　　❑ Writing Style
❑ Accuracy　❑ Examples
❑ Listings　　❑ Design
❑ Index　　　❑ Page Count
❑ Price　　　❑ Illustrations

What do you like least about this book?
Check all that apply.
❑ Content　　❑ Writing Style
❑ Accuracy　❑ Examples
❑ Listings　　❑ Design
❑ Index　　　❑ Page Count
❑ Price　　　❑ Illustrations

What would be a useful follow-up book to this one for you?_____

Where did you purchase this book?_____

Can you name a similar book that you like better than this one, or one that is as good? Why? _____
_____
_____

How many New Riders books do you own? _____

What are your favorite computer books?_____
_____

What other titles would you like to see us develop? _____
_____

Any comments for us? _____
_____
_____
_____
_____

Fold here and scotch tape to mail

New Riders Publishing
201 W. 103rd St.
Indianapolis, IN 46290